Exploring Spirituality from Post-Jungian Perspective

CW00923212

Derived from Ruth Williams' more than 40-year immersion in spiritual practice, as well as her clinical experience as a Jungian analyst, this thought-provoking volume explores the nature of spiritual paths and trajectories in practical ways, incorporating personal anecdote and ground-breaking academic research and providing a window into how Jungian practitioners work with soul and spirit.

Williams explores the nature of being a human using the Yiddish idea of a person being a 'mensch', which means being a decent human being, having humanity and living ethically with integrity. The idea of 'grace' is the thread that runs through the book—the mystery that binds things together and makes life meaningful, purposeful, potentially joyful and spiritually fulfilling. Williams sees 'grace' as being that which underpins and lies behind synchronicity and divinatory practices and as a force by which we can learn to be guided.

Rooted in clinical work, *Exploring Spirituality from a Post-Jungian Perspective* is fascinating reading for Jungian analysts, therapists and academics, as well as for general readers interested in a spiritual journey, both personally and for clinical purposes.

Ruth Williams, MA (Jungian and Post-Jungian Studies), is a Jungian analyst-analytical psychologist, integrative psychotherapist and supervisor based in London, England. She is the author of *Jung: The Basics* (Routledge 2019). See: www.RuthWilliams.org.uk.

'Ruth Williams has a feel for what matters, and in this set of engaging reflections on what spirituality means, or might mean, in the contemporary world, she homes in on a range of challenging but vital topics: ecological responsibility, the purpose of life, destiny, the ineffable, and many more. As a psychotherapist, Williams is far from unfamiliar with the darker side of life; but she also attends to the struggles involved in facing the light. Through a deft choice of anecdotes and vignettes drawn from spiritual traditions, popular culture, and above all her own personal and professional experience, she champions the pursuit of one's individual path. And her vivid, personable style helps to make all the addressed issues emotionally as well as intellectually accessible. Exuding courage and generosity, this book should be helpful to a wide readership.'

Professor Roderick Main, *Department of Psychosocial and Psychoanalytic Studies, University of Essex*

'I am overjoyed to find in *Exploring Spirituality from a Post-Jungian Perspective: Clinical and Personal Reflections* a uniquely welcoming voice and distilled wisdom. Whatever our religious or secular background, this book invites us to celebrate being human by becoming spiritual. Williams writes with the accessibility and experiential depth to include everyone with a questing spirit, whether familiar with Jungian psychology or not. Superbly grounded in the personal, this book is a deep dive into dimensions of being often labelled religious, mystical, esoteric, paranormal, or transpersonal. It shows us how to live more fulfilled lives in this troubled twenty-first century. Buy it!'

Susan Rowland (PhD), *Core Faculty, Pacifica Graduate Institute*

'This important work captures the essence of a spiritual approach to the unconscious: continually grounding experience by reality testing, watching what your Shadow is doing, and having a sense of humour. Ruth explains this with clarity, vision and, above all, warmth of heart.'

Dr Dale Mathers, *IAAP*

Exploring Spirituality from a Post-Jungian Perspective

Clinical and Personal Reflections

Ruth Williams

LONDON AND NEW YORK

Designed cover image: **The Black Pine** by Arts4Giving artist © Sandy Damon 2021

First published 2023
by Routledge
4 Park Square, Milton Park, Abingdon, Oxon OX14 4RN

and by Routledge
605 Third Avenue, New York, NY 10158

Routledge is an imprint of the Taylor & Francis Group, an informa business

© 2023 Ruth Williams

The right of Ruth Williams to be identified as author of this work has been asserted in accordance with sections 77 and 78 of the Copyright, Designs and Patents Act 1988.

All rights reserved. No part of this book may be reprinted or reproduced or utilised in any form or by any electronic, mechanical, or other means, now known or hereafter invented, including photocopying and recording, or in any information storage or retrieval system, without permission in writing from the publishers.

Trademark notice: Product or corporate names may be trademarks or registered trademarks, and are used only for identification and explanation without intent to infringe.

British Library Cataloguing-in-Publication Data
A catalogue record for this book is available from the British Library

ISBN: 978-1-032-25673-3 (hbk)
ISBN: 978-1-032-25681-8 (pbk)
ISBN: 978-1-003-28455-0 (ebk)

DOI: 10.4324/9781003284550

Typeset in Times New Roman
by MPS Limited, Dehradun

To the love behind each breath.

There are things I must record,
Must praise.
There are things I have to say about the
fulness and the blaze Of this beautiful life.
(Extract from "Grace" by Kae Tempest 2022)

Contents

Figures

Acknowledgements

I am grateful to Sandy Damon who so generously created the artwork for the book cover.

I am grateful to Professor Andrew Samuels for pointing me in the direction of F.W.C. Myers which proved to be such an interesting and fruitful direction to explore.

Thanks to Dr Terence Palmer for generously giving of his time to discuss the world of spirits and the work of Frederic Myers including his permission to print the transcript of our conversation. I was sad to learn that Dr Palmer died on New Year's Eve 2021 before I had a chance to send him a copy of this book which I know he would have been delighted to see. RIP.

I am grateful to Professor Roderick Main for his help on certain queries I had with regard to synchronicity and the *I Ching*.

I am grateful to Professor Sonu Shamdasani for his assistance in establishing a particular point regarding synchronicity.

Thank you to Dr Carola Mathers for allowing me to use her unpublished notes on the Fool.

Thank you to Dr Liz Greene for allowing me to quote from her letter to the IAJS Discussion List (in August 2020) in chapter 7.

Thank you to Dr Martin Stone for his assistance with details of Gerhard Adler.

I thank Lucy Adler for her kind permission to recount certain stories she related to me.

I am grateful to Dr Jules Cashford, Dr Dale Mathers, Elizabeth Scharsach and Dr Evangeline Rand who read draft chapters and provided such helpful comments. Thank you all.

Sincere gratitude to all the colleagues who so generously responded to my research questionnaire.

I am most grateful to Alexis O'Brien, my editor at Routledge, for her kindness, generosity and patience. As well as to Katie Randall and all the other wonderful staff at Routledge who have been such a pleasure to work with.

I want also to express my appreciation to the many writers I have quoted here and from whom I have learnt so much and drawn such inspiration. Many have expressed exactly what I wanted to articulate and did so far better than I could do.

Anonymous gratitude only can be expressed to the patients who have generously agreed that their stories may be included here. All identifying details have of course been obscured to protect the patients' confidentiality.

List of permissions

I am grateful for the following permissions to reprint material which have kindly been granted:

With thanks to Domino Publishing Company Limited for use of the Kae Tempest quotation from *Grace*.

Introduction
'Anthem' from STRANGER MUSIC by Leonard Cohen. Copyright © 1993 Leonard Cohen and Leonard Cohen Stranger Music, Inc., used by permission of The Wylie Agency (UK) Ltd.

Chapter 1
Princeton University Press have kindly given permission to quote from Ai Weiwei's Humanity.

Chapter 2
Faber & Faber for generously allowing me permission to quote from T.S. Eliot's *The Waste Land* in chapter 2.
   HarperCollins New York for generously allowing me permission to quote from T.S. Eliot's *The Waste Land* in chapter 2.

Chapter 3
I am grateful to Harvard University Press for allowing me to quote extracts from: THE FALLING SKY: WORDS OF A YANOMAMI SHAMAN by Davi Kopenawa and Bruce Albert, translated by Nicholas Elliott and Alison Dundy, Cambridge, Mass.: The Belknap Press of Harvard University Press, Copyright © 2013 by the President and Fellows of Harvard College. Used by permission. All rights reserved.
   Princeton University Press have kindly given permission to quote from Ai Weiwei's Humanity.

Chapter 4
Rumi's poem in chapter 4 is reprinted by permission of HarperCollins Publishers Ltd © Maryam Mafi and Azima Melita Kolin (1999).

Taylor & Francis for Natalie Pilard table in chapter 4.

Chapter 5
Taylor & Francis for Murray Stein quote from Minding the Self in chapter 5.

Chapter 8
I grateful to Eastern Daily Press for their permission to quote their article about Caroline Flack in chapter 8.

Curtis Brown have kindly given worldwide permission to quote extracts from Alistair Campbell's Living Better: How I Learned to Survive Depression. London: John Murray.

Chapter 10
Illustration from the Jungian Tarot deck in chapter 10 reproduced by permission of U.S. Games Systems, Inc., Stamford, CT 06902 USA. © by U.S. Games Systems, Inc. Further reproduction prohibited.

A note on references

All references to the works of Carl Gustav Jung are to his 20 volume *Collected Works* (Edited by Sir Herbert Read, Michael Fordham and Gerhard Adler) (Translated from the German by R.F.C. Hull). London: Routledge. Princeton, NJ: Princeton University Press. (1953–77).

References to volumes are referred to as "CW" followed by the volume number.

I have used paragraphs rather than page numbers for ease of reference.

Introduction

I've looked into the face of darkness, and I've looked into the face of light. I cannot say I loved looking into the face of darkness, but I have and I have survived. Indeed survived and flourished as a result of looking into the abyss whenever I have needed to. It does take courage. In Jungian terms, this is called facing the Shadow.

I remember as a young adolescent, looking into the mirror to look deep within my eyes until I absolutely freaked myself out. I remember feeling de-stabilised, not knowing who was looking at whom. In retrospect I was looking for my 'Self' (capitalised as Carl Jung sometimes does to indicate something greater than a mere personal self). This was before I knew what spiritual searching meant and before I had any notion of examining an interior existence. Perhaps that was the beginning. A more conscious step was when Peter Brook released his film about Gurdjieff/Ouspensky called *Meetings with Remarkable Men* (Dir: Brook 1979) which I eagerly devoured, although consciously more because of my interest in Peter Brook's stellar reputation in theatre. But this inched me further towards a spiritual path which became my *raison d'etre*.

After my father died we would go to spiritualist meetings led by a man called Joe Benjamin in Kentish Town in North London. Benjamin was a medium who would commune with the dead. Some saw these evenings as a bit of entertainment; others had a deep faith that he was genuinely bringing messages from their loved ones. Sometimes we would see Benjamin for individual sessions and these were, in a way, my first 'therapy' sessions. It became somewhere to open up and confide in someone who seemed to have the capacity to deal with deep meaningful questions and emotions.

I began to encounter different forms of healing. A dear friend in my 20s was a gifted healer who would tell me stories of how, tragically, when her husband committed suicide when she was very young, she went to live in the woods as a hermit and began to commune with animals. The trauma opened up her energetic sensitivities and she became a highly gifted healer of humans and animals. Hers were also the first accounts of abuse I ever heard

DOI: 10.4324/9781003284550-1

which laid the ground for the work I was eventually to take up and prepared me for horrific tales I would hear. I am deeply indebted to her for her friendship and healing energy which I was never able to appreciate in person as deeply as I would have liked. She was also the first person to introduce me to Jung's writings when she gave me a copy of the *I Ching: or Book of Changes* (Wilhelm 1951) and this subsequently became my first incarnation as a proto therapist (years before I trained) when people would ask me for readings of the *I Ching*. There have subsequently been a number of important teachers and guides who have made an indelible impression on me and who have helped to align me to my own path in life which Carl Jung (1875–1961) called Individuation (Williams 2019).

This encounter through personal experience is a route I have travelled in my own unique ways, as we all must do. The most terrible experiences are often of great value and ultimately lead to growth and deepening as a person. You don't think that when you are in the depths of grief or trauma or abuse. But for many, this can indeed be the result. Having these experiences primes the soul. There are times when encountering the Shadow is a profoundly frightening experience and the visceral impact can be shattering. It is no mean feat; not for the faint-hearted. But, without acknowledgement of the Shadow, the result can be a rather shallow personality and in a need to be liked by others. It is often by incorporating these unwanted factors that depth is discovered and the ability to cope with difficulties in life and in our relationships.

This is the nub of the project of psychotherapy and psychoanalysis which has exploded exponentially over recent decades. For many therapists (or analysts in particular), the route to such work (and the root) is via our own trauma and pain. This is the story of the Wounded Healer (Sedgwick 2017) known in Greek mythology as Chiron. Chiron was a centaur who was accidentally shot by a poison arrow. This wound was the guiding force which taught Chiron healing. The notion of the Wounded Healer is predicated on the dual nature of life whereby poison and healing are inextricably linked because paradoxically poison can also heal.

The notion of the Wounded Healer conjures up the image from a poem by Sufi mystic poet Rumi when he talks of the light entering through the wounded place. This idea is echoed eight centuries later by Leonard Cohen in his "Anthem": "There is a crack, a crack in everything. That's how the light gets in" (Sony Music 1992). Perhaps it is sentiments like these which help us all stagger on when life feels too tough. We sense that there is some meaning in the pain we are experiencing.

The concept of being a Wounded Healer can sometimes be rather idealised. In fact, the truth is that, although many analysts would identify with such an appellation as for many becoming a therapist is a deep soul journey, the sad truth is though that we give the best of ourselves to our patients and often treat each other badly. We all know what families are like! And the adage that familiarity breeds contempt. I think that is partly why there is such a tendency for analytic organisations to split. (There is a long history of this in the Jungian world.) We characterise these splits as being along theoretical lines (and it's true) but there is also considerable personal animosity in the mix which is rarely discussed.

Some therapists become inflated in seeing themselves as healers rather than being a channel for healing. This might seem like a subtle distinction but it is of the utmost significance in that it is not the individual ego which heals. And acknowledging that, being conscious of that, enables the therapist to *serve* rather than seeing themselves as being a magical creature, as if healing were their personal doing.

You might notice I am highlighting a 'spiritual' aspect, and then I ground it with a dose of 'reality' to keep it earthed and authentic. This is an important aspect of relationship with spirituality which I am purposefully doing to model by example how to live in relationship with spirituality. Without that grounded ingredient, you end up flying too close to the sun. The ego becomes inflated. It is also simple reality.

I will always remember a day when I meditated particularly deeply many years ago. For some reason on that day my concentration was really constant and I did not move for a number of hours. I experienced the source inside myself so deeply that I realised the realms within are equidistant to those without as far as the mind – or consciousness – can travel. This is a realisation, an experience, which has lived with me through all the subsequent decades and remains a guiding light. Many years later I came across the following in the works of Carl Gustav Jung which resonated powerfully with the experience I remembered: "the only equivalent of the universe within is the universe without; and just as I reach this world through the medium of the body, so I reach that world through the medium of the psyche" (1930 par. 764). Jung also refers to the legendary Renaissance alchemist Solomon Trismosin (who taught alchemy to Paracelsus) and who in the 1500s wrote: "All that is without thee, Also is within" (quoted in Jung 1937 par. 153) which, again, resonated with my intuitive realisation.

Psychotherapy and analysis are often associated with coping with difficulties and tragedies in life. In fact, I think people struggle with the light as much as the darkness. Allowing the heart to be full in the midst of the Maya (a Sanskrit word used in Hindu Vedanta meaning the illusory nature of this world), can be a real struggle which is constantly challenged by bumping into the daily grind and rage and frustration which is arguably particularly prevalent in the West. (And of course I do not exclude myself from this at all!)

I will not be recommending any particular spiritual path as we must all find our own. I can help you understand the yearning to find your path, and to align to it, but what it is must come from you as a unique soul. If your heart is open, you are more likely to be able to sniff out your own path.

You will already have encountered some contested terms which might encourage or discourage you from reading further. What I mean by spirituality may be different to how you relate to it. What I mean by 'soul' and 'spirit' equally may cause you to pause and consider if you relate to these terms at all and whether my use of them sits comfortably with you. This will be particularly the focus of my research which appears in chapter eleven.

> In this book I will be exploring the deeper meanings of life and how we navigate them. It is about being human in the Yiddish sense – being a 'mensch' – which means being a decent human being, having humanity, living ethically with integrity. It is about 'being' rather than 'doing' (which can so easily become a tyranny of consumption, of over-rationality and one-upmanship which stimulates so much disharmony. (Fuller 'being', de Chardin suggests, "*is* closer union" (1965 pp. 31) (emphasis added)). Grace is the thread – the mystery – behind it all which binds it together and makes life meaningful, purposeful and potentially joyful and spiritually fulfilling.

In the chapters that follow, I have taken some big subjects, some of which are explored in more personal ways; others in more heuristic academic style. Rather than being gratuitously 'personal' in a flamboyant narcissistic manner, this stance is known as autoethnography, an anthropological form of qualitative research methodology which I encountered through the work of Dr Kevin Lu of the University of Essex in his paper on racial hybridity (2020 pp. 11–40). This methodology uses self-reflection and self-narrative to explore anecdotal and personal experience, connecting autobiographical story to wider cultural, political, and social circumstances. One of the arguments put forward by the Scientific and Medical Network is the need to develop a new methodology of "radical introspection or inner experience" (Walach 2019 pp. 6) to work towards what the Network terms post-materialist or spiritually informed science (ibid. pp. 86). This work is intended as a modest step in that direction.

Some may see *Exploring Spirituality* within the field of New Age thinking (although I am not sure it really exists as a movement any longer). The so-called New Age grew out of a sense of many people feeling empty and alienated by religion, religious dogmatism and fundamentalism, while retaining a sense that spirituality contained something important and vital. Rather than being a "pick and mix" approach (which is how the New Age is/was often disparaged), it is a path of individuation by which we may explore and develop our own spiritual nature in a way that feels truly authentic and embodied. Following or finding your own spiritual path is less *laissez faire*, than taking responsibility for what truly resonates within your own soul and spirit as a 'home'; feels like an authentic fit, and is experienced as fulfilling. It is a deep, sometimes painful and difficult path which perhaps ironically may be lonely if it creates a separation from those you love who may be on a different [spiritual] path. But as James Hillman (1926–2011) puts it, the source of this deep loneliness seems to be: "the solitary uniqueness of each daimon, an archetypal loneliness" (1996 pp. 54). (Hillman, the originator of Archetypal Psychology which is an offshoot of Jung's Analytical Psychology, was hailed as the most important US psychologist since William James in the nineteenth century. We shall come to Hillman again in the chapters that follow.) We arrive on this planet alone and leave alone. The path to find or follow our own star is but single track.

You may intuit that your spiritual path is calling to you. It takes guts to take that seriously and try to attune your senses to that call. As Australian Jungian academic and public intellectual David Tacey so poetically puts it:

> The spirit of the holy has fallen into the unconscious, and we can no longer find this light by the official means, but only by arduous and difficult dialogue with the unconscious … . It is as if the sun had been extinguished and instead of the gleam of Apollo or Phoebus, we have a new kind of radiance, a galaxy of little lights, a night sky of stars. To see these lights we must learn to see in the dark, discern glimmers of myth in dreams and moments of grace in the ordinariness of our lives. The divine light has been humbled and we have to humble ourselves to recover it.
>
> (Tacey 2013 pp. 4)

This chimes with Murray Stein, prolific Jungian writer, graduate of Yale Divinity School and senior Jungian analyst in Zurich, when he advocates: "an individual path to spirituality that is grounded in personal experiences and lived by reflecting upon them using a psychological perspective. It exists outside of all religious organizations and structures" (2014 pp. 4).

Williams James (1842–1910) (Harvard Professor of Philosophy, 'father' of American psychology and brother of writer Henry James) in his *magnum opus,* wrote of the noetic quality of personal experience (that is, bridging scientific exploration and experiential discovery to better understand the deeply interconnected nature of our universe):

> Although so similar to states of feeling, mystical states seem to those who experience them to be also states of knowledge. They are states of insight into depths of truth unplumbed by the discursive intellect. They are illuminations, revelations, full of significance and importance, all inarticulate though they remain; and as a rule they carry with them a curious sense of authority for after-time.
>
> (1985 pp. 380–381)

There are many great minds turning to address this field of exploration, challenging the scientific materialistic view of the world and who see the limitations of such a philosophy, even in the face of the perceived legitimacy with which science is culturally endorsed. In her *Call for a Renaissance of the Spirit in the Humanities,* Dr Athena D. Potari from Harvard University urges theorists to:

> open to greater levels of dialogue and consideration of nonmaterialist worldviews, by also expanding the scope of permissible epistemological approaches to include non-discursive methodologies, self-reflexive, participatory and action research methods that evolve and transform not only knowledge, but the practitioners as well.
>
> (see: Renaissance-Call.pdf (galileocommission.org) – accessed 2 May 2022)

One of her goals is to: "Re-emphasize the more contemplative and experiential ways of knowing by demonstrating how 'the experiential can be academic'" (ibid.). Potari is writing on behalf of the Galileo Commission who have published a Report which seeks to open public discourse to expand the scope of science from the constraints of outmoded views of 'matter' and to incorporate evidence indicating consciousness may go beyond the brain (see: https://galileocommission.org/report/#renaissance – accessed 2 May 2022) (Walach 2019).

A fable

Setting out on a new path, or deepening an approach to a path, can be scary. The following ancient fable might help put you in a receptive frame of mind as you read:

> According to the story, a village was frozen in fear and mourning because it knew that a dragon was planning to devour every person in it. Everyone could see the dragon on a far-off mountain, looming as large as fear itself. They could hear its horrible roar louder than the crack of thunder. Now, a young stranger happened by and decided to confront the dragon, so off he went to climb the dreaded mountain. Curiously however, the closer he got to the dragon, the smaller it appeared. When he finally reached the monster, it was no larger than a cat and its fearsome roar had diminished to something like purring. The stranger tucked the creature under his arm and returned to the village. Everyone was amazed at his story and marveled at the cute little dragon that they'd held in such dread. Eventually someone asked the dragon's name, whereupon – to everyone's amazement – the dragon itself spoke: "I am known and feared by many names throughout the world, but ultimately all know me as 'what might happen'.
>
> (Thurston and Fazel 1992 pp. 102)

During my research for this book I have come across the offspring of some of the originators of important work in this field whose children have now begun to take the work forward. I refer herein to the work of Laurence Hillman (son of James Hillman), Merlin Sheldrake (son of Rupert Sheldrake); in looking into astrology I have come across the work of Becca Tarnas (daughter of Richard Tarnas). Mark Watts (son of Alan Watts) produced a radio series with his (now late) father entitled *The Love of Wisdom*. I think this is a hopeful sign, not only of good relationships in those families, but of the inspiration being carried forward to another generation.

My hope is this work might be a modest contribution to opening this field of exploration further. This book is aimed at all those who are interested in spirituality, mysticism, esoterica, personal search, incarnating their potential and developing spiritual practice, as well as psychotherapists and analysts who may, or may wish to, incorporate such an approach into their practice. I have done my best to use language which both the seasoned practitioner and those new to this field may find accessible. We are all as seekers somewhere along a continuum that is not defined by intellect or qualifications. The journey of the soul knows no barriers of class, education, culture or wealth. Wisdom is available equally to all.

The broad span of this book ranges from introducing practices to the novice, to looking at spiritualism and the possible life beyond this realm. I have divided the book into four parts:

In Part 1 (chapters 1–3), I take a personal tack to look at spirituality itself, how it may be accessed, practised and experienced, as well as how it manifests in nature and ecology, looking at our responsibilities to this precious planet. Part One sets the scene with an overview of the spiritual perspective at the heart of this work.

In Part 2 (chapters 4–8), I look at dilemmas we encounter in life, covering deep questions around the purpose of life and existence and how we intuitively 'know'. In this section we look at some vital components of a spiritual perspective, as well as addressing some of the deepest questions in life.

In Part 3 (chapters 9–10), I examine various puzzles such as predestination, destiny and fate, synchronicity and look at three mantic (divinatory) practices: Tarot, I Ching and Astrology, each of which is linked to synchronicity and grace.

Part 4 (chapters 11–13), looks at the ineffable. In this final section, we look at some of the most challenging matters we may ever face: questions of the limits of existence, phantoms, the transcendent, the sacred and the deeply mysterious. I begin with a piece of qualitative research to ground the ineffable in the day-to-day experience of contemporary practitioners.

Finally (in the Endplate), I close with some humour. Although I have addressed some heavy matters throughout this book, I think it is important not to be too pompous.

References

Brook, P. (1979) (Director) (Co-written by P. Brook, G.I. Gurdjieff and J. Salzmann). *Meetings with Remarkable Men.* Remar.

Cohen, L. (1992) Sony BMG Music Entertainment/Sony Music Entertainment.

de Chardin, T. (1965) *The Phenomenon of Man.* New York & San Francisco: Harper Colophon Books.

Hillman, J. (1996) *The Soul's Code: In Search of Character and Calling.* New York: Warner Books, 1997.

James, W. (1985) *The Varieties of Religious Experience.* London: Penguin Classics.

Jung, C.G. (1930) "On Kranefeldt's 'Secret Ways of the Mind'" in CW4.

Jung, C.G. (1937) "Psychology and Religion" in CW11.

Lu, K. (2020) "Racial Hybridity Jungian and Post-Jungian Perspectives" in the *International Journal of Jungian Studies.* Vol. *12.* Brill Publishing.

Sedgwick, D. (2017) *The Wounded Healer: Countertransference from a Jungian Perspective.* London & New York: Routledge Mental Health Classic Edition.

Stein, M. (2014) *Minding the Self: Jungian Meditations on Contemporary Spirituality.* London and New York: Routledge.

Tacey, D. (2013) *The Darkening Spirit: Jung, Spirituality, Religion.* London and New York: Routledge.

Tempest, K. (2022) "Grace" in *The Line is a Curve.* Republic Records.

Thurston, M. and Fazel, C. (1992) *The Edgar Cayce Handbook For Creating Your Future.* New York and Toronto: Ballantine Books.

Walach, H. (2019) *Beyond a Materialist Worldview: Towards an Expanded Science.* Lulu.com.

Wilhelm, R. (1951) (Trans.) (rendered into English by C.F. Baynes and with a foreword by C.G. Jung) *I Ching: or book of changes.* London: Routledge & Kegan Paul.

Williams, R. (2019) *Jung: The Basics.* London & New York: Routledge.

Part I

Spiritual perspective

This section sets the scene with an overview of the spiritual perspective at the heart of the work, encompassing personal experience, path and the connection with the more-than-human world.

DOI: 10.4324/9781003284550-2

Part 1

Spiritual Perspectives

Chapter 1

Overview

A spiritual perspective could be described as transpersonal, which is a term meaning it is beyond the personal, inter-personal or mundane realm. Spirituality is not the same as religion although it is often the goal of religious practice. A new term has come into existence, which is SBNR – spiritual but not religious – and increasing numbers of people find they identify with this designation.

Where you put your attention – what you practice in your day – is what you get good at. If it is on nit-picking, that will be your experience of life. If it is prioritising harmony and contentment, then they become more accessible. Not fixed; not guaranteed. Nothing is. But more within your grasp. It is on your radar. Of course, it needs to be more than an intellectual idea, but rather an experience to have a real impact; a genuine encounter with the sublime. So, I am not talking about sentimental ideas; not breathless piety; not religion (socially/culturally constructed systems of rules on one level. N.B. the etymology of 'religion' stems from 'religare' meaning 'to bind' as in ligature). I have no interest in 'positive thinking', which is often denial in another guise. Or 'false peace', as the former Archbishop Rowan Williams called moving on prematurely without genuinely resolving issues. We can – and need to – experience more than this in life. Our depths yearn for more.

Far from being from 'above', having a spiritual attitude entails engagement with gritty reality; a grounded embodied spirituality, incorporated in daily existence. It is concerned with wholeness, encompassing all aspects of life – wanted or not! As Carl Jung (1875–1961) (father of Analytical Psychology) puts it: "One does not become enlightened by imagining figures of light, but by making the darkness conscious" (1945/54 par. 335).

The path of spirituality is about incarnating our potential. It is about doing our best to live alongside others with integrity and generosity. I often fail, but on the whole I attempt to make reparations and heal any damage I may have caused by word or deed. I have written elsewhere (2014) about atonement and forgiveness, which are profoundly important concepts that play a vital part in living a life with integrity which is the *sine qua non* of a spiritual path.

DOI: 10.4324/9781003284550-3

Many people come unstuck when they try to adopt a spiritual attitude defensively (whether consciously or not) as a hiding place from the more challenging aspects of life. It simply does not work. It's the grit in the oyster that makes the pearl. I realised a more all-encompassing approach was required and this is how I came to enter psychotherapy in the first place. I came to see that the people around me (including me) in my spiritual community were predominantly not able to engage with the more challenging or 'negative' sides of life such as envy, rage, rivalry, competitiveness and mis-dealings. I went and faced those things in therapy and this opened up a fathomless pool which enabled me to encompass and embody these difficult facets of life which we all must necessarily encounter and deal with. Otherwise life becomes one-sided, superficial and unsatisfying. You don't have to live in an ashram to experience a spiritual connection (although I did for many years). *Spirituality is available to all of us, all the time.* The numinous is not an intellectual concept. It is not a luxury or privilege available only to initiates or priests. You just need a pulse. Every human has the potential to connect with spirituality which you might find in:

- A connection with the wonder and energy of all life
- Spiritual values
- Development of heart, compassion and consciousness
- A mindful, solid and inspiring strength to carry us through good and bad times
- A sense of meaning, personal integrity and purpose independent of material success and the opinion of others
- An embedded sense of wellbeing to support physical and mental health, and
- A deep enjoyment of life that is also fully present to its challenges and suffering.

(This is a slightly adapted list taken from Bloom 2011 pp. 6.)

David Tacey in Australia, writing about his engagement with the Aboriginal peoples, articulates the synthesis which is required:

If we take the mystical element from animism and the intellectual element from rationality, we end with a discerning or watchful mysticism, a mysticism on the alert for implausible claims and a capacity to detect nonsense, yet always open to wonder and revelation.

(2009 pp. 155)

Carl Jung was the pioneer of the transpersonal approach psychotherapeutically and many humanistic schools such as psychosynthesis have drawn on his teachings. Famously in a BBC *Face to Face* interview with John Freeman in 1959 (accessible on YouTube), Jung replied he did not believe in God – he knew. It is important to note that this is not said with arrogance, but rather a confidence which is visibly convincing. Jung writes of his engagement with the deep, spiritual realms throughout his *Collected Works*. Jung saw neuroses as being teaching moments, in some cases. He sees a neurosis as having a purpose:

> We should even learn to be thankful for it, otherwise we pass it by and miss the opportunity of getting to know ourselves as we really are. A neurosis is truly removed only when it has removed the false attitude of the ego. We do not cure it – it cures us. A man is ill, but the illness is nature's attempt to heal him. From the illness itself we can learn so much for our recovery, and what the neurotic flings away as absolutely worthless contains the true gold we should never have found elsewhere.
>
> (1934 par. 361)

Many others have felt and feel – or intuited – the same. Edgar Cayce (1877–1945) known as the 'sleeping prophet' had the ability to put himself into a sleep-like or perhaps trance state by lying on a couch and tuning in to all of time and space (ie past, present and future) which he saw as universal consciousness. In this way, he would give psychic readings and became the most documented psychic of the twentieth century. He was also the father of holistic medicine. Cayce saw God as responsive to individual prayer and as active in human affairs. (So, no 'old man with a beard' in the sky for him.) This accounts for the ideas put forward in chapter 10 about the grace which is the guiding element behind mantic (divinatory) practices.

Consciously or not, I believe we all crave connection with a deeper, more meaningful, realm. We feel separated when we are cut off from it as it is our deepest nature. This may manifest in needing soulful relationships, contact with the natural world, having an animal companion or studying astronomy or astrology to look out into the deepest recesses of space. In the midst of the crazy busy worlds many of us inhabit, it can be difficult to remember that we are not our problems.

I am often reminded of a parable from the Kabbalah. It tells us we are born on the understanding that we 'forget' where we came from, ie the lap of G-d (spelt in this way because in Jewish law you are not supposed to write or speak the name of God), which leaves us forever with a longing to return but not being able to locate the source of that yearning. The teaching is called the *Aggadic Midrash* based on a passage in *Talmud Masechet Nidah*:

> Before a child is born, a light is held behind its head, with which it can see from one end of the world to the other, and they teach it the whole of Torah. But at the moment of birth an angel touches it on the lips and it forgets all. So all of life is spent remembering what we once knew.
>
> (Assembly of Rabbis of the Reform Synagogues of Great Britain 1977 p. 367)

The story continues: "Therefore we all have a dent below our nose which is where the angel touched us" (with thanks to Rabbi David Freeman for the full quote and reference; Williams 2019 pp. 28).

There is a remarkably similar myth in the Shamanic lore of the Dagara tribe in Burkino Fasso. In a description of their initiation rite, we are told:

> Each one of us possessed a center that he had grown away from after birth. To be born was to lose contact with our center, and to grow from childhood to adulthood was to walk away from it/'The center is both within and without. It is everywhere. But we must realize it exists, find it, and be with it, for without the centre we cannot tell who we are, where we are from, and where we are going'.
>
> (Somé 1994 pp. 198)

These myths also chime with Plato's concept of anamnesis (see his Dialogues *Meno* and *Phaedo* in Plato 2010 pp. 95–256). Plato believed humans possess innate knowledge (perhaps acquired before birth) and that learning consists of rediscovering knowledge from within.

The longing for a 'home' many of us experience (be it physical, familial or professional), relates to these stories of having come from the lap of God. That yearning to find where we belong is deep. It is an archetypal need. Perhaps that is even what has brought you to this moment, to read a book exploring these issues.

We will return to these ideas in chapter 9 where I look at destiny and fate.

Alchemy

One of the unique features of Jung's approach is his use of alchemy (which falls within the spiritual/esoteric tradition). At first glance, it might seem as if this is a peculiar 'way-out' angle to adopt, but it has proved to have great value as a metaphor in psychotherapeutic practice and in the literature. Jung saw alchemy as an historical counterpart to his psychological work on the unconscious and used a series of ancient woodcuts to draw a link between how alchemy works and the relationship between analyst and analysand in the process of psychoanalysis. I discuss the topic at greater length in *Jung: The Basics* (2019) and in my chapter on Atonement in *Alchemy and Psychotherapy: Post-Jungian Perspectives* (2014 Ed. Mathers). Rather than over-complicate matters here by going into what is quite a dense, complex system, I will simply focus on the final phase of the alchemical process to show how it relates to the spiritual connections I am laying out: The final phase of the alchemical work is known as the *rubedo* or reddening, or the *coniunctio* (reunification). This refers to the reunion of body, soul and spirit, which is the pinnacle of the work. Inner conflict lessens at this stage of the process bringing a more peaceful resolution to the relationship between the body, soul and spirit and a longed-for calming of conflicting demands. The reddening evokes the sky at sunrise and the dawn of new possibilities. Red in *rubedo* symbolises the completion of the cycle, represented by the phoenix rising from the ashes of our old ways. (Incidentally, for anyone interested in the colour red, there is an outstanding scholarly paper amplifying the colour and associated imagery by a Jungian Analyst called Deborah Fausch which may be accessed free online via the Archive for Research in Archetypal Symbolism -ARAS) (2019). (See: https://aras.org/articles/red-amplification-color accessed online 12 June 2020.)

The alchemical phases have to be repeated as many times as need be, as in therapy and analysis. It is a circular process; or more accurately a spiral process so matters are revisited from different perspectives. Perhaps like the planets (complexes?) rotating around the sun, each at their own distance and with their own qualities. The Ancient Greek philosopher Plotinus thought our souls travel in circles, so perhaps it is simply the way we function. My Jungian colleague, Ann Baring (who has explored Jung's alchemical works for over 50 years) gives us a salutary reminder:

> We grow through the *Nigredo* and *Albedo* phases of alchemy into the *Rubedo*. We cannot force entry into it by spiritual exercises or any formulation of goals. It may happen to us ... or we can grow into it through the expansion of the heart, the instinctive capacity to love, to give to others, to serve life through an awakened compassion.
>
> (2013 pp. 482–3)

Note – this is an exercise of the heart. This is so important. It may be that the heart muscle (metaphorically) needs to be exercised - or strengthened - in order to engage with this level.

Psychologically, alchemy is about re-finding spirit in matter; about healing the split between spirit and matter so our nature may be linked back together where it belongs. In entering into the work of alchemy, we join with spirit to release its energy. And in healing ourselves, we heal the world since we are connected. We all stem from the same source. So, exploring oneself in therapy is more than a private matter. It has ramifications for our families, communities and society. Jung captures this idea:

> For two personalities to meet is like mixing two different chemical substances: if there is any combination at all, both are transformed. In any effective psychological treatment the doctor is bound to influence the patient; but this influence can only take place if the patient has a reciprocal influence on the doctor.
>
> (1929 par. 163)

This idea is also expressed by the artist Ai Weiwei:

> My conclusion is we are one humanity. If anyone is being hurt, we are all being hurt. If anyone has joy, that's our joy.
>
> (2018 pp. 2)

The search for the philosopher's stone in alchemy – the gold of insight psychotherapeutically – symbolises the stages in the journey of analysis, through the struggles to heal and to reunite body, soul and spirit within the Self. To end this section and this chapter, I leave you with Ann Baring:

> Alchemy flows beneath the surface of Western civilization like a river of gold, preserving its images and its insights for us so that we could one day understand our presence on this planet better than we do. Alchemy builds a rainbow bridge between the human and the divine, the seen and unseen dimensions of reality, between matter and spirit. The Cosmos calls to us to become aware that we participate in its life, that everything is sacred and connected: one life; one spirit. Alchemy responds to that call. It asks us to develop cosmic consciousness, to awaken the divine spark of our consciousness and reunite it in the invisible Soul of the Cosmos. It changes our perception of reality and answers the questions: 'who are we?' and 'why are we here?' It refines and transmutes the base metal of our understanding so that we – evolved from the very substance of the stars – can know that we participate in the mysterious ground of spirit while living in this physical dimension of reality.
>
> (2013 pp. 457–8)

References

Assembly of Rabbis of the Reform Synagogues of Great Britain (Eds) (1977) *Forms of Prayer for Jewish Worship* (seventh edition). London: The Reform Synagogues of Great. Britain.

Baring, A. (2013) *The Dream of the Cosmos: A Quest for the Soul*. Dorset: Archive Publishing.

Bloom, W. (2011) *The Power of Modern Spirituality: How to Live a Life of Compassion and Personal Fulfilment*. London: Piatkus.

Fausch, D. (2019) *Red: Amplification of a Colour*. ARAS Connections. Issue 4.

Jung, C.G. (1929) "The Problem of Modern Psychotherapy" in CW16.

Jung, 1934: "The State of Psychotherapy Today" in CW10.

Jung, C.G. (1945/54) "The Philosophical Tree" in CW13.

Mathers, D. (Ed.) (2014) *Alchemy and Psychotherapy: Post-Jungian Perspectives*. London and New York: Routledge.

Plato (2010) *Dialogues of Plato*. New York: Simon & Schuster.

Somé, M.P. (1994) *Of Water and the Spirit: Ritual, Magic and Initiation in the Life of an African Shaman*. New York: Penguin Books.

Tacey, D. (2009) *Edge of the Sacred: Jung, Psyche, Earth*. Einsiedeln: Daimon Verlag.

Weiwei, A. (2018) "Humanity" (Ed. Warsh). New Jersey and Woodstock, Oxon: Princeton University Press.

Williams, R. (2014) "Atonement" in *Alchemy and Psychotherapy: Post-Jungian Perspectives* (Ed. Mathers). London and New York: Routledge.

Williams, R. (2019) *Jung: The Basics*. London & New York: Routledge.

Chapter 2

Spiritual attitude

The key to developing a spiritual attitude is establishing a genuine connection to one's own spiritual nature. It has to come from a deep engagement to be meaningful and this can be facilitated by creating a daily practice. This could take many forms:

- A routine of meditating.
- Immersing yourself in spiritual poetry (particularly the mystic poets such as Kabir, Rumi, Mirabai, Hafiz, or Mary Oliver for a contemporary Christian perspective) may help.
- Spending time in wild nature in all its manifold manifestations. (We will come to ecopsychology in the next chapter.)
- Sharing deeply with friends.
- Even holding a pebble in the palm of your hand might connect you to your shared origins on this planet earth. The Ancient Greeks saw this idea as pantheism, meaning God is in everything. Stones, as Jung knew, have soul and, when we touch them (in the right frame of mind) we vibrate to the same wavelength and recognise we share something fundamental. This relates of course to every aspect of nature, each element or living being having its own vibration. (For those of a scientific bent, this idea can be found in string theory in physics). Every part of the world and the life upon it is sacred with no one having greater intrinsic value. (Humans are made of the same materials as the earth and the stars. According to Yanomami (indigenous population of the Brazilian Amazon) shamanic lore: "What the white people call "minerals" are the fragments of the sky, moon, sun and stars" (Kopenawa 2013 pp. 283). Their word for stars derives from the word for a shiny metal). This may give you a sense of how precious each life is.
- For others smells are evocative, or different sounds such as bells or indeed any instrument which can resonate deeply within the body and soul. This is why bells, drums and singing bowls are used in many spiritual rituals. The extraordinary, deaf percussionist Evelyn Glennie so beautifully articulates this: "to truly listen we must use our bodies as

DOI: 10.4324/9781003284550-4

resonating chambers (Glennie 2017, in Hopenwasser 2017 p. 60). My Jungian colleague, Dr Martin Stone, expresses the same idea when he writes of our bodies being like tuning forks (2006), a metaphor I have used myself over many years. This is the key to empathy. We can literally tune in to other people. (This links to the idea of mirror neurons which is beyond the scope of this work but is well worth exploring.) This is incidentally how many therapists and analysts work, by attuning to the person we are sitting with and using what we call our counter transference (which is the reciprocal relationship with an analysand where the analyst will experience feelings touched off by the analysand's transference to the analyst). By using these practices, we can tune in to the tonal vibrations of the universe, including within ourselves, which can transport your spirit.

- Even noticing the weather can put you in touch with something greater than the personal realm. You can feel quite lifted by simply soaking up the rays of the sun; or by getting drenched. This can bring about a sense of belonging to – or being a part of – the natural world. A child's first encounter with snow is often enchanting as they fathom what this mysterious substance is. In the tale of a Dagara elder from Burkino Faso we are told the grandfather:

> used to call rain 'the erotic ritual between heaven and Earth'. The rain represented the seeds sown in the Earth's womb by heaven, her roaring husband, to further life. Rainy encounters between heaven and Earth were sexual love on a cosmic scale. All of nature became involved. Clouds, heaven's body, were titillated by the storm. In turn, heaven caressed the Earth with heavy winds, which rushed toward their erotic climax, the tornado.
>
> (Somé 1994 pp. 75)

- Having fresh flowers not only creates an aesthetically pleasing environ-ment which in itself is nourishing of soul, but may infiltrate our nostrils and senses in a way that fills us with joy, feels enlivening, enriching and reminds us we are a part of the natural world. Smell directly connects us within our physical bodies to what can be an exhilarating experience. Our bodies are not simply a clothes horse to primp and preen (as much as that can be fun). Our bodies are the gateway through which we experience both the spiritual and the mundane worlds.
- The world of the senses takes us deep within ourselves. This might involve Tantric sex which channels the energies through very slow coupling with an emphasis on synchronised breathing, touching and eye contact. Orgasm is not regarded as a goal; rather it is about enhancing the intimacy with your lover and expanding the spiritual connection.

- Simply being in touch with your breath can bring a deep appreciation of the value as well as the fragility of life. (This has been brought starkly into our consciousness in the period of the Coronavirus pandemic.) Each breath is a gift over which we have no power (apart from artificially holding your breath which can only be done for strictly limited periods). Each breath taken consciously helps to soften the tensions held in the body and mind, creating a more open heart. We begin life with a breath in, and it all comes to an end with a breath out. Being witness to either one of these events is a profound and unforgettable experience. And yet, in the ordinary busyness of life, we take millions of breaths which we do not even notice. How often do we stop to appreciate the gift that is the breath which keeps us alive? Gratitude is a quality which naturally arises when we are in touch with our spiritual nature, when the heart is full. And the more gratitude you can allow, the more supple and ample the heart becomes. Heart in this context is synonymous with soul.
- For some a candle evokes the divine light we each embody and which shines through as charisma when someone is aligned to their path. There are many reports of this light in near death experiences (see Chapter twelve). There is a wonderful story in a Martin Scorsese documentary about the light. The documentary, on the life of George Harrison, is an investment of time running at three and a half hours. The final anecdote is from his wife, Olivia, talking about Harrison's 'death'. She tells us how dedicated he was to his spiritual life and explorations and, when he knew he was dying, he sincerely wanted to die as he had lived, so he meditated deeply unto his final breath. As he exhaled his last, she tells us, the entire room filled with light (Dir: Scorsese 2011).

Humility must be mentioned here. There is no place for hubris in a spiritual journey. Being in awe (in the original sense) automatically creates a sense of one's proportion in the scheme of life which naturally generates humility. Neither under-estimating your 'importance' nor over-estimating it. Perhaps seeing humans as grains of sand who have the fortune to pass through this world for the shortest time is a useful corrective to our sometimes inflated sense of significance.

Dreams can be the gateway to spiritual experience. While steeped in research on the African and Brazilian shamanic tribes I have referred to, I dreamt of an elephant:

The elephant was in an empty whitewashed room. Perhaps like a farm outbuilding. It was my environment; not hers. There was something about the elephant helping me by 'milking me' which meant me giving the elephant my ear (which I realised meant listening to me). There was some consideration about whether to take this seriously or if I should consult someone human as it was quite scary to be so vulnerable with the elephant. (She was an adult female elephant.) She lay down on the floor on her side to show me she was not threatening and to encourage me to have the courage to go ahead and lay down next to her if I liked, and which I did. This was deeply comforting.

She became a spirit animal who would calmly accompany me in some of my explorations during the writing of this work. She was later joined by a beautiful wolf with remarkably bright blue eyes, and then subsequently by a stag. I've been gathering quite a menagerie!

I had a similar experience with a spirit called "the Mandarin" much earlier in life which I describe in chapter twelve.

Living a life of service is the ultimate. For some this means dedicating one's life to living in a religious order, or it may be tithing a percentage of your earnings to charity. For others it is doing work which is experienced as service or vocation. We talk of public service and civil service, but not often of spiritual service. If you are lucky enough to do work experienced as service, it is a great boon. We do not all have to toil at the capitalist wheel even though we all need to support ourselves. Viewing the graft many of us in the West undertake on a daily basis and the values this promotes through the perspective of the African shaman I mention is a genuine eye-opener. Finding a way of straddling both these worlds – integrating these perspectives – can be deeply rewarding and empowering.

Spirituality is not necessarily a solitary activity. It relates to *how* we live our life with others too, whether in a community or family or alone. We radiate an energy which communicates our inner state. This can be a humbling – or humiliating – realisation. Even if you are preaching sweetness and light, if you are generating negativity or inauthenticity, people know; they sense it.

A word of caution. Summoning spiritual aid needs to come from a humble place; not one of control. There was a fad some years ago known as 'cosmic ordering' where people would call up all manner of desires, be it for a partner, for abundance, for this, that and the other. And it worked! I remember creating a map of the man I wanted to attract at the time using scraps of words and images from magazines and so forth. And I got exactly what I asked for. But the fatal flaw in the plan was that I failed to include one vital ingredient. The profound learning for me was my prayers need to hand over the power to the source of wisdom who knows better than I do what I need. T.S. Eliot encapsulated this idea when he suggested: "I said to my soul, be still and wait without hope, for hope would be hope for the wrong thing" (1959, pp. 28).

Putting things into perspective

Seeing ourselves in right proportion to the world around us was brought home to me powerfully in 2006 when Pluto was demoted from being a planet and was recategorized as a dwarf planet (which does not have the same status as a planet).

Astrologer Jonathan Cainer published a set of images to put this into perspective showing that, although Pluto might be seen as small, it really was a matter of how far back you pull the focus as earth, and even our sun, appear 'small' when compared to outer planets which are gigantic in comparison to them. As with many things in life, it really is a matter of perspective. (These images may be viewed on my website at www. RuthWilliams@msn.com).

Perspective can shift in less than the blink of an eye. There is a set of famous images used in Gestalt psychology where the pictures convey two utterly different images according to how you look at them. There is one which is the face of a witch, or alternatively from another perspective a young woman looking over her shoulder. (The hag's nose can be seen as the young woman's jawline.) A second can be seen as a duck, or alternatively as a hare. (The beak becomes the hare's ears.) Another is either a vase, or two people looking at each other in profile. No squinting is required. It is simply a flick of a switch in the brain which perceives something utterly different. (These can easily be found with an online search or at www.RuthWilliams.org.uk). Or if you simply close one eye and then the other, your perspective subtly shifts.

Some of us, like the Dagara tribe (mentioned in chapter one), see every individual as a spiritual incarnation. That perspective sees us not as humans having a spiritual experience, *but rather we are spiritual beings having a human experience*. Malidoma Patrice Somé (who sadly died in December 2021 as I was writing about him) in writing of his experience between two worlds (the Dagara tribe into which he was born and the white Catholic world into which he was kidnapped) provides a deeply effecting perspective on how the world of white people in so-called advanced societies are perceived from a shamanic perspective grounded in the world of spirit. He tells us: "To a Dagara man or woman, the material is just the spiritual taking on form" (Somé 1994 pp. 8).

References

Eliot, T.S. (1959) *Four Quartets: East Coker*. (London: Faber and Faber).

Hopenwasser, K. (2017) "The Rhythm of Resilience: A Deep Ecology of Entangled Relationality" in *Wounds of History: Repair and Resilience in the Trans-Generational Transmission of Trauma* (Eds. J. Salberg and S. Grand). London & New York: Routledge.

Kopenawa, D. (2013) (with B. Albert) (Trans. Elliott and Dundy) *The Falling Sky: Words of a Yanomami Shaman*. Cambridge, Massachusetts and London: Belknap Press of Harvard University Press.

Scorsese, M. (2011) *George Harrison: Living in the Material World* [DVD]. Grove Street Pictures.

Somé, M.P. (1994) *Of Water and the Spirit: Ritual, Magic and Initiation in the Life of an African Shaman*. New York: Penguin Books.

Stone, M. (2006) "The Analyst's Body as Tuning Fork: Embodied Resonance in Countertransference" in *Journal of Analytical Psychology* 51(1):109–124.

Chapter 3

Gaia/ecology, indigenous perspectives and animals

Gaia/ecology

The sort of perspective the planets provide in the images just mentioned in chapter two puts us all in right proportion to our environment, to each other, to all of humanity and to our place on earth, ("this orbiting psychiatric ward" as Woody Allen so deftly calls it (2020 pp. 332)).

This might give us a sense of our responsibilities to do as little damage to the planet and the environment as we possibly can while we are here. We are merely the custodians of the planet for our brief stay. We might see ourselves as honoured visitors. A whole field of ecopsychology has been established over recent decades which can be explored in for instance (Roszak *et al* (1995) and Mathers (Ed.) (2021)).

The artist Ai Weiwei reminds us what makes this collective problem so difficult:

> It is human nature to believe that we are so smart, that we control the universe. But, at the same time, human nature is suicidal, because we never fully appreciate how temporary and ephemeral our fate really is.
> (2018 pp. 10)

Gaia is a word adopted by biochemist James Lovelock (1979) (from the ancient Greek term for earth mother) when he was exploring the idea the earth is regulated homeostatically. He saw the whole of nature is itself a self-regulating system, finely balanced to promote our wellbeing and conditions to survive.

Ecology is the study of connectedness. Attuning to the living, 'breathing' planet upon which we depend may help us understand the Indigenous concept of reciprocity with the earth; the need to honour that which we take from the earth, give thanks for the gifts we consume each day and be conscious of how we can give back.

If anyone has doubt about the wisdom of nature and how connected we truly are, I would refer you to the work of Peter Wohlleben, a forester who has written about how trees (which filter our air) communicate with each

DOI: 10.4324/9781003284550-5

other through a sophisticated root system – the wood wide web (2017)! This term was coined by Sir David Read who in 1984 was the first (with colleagues) to show carbon could pass between plants through fungal networks (M. Sheldrake 2020 pp. 168). He wrote a commentary on a paper in the journal *Nature* on the ground-breaking work of Dr Suzanne Simard who wrote an afterword to Wohlleben's book where she touches on her research which reveals:

> The wood wide web has been mapped, traced, monitored, and coaxed to reveal the beautiful structures and finely adapted languages of the forest network. We have learned that mother trees recognise and talk with their kin, shaping future generations. In addition, injured trees pass their legacies on to their neighbors, affecting gene regulation, defense chemistry, and resilience.
>
> (ibid. pp. 249)

Similar findings are coming forth about fungi too. (See the work of Merlin Sheldrake 2020, son of Rupert Sheldrake whom I mention elsewhere in this chapter). Wohlleben tells us that fungi have an: "underground cottony web, known as mycelium … There is a honey fungus … in Oregon … estimated to be 2,400 years old, extends for 2,000 acres, and weighs 660 tons. That makes the fungi the largest known living organisms in the world" (2017 pp. 50). The trees and fungi collaborate for their mutual survival. Wohlleben tells us:

> With the help of mycelium of an appropriate species for each tree … a tree can greatly increase its functional root surface so that it can suck up considerably more water and nutrients. You find twice the amount of life-giving nitrogen and phosphorus in plants that cooperate with fungal partners than in plants that tap the soil with their roots alone (ibid).

Have humans got a lot to learn about collaborating! Trees can not only share nutrients, they share information about impending insect attacks. Wohlleben reports trees have a form of brain in their root tips which 'feel'. Electrical impulses have been measured. Researchers from the University of Bonn discovered:

> In addition to the signalling pathways, there are also numerous systems and molecules similar to those found in animals. When a root feels its way forward in the ground, it is aware of stimuli. … If the root encounters toxic substances, impenetrable stones, or saturated soil, it analyses the situation and transmits the necessary adjustments to the growing tip. The root tip changes direction as a result of this communication and steers the growing root around the critical areas.
>
> (Wohlleben 2017 pp. 83)

This interconnection between the trees has a downside. Wohlleben recounts a lightning strike he witnessed of a particular Douglas fir resulting in the death of the surrounding firs within a radius of 50 ft, from which he inferred that: "instead of the life-giving sugar" they would normally share via the roots, "what they received was a deadly serving of electricity" (ibid. pp. 206).

Jung wrote a great deal about how we are interconnected. Nathan Field (Jungian analyst in the UK) writes about this when discussing thought transference between analyst and patient, and the unexpected unconscious happenings and synchronicities which can arise. Field tells us:

> [Jung] compared individual consciousness to islands standing up in the sea; if we look below the surface we realise that at the level of the sea bed we are joined. Somehow we have to entertain the paradoxical notion that, as living beings, we are both separate and united.
>
> (1996 pp. 42)

Jungian analyst Dale Mathers in London envisages our minds as being metaphorically like: "complex eco systems – neural forests, each with over ten billion interconnected trees" (2021 pp. 162) which he sees as the network of connections enabling us humans to communicate via the collective unconscious. Patterns in nature can be seen everywhere.

M. Sheldrake describes the electrical system in fungi through their mycelial networks as being akin to the electrical impulses in animal nerve cells (2020 pp. 7). (Sheldrake comes out with some absolute corkers (awesome facts), such as we have more bacteria in our guts than there are stars in the galaxy (ibid. pp. 18)).

Fungi also have the potential to repair some of the harm we humans have perpetrated on earth as they have the ability to transform pollutants in soil and waterways; they can degrade pesticides, crude oil, some plastics and the detritus from various chemicals we scatter in our waste (ibid. pp. 205–6). Pretty smart! The caveat is this is absolutely at the cutting edge and still awaiting institutional adoption and academic scrutiny which means, partly, overcoming vested interests who profit from *not* pursuing such a radical agenda.

My interest in these networks is not purely love and awe of the beauty of nature. It is the awareness of our non-separation from all other forms of life which is encapsulated well by Professor Michael C. Kalton of University of Washington (whose speciality is Korean Neo-Confucianism):

> Concern for the well-being and relative continuity of the life community with which we co-evolved requires no altruism; we understand now that we ultimately interdepend in the web of biotic life so that concern for other creatures operates in synergy with self-concern. This is the spiritual dynamic of systemically grounded horizontal transcendence, where the part and the whole are never two.
>
> (2000 pp. 196–7)

By horizontal transcendence he means we belong to the universe as opposed to needing to transcend vertically to an Absolute.

Coming back to trees, they communicate with us too. Wohlleben tells us standing underneath conifers raises the blood pressure, whereas standing under an oak lowers it (2017 pp. 223). Most extraordinary of all, Wohlleben mentions a study in California which has discovered fruit flies might dream (ibid. 242)! (This research is contained in a German paper entitled (in translation) "A fly's eye view of the world") in the Süddeutsche Zeitung of 19 May 2010, available at www.sueddeutsche.de/panorama/forschung-die-welt-aus-sicht-einerfliege 1.908384 accessed January 21, 2016.)

I want to mention another book about trees which is *The Oak Papers* by James Canton (2020). He focuses predominantly on one single oak tree which he spent a year 'visiting' and where he recorded the changes around him and within himself. He found it was nourishing to his soul to be close to trees (which I am sure many of us can attest to for ourselves). He touches on the depth of feeling which arises when you touch a tree; the connection to the more than human world this elicits. He saw his daily ritual of visiting the oaks like a meditative or religious practice. I learnt from Canton there is a team at the University of Murcia in Spain studying the ecological and philosophical basis of plant intelligence.

Even the Dalai Lama has made public he is in favour of large-scale tree planting to help tackle climate change and says he would vote Green, declaring, if Buddha returned to this world, "Buddha would be green"! (See: 'Buddha would be green': Dalai Lama calls for urgent climate action | Dalai Lama | The Guardian accessed 15th April 2022.)

I used at one time to photograph trees which seemed to have faces in the pattern of their bark. I guess it was my way of having a proto interaction with the trees as I intuitively sensed they were animated (ensouled). And who does not love to hug a tree if no one is watching?! Every child knows there is something precious and fascinating about trees, loving the physical contact of climbing them. It is a pity, as we become adults, many lose that uninhibited connection. Many of us have connections to particular trees and even have tattoos of them. Traditional harvesters (from Indigenous communities) see trees as non-human 'persons' to be approached with humility. Permission is asked in those communities before chopping a tree. This becomes a mindful practice.

Indigenous perspectives

Davi Kopenawa, a shaman from the Yanomami community in the Brazilian Amazon, tells us of their ancient indigenous belief system which appears prescient:

> The white people probably think that *Teosi* [God] will manage to make the *xawara* smoke from their factories disappear from the sky?

They are wrong. Carried very high into its chest by the wind, it is already starting to soil and burn it. It is true, the sky ... is getting as sick as we do! If all this continues, its image will become riddled with holes from the heat of the mineral fumes. Then it will slowly melt, like a plastic bag thrown in the fire, and the thunders will no longer stop shouting in anger. This has not happened yet because the sky's *hutukarari* spirits are constantly pouring water on it to cool it down. But we shamans fear this disease of the sky more than anything. The *xapiri* [spirits] and all the other inhabitants of the forest are also very worried about it because if the sky catches fire, it will fall again. Then we will all be burned, and we will be hurled into the underworld like the first people in the beginning of time.

(2013 pp. 295–6)

I do not know what the Yanomami know of the latest research into the ozone layer or global warming, but it appears in their native cosmogony. Their wisdom is gleaned via spiritual journeying and dreaming. Kopenawa relates his story as he is concerned we will all perish if action is not taken to reverse the damage mankind is doing to the planet. Kopenawa had to travel far and wide beyond his community in an effort to resist the incursions made by gold prospectors, loggers and cattle ranchers cutting down swathes of the ancient, untouched Amazon forests.

As an aside, in stark contrast to our Western materialist frenzy which has caused the havoc and destruction to the earth, the Yanomami destroy all the personal belongings of a person when they die which means there is none of the egregious clamouring to inherit when a person dies. The Yanomami see possessions belonging to a deceased as carrying the imprint of the person which will cause sadness to their loved ones. Destroying these objects is part of the mourning process for them. Kopenawa:

We think it is bad to own a dead man's goods. It fills our thoughts with sorrow. Our real goods are the things of the forest: its waters, fish, game, trees, and fruit. Not merchandise! This is why as soon as someone dies we make all the objects he kept disappear. We grind up his bead necklaces; we burn his hammock, his arrows, his quiver, his gourds, and his feather ornaments.

(2013 pp. 330)

Traditional Roma families do the same. They burn the body in the deceased's Vardo (vehicle like a caravan), along with all their possessions, considering it bad luck if you do not do this (Dr Dale Mathers, personal communication 22 April 2022).

Later, Kopenawa tells us:

> I do not have a taste for possessing much merchandise … In the beginning it is attractive, yes, but it quickly gets damaged and then we start to miss it. … For me, only the forest is a precious good. Knives get blunt, machetes get chipped, pots get black, hammocks get holes, and the paper skins of money come apart in the rain. Meanwhile, tree leaves can stiffen and fall, but they will always grow back, as beautiful and bright as before. The small amount of merchandise I possess is sufficient and I do not desire more.
>
> (ibid. pp. 337)

Kopenawa struggles to relate to the Western way of thinking we need bigger, faster, more and nothing is ever enough. As do many Westerners! (See Paul Watchel's *The Poverty of Affluence,* 1989). Capitalism wants unhappy people as they spend more money! There seems to be no limit to people's desires and addictions; rivalries to obtain the latest/best/shiniest/most aspirational goods and lifestyles), even parading their imagined perfect family (as defined by the advertising industry and social media). These attempts cannot fill the existential void, though, which people must face at some point in life. And, as difficult as that is, it is also a good thing. We need to learn consumption cannot satisfy spiritual hunger. The secret of life does not lie in consumerism.

Robin Wall Kimmerer (2020), member of the Citizen Potawatomi Nation, (American Distinguished Teaching Professor of Environmental and Forest Biology; Director, Center for Native Peoples and the Environment, at the State University of New York College of Environmental Science and Forestry) penned a guideline to encapsulate the teachings she has learned from her Indigenous community as a rule of thumb for how to approach the gifts the earth offers which they refer to as the Honourable Harvest. It is deeply respectful and modest, encouraging us to be in a relationship with nature and treat it with honour. She talks of only taking what we need; what is given by the earth. There is no need to be greedy and acquisitive. There is plenty. The community encourage a modest stance, perhaps as you might treat an honoured guest in your home – except that, here, we are the guest!

Even Bill Gates, then the wealthiest man on earth, realised he had made enough and turned to philanthropy, an example some have been inspired to emulate.

Kopenawa forces us to think about many Western ways we take for granted. For instance, he was taken to a museum in Paris and shown the remains of early indigenous people preserved alongside their arrows and tools and beads which would normally have been destroyed (see above). Kopenawa was angry to see beings and their belongings so disrespected for our entertainment. Later he talks of visiting New York (where Kopenawa had been invited to speak in defence of his people) and not being able to fathom the discrepancy between the rich at the centre of the metropolis and the poor at the outskirts. From his perspective it was truly an alien way to live. He notices how disturbed his sleep and dreams are in a city; how people rush around looking at the ground without making eye contact with each other. He cannot help but notice the pollution, the roaring of the noises at every turn, the adrenaline fuelled and empty way of life which has become normalised in the industrialised West.

In Yanomami mythology *Omama* (the Creator) is central to ecology. Humans are seen as part of ecology alongside the spirits, game, trees, rivers and everything natural. This is fundamental to their worldview. They are guided by the spirits of the forest in all they do. Their interest however is not simply in protecting their forests, but the whole of the planet (ibid. Chapter 23).

David Tacey encapsulates his own concerns:

> [i]t may be easier for us as a nation [Australia] to approach the task of resacralizing through environmental and social ecology ... ecology almost looks like a pragmatic and secular activity, and devotion to the needs of the environment may not cause the same embarrassment that devotion to the spirit would generate. Through ecology we attend to the most urgent practical issues in the world, and yet, within the practice of ecology there is the romantic and mythopoetic impulse, eros itself, engaged in its vital task of binding, weaving and connecting us to the other. Through ecology we strive to heal the world and ourselves, to transcend the contemporary condition and link our souls vitally to the soul of the world.
>
> (2009 pp. 139–140)

Arthur Machen

It is not of course only indigenous people who possess this perspective on man's relationship to our natural environment. The Edwardian Welsh writer Arthur Machen (1863–1947), known for his supernatural fantasy and horror fiction, describes:

> the impact of a particular landscape on an individual, and suggests that the landscape and the individual have conjoined in a way that constellates particular qualities in the human because the same qualities, in a nonhuman form, are inherent in the landscape.
>
> (Letter from Liz Greene to the IAJS Discussion Seminar 9 August 2020)

Greene goes on to cite the following from the end of Machen's story (originally in an anthology called *The Children of the Pool and Other Stories* (Hutchinson, London, 1936):

> The things which we distinguish as qualities or values are inherent in the real environment to make the configuration that they do make with our sensory response to them. There is such a thing as a "sad" landscape even when we who look at it are feeling jovial ... That is not imputing human attributes to what are described as "demand characters" in the environment, but *giving proper recognition to the other end of a nexus, of which only one end is organised in our own mind.* (emphasis in original).
> (Machen 1964 pp. 334)

These approaches are all bridging difference.

Ecocide

The problems I have been drawing attention to around the despoilation of the earth which is creating the climate crisis, is garnering increasing attention and there are moves afoot to establish an international crime known as ecocide. World leaders are being called upon to make ecocide the fifth crime against peace, alongside genocide, war crimes, crimes against humanity and the crime of aggression. This would make it easier to hold those responsible to account in a concrete way. Ecocide is a crime against the living, natural world. I refer you to the work of Scottish barrister and ardent campaigner Polly Higgins who pioneered this movement and who describes ecocide as "a missing atrocity crime of corporate and State responsibility, a missing international crime against peace" (See https://pollyhiggins.com/ accessed 23rd April 2022).

Conscious choice

Much of what I touch on here is about how we relate to each other and reaching more intimate, meaningful, spiritual depths.

If you follow a spiritual path, you need to be sure this is what you really want. It can be a solitary path as for each of us it will be unique and one we need to tread as individuals. A spiritual or religious community can be a comforting confraternity, but we arrive alone and must needs leave this life alone. You may break collusions you have with friends or relatives which you might find do not hold as you strive to be true to your authentic self. This is not easy. Many end up compromising their individual path to retain the company of their friends and family. No blame there. We are social creatures. For introverts it is perhaps easier to dedicate life to a solitary path which some may experience as sacrifice as the inner world is the primary focus in life. (See my *Jung: The Basics* for an exposition of Jung's psychological types of which introversion and extraversion are an aspect (Williams 2019 pp. 85–104.) Couples who continue to grow both individually and together while both pursuing a spiritual path are fortunate indeed. And quite rare I would venture.

Man's connection with animals (and New Physics)

Finally, I want to touch on man's connection with animals which I wrote about elsewhere (2021). In that chapter I touch on how we are connected with animals and the universe through multiple systems (such as psychology, symbols and spirituality making links with the New Physics). Many of us have experienced uncanny connections with our pets and I suggest these are not random. We are connected by energy fields known variously as Morphic Resonance (R.Sheldrake 2009 and 2011); the Akashic Field (Laszlo 2004); the Implicate Order (Bohm 1980/2002); or holograms (Talbot 1991). These approaches all help us understand our connections with animals as well as each other. They show us how we are linked on subtle levels so that it is no wonder we affect each other and cherish time we can spend with animals. For children it may be a first experience of loving and learning about re-sponsibility to another creature.

Many of us may have experienced inexplicable phenomena with animals. How do they know when their owners are about to arrive home? Because they do. How do they know when their owners are ill? It is well-known dogs can detect when their owners are sick and have even saved lives by alerting the owner to seek medical attention. For example, the animal is drawn to a changed smell in an area where cancer has not yet been medically detected. Or when they intuit an owner is about to have an epileptic fit. It is worth quoting biologist Rupert Sheldrake who cites an impressive anecdote from his research:

> [the dog] can sense, up to 50 minutes before, that I am going to have an attack and taps me twice with his paw, giving me time to get somewhere safe. He can also press a button on my phone and bark when it is answered, to get help, and, if he thinks I'm going to have an attack while I am in the bath, he'll pull the plug out.
>
> (2011, p. 196)

Anna Breytenbach in South Africa is an extraordinary sensitive who has become an animal communicator creating a communicative bridge between human and non-human animals. She tells us:

> By connecting with our intuition, we can engage in meaningful dialogue and remember how to hear the subtle messages from those whose space we share in our lives and our natural environment. Coming from a

place of respect and reverence for all life, we can learn to understand our wilder relatives, honour their truths and live in greater harmony.
(See https://www.animalspirit.org/ accessed 14th September 2020)

There are many stories of Breytenbach communicating with animals. The most striking one is of her being called in to an animal sanctuary where a black leopard has been behaving in an aggressive and upset manner. She sits with him and discovers that he is unhappy with being called Diablo with all the negative connotations that entails. She understands from him that is not his true nature and tells the keepers what she has learnt. After she leaves, the keeper goes to 'talk' with Diablo and apologises, saying he realises this name is not true to his spirit, they will leave him in peace and will now call him Spirit. The leopard came out of his hiding place for the first time in months and was now at peace and ceased his aggressive behaviour. I realise this story may sound far-fetched. I would encourage you to search on YouTube where you can actually see this filmed encounter taking place.

In this era where humans have had such a destructive impact on our precious planet, I think this becomes increasingly important. The animals are letting us know, I believe, that they are in distress. There was a case reported in the press at the time of writing which tells us of a group of orcas – killer whales – making an apparently unprovoked attack on a sail boat in the Straits of Gibraltar. This just does not normally happen. The pod kept ramming the boat for more than an hour. See: https://www. theguardian.com/environment/2020/sep/13/the-tale-of-the-killer-whales (accessed 15th September 2020). There have since been other similar reports. We can only speculate on the cause of such attacks, but humans are responsible for depleting the food stock required for their survival which is also causing them to lose babies. We probably all know now of the gargantuan volumes of pollution mankind has mindlessly emptied into the oceans such as both plastics and oil spills. Perhaps nature is fighting back.

Animals are now even at the forefront of scientific research at this time of global pandemic. Scientists in Helsinki have been trialling a pilot project where they train sniffer dogs to identify cases of Covid-19 and the success rate has been close to 100%. (https://www.theguardian.com/world/2020/sep/24/close-to-100-accuracy-airport-enlists-sniffer-dogs-to-test-for-covid-19?CMP=Share_iOSApp_Other accessed 24th September 2020).

If you think of all beings as manifestations of the same basic energy (both human and more-than-human), I wonder how it might change our perspective and our reverence and respect for each other? I wonder how we might feel about eating animal flesh if we really experienced that perspective? The need to radically reduce meat consumption in order to counteract some of the effects of climate change is now well-known, so that such a shift would have beneficial effects on both personal and collective levels; for our 'individual' souls and the *anima mundi*.

Sensitivity

Many of us will probably have experienced the odd sensation of walking down a road to 'feel' someone's gaze behind you. Or having picked up the phone only to find the person you were ringing already on the line to you. These things happen all the time (see R. Sheldrake 2004). We are connected via the same invisible threads touched on above in relation to animals, and it is when we lose sense of these deep links that we are more likely to treat each other like strangers and even enemies.

I am referring now to matters that might more precisely be termed uncanny rather than spiritual. However, my point is that there is more on heaven on earth than meets the eye and these experiences connect us to a realm which is more than the concrete, humdrum or temporal dimension. We can develop this connection – this sensitivity. You might find this enrichens your connections with others and the world around you. It takes conscious effort to do this and might be facilitated by some of the methods I mentioned in chapter two. A deeper and more attuned connection to your own interiority and the gifts you may find there, tends to engender greater harmony and connection not only internally, but with the world around us and those who cross our paths. (The flip side of this would be greater [over]sensitivity in a neurotic/Borderline way – tends to create disharmony and disunity with the world around us and those we encounter.)

☯

If the notions covered in this chapter strike you as implausible, I would encourage you to refer to your heart. It has its own wordless wisdom. Rationality is a good servant, but a bad master. We are so much more than our rational minds and I suspect that, if you are reading this, you will have at least an inkling of this for yourself. Perhaps I can invite you to read on with an open mind and heart. As Susie Orbach has it, in referring to what she calls the epic work on consciousness of Mark Solms:

> [he] resituates psychoanalysis on the ground of affects ... . We could summarize this as: We are because we feel. We feel therefore we are. We know because we feel.
>
> (Hilty (Ed.) 2022 pp. xiii)

So, you might find it helpful to engage your feeling and intuitive capacities as well as your intellectual powers when trying to grasp these ideas. You might find you are more sensitive to the subtle energies we have looked at than you ordinarily admit in daily life, and this may be something that might be welcomed.

I will end this chapter with an important question which might arise in the quest you may follow in these chapters and which might require some quiet reflection:

> Is it possible to embrace spiritual meaning and not become either childish or irrational, while increasing one's genuine awe, inspiration, gratitude, *and* intellectual appreciation of living now in this period of scientific skepticism?
>
> (Young-Eisendrath and Miller 2000 pp. 2)

References

Allen, W. (2020) *Apropos of Nothing*. New York, New York: Arcade Publishing.

Bohm, D., (1980/2002) *Wholeness and the Implicate Order*. London and New York: Routledge Classics.

Canton, J. (2020) *The Oak Papers*. Edinburgh: Canongate Books.

Field, N. (1996) *Breakdown & Breakthrough: Psychotherapy in a New Dimension*. London and New York: Routledge.

Kalton, M. (2000) "Green Spirituality: Horizontal transcendence" in *The Psychology of Mature Spirituality: Integrity, Wisdom, Transcendence*. (Eds. Young-Eisendrath and Miller). London and New York: Routledge.

Kopenawa, D. (2013) (with B. Albert) (Trans. Elliott and Dundy) *The Falling Sky: Words of a Yanomami Shaman*. Cambridge, Massachusetts and London: Belknap Press of Harvard University Press.

Laszlo, E. (2004) *Science and the Akashic Field: An Integral Theory of Everything* Rochester, VT: *Inner* Traditions.

Lovelock, J. (1979) *Gaia: A New Look at Life on Earth*. New York: Oxford University Press.

Machen, A. (1936) "The Children of the Pool" in *Tales of Horror and the Supernatural*. London: John Baker, 1964.

Mathers, D. (2021) "Time, Intuition and Imagination" in *Depth Psychology and Climate Change: The Green Book*. London and New York: Routledge.

Mathers, D. (Ed.) (2021) *Depth Psychology and Climate Change: The Green Book*. London and New York: Routledge.

Orbach, S. (2022) "Foreword" to Hilty, R. (Ed.) (2022) Primitive Bodily Communications In *Psychotherapy: Embodied Expressions of a Disembodied Psyche*. London: Karnac Books.

Roszak, T., Gomes, M.E., Kanner, A.K. (eds) (1995) *Ecopsychology: Restoring the Earth, Healing the Mind*. San Francisco: Sierra Club Books.

Sheldrake, R. (2004) *The Sense of Being Stared at: And Other Aspects of the Extended Mind*. London: Arrow Books.

Sheldrake, M. (2020) *Entangled Life: How Fungi Make Our Worlds, Change Our Minds and Shape Our Futures*. London: The Bodley Head.

Sheldrake, R., (2009) *Morphic Resonance: The Nature of Formative Causation*. Rochester, VT: Park Street Press.

Sheldrake, R., (2011) *Dogs That Know When Their Owners Are Coming Home: The Unexplained Power of Animals*, London: Arrow Books.

Tacey, D. (2009) *Edge of the Sacred: Jung, Psyche, Earth.* Einsiedeln: Daimon Verlag.
Talbot, M., (1991) *The Holographic Universe.* London: Harper Collins.
Wall Kimmerer, R. (2020) *Braiding Sweetgrass: Indigenous Wisdom, Scientific Knowledge and the Teachings of Plants.* London: Penguin Books.
Watchel, P.L. (1989) *The Poverty of Affluence: A Psychological Portrait of the American Way of Life.* New York, New York: Ig Publishing.
Weiwei, A. (2018) "Humanity" (Ed. Warsh). New Jersey and Woodstock, Oxon: Princeton University Press.
Williams, R. (2021) "Our Connection with Animals and the Universe: Psychology, Symbols, Spirituality and the New Physics" in (Mathers (Ed.) (2021) *Depth Psychology and Climate Change: The Green Book.* London and New York: Routledge).
Williams, R. (2019). *Jung: The Basics.* London & New York: Routledge.
Wohlleben, P. (2017) *The Hidden Life of Trees: What They Feel, How They Communicate.* London: William Collins.
Young-Eisendrath, P. and Miller, M. (2000) *The Psychology of Mature Spirituality: Integrity, Wisdom, Transcendence.* London and New York: Routledge.

Resources

Ecopscyhology UK website: https://ecopsychologyuk.ning.com/
Viridis Graduate Institute, Ecopsychology and Environmental Humanities website: https://www.viridis.edu/

Part 2

Dilemmas

In this section, we look at some vital components of a spiritual perspective, as well as addressing some of the deepest questions and dilemmas in life.

DOI: 10.4324/9781003284550-6

Chapter 4

How the heart knows

The heart is like a candle
longing to be lit.
Torn from The Beloved
it yearns to be whole again,
but you have to bear the pain.
You cannot learn about love.
Love appears on the wings of grace.

Jallāledīn Mohamad Rumi.
    (thirteenth century Persian poet) (1999 pp. 77)

Your heart yearns to be full, to be satisfied, to feel love, to feel connected to both others and to the divine (as in the Rumi poem above). This is not a psychic prediction! It is what hearts yearn for. Hearts guide us throughout our life towards what the heart needs, although can be notoriously unreliable when it comes to choosing love matches. It can so easily get mixed up with what the mind wants and what the body desires. They are very different things!

The heart is where compassion lives. And joy and kindness. All the good stuff. As Antoine de Saint-Exupéry puts it: "One sees clearly only with the heart. Anything essential is invisible to the eyes (1943 pp. 63).

Love of money – does not come from the heart. It is a desire of the mind, like greed and addictions of all sorts.

Let's do a quiz for some fun. Tick the boxes below (Fig. 4.1).

DOI: 10.4324/9781003284550-7

Question: What comes from the heart, the mind, or from either/both?

	Heart	Mind	Either/both
1. Love of your children			
2. Love of your partner			
3. Love of God			
4. Love of art			
5. Love of food			

Figure 4.1 Quiz: Heart, mind, either/both.

Key to watch out for: the heart does not speak in words. It speaks in feelings. If words accompany your 'love', it is from the mind. If you think "I feel *that* ...", it is a thought from your mind.

The fact is that most of the quiz answers can be from either or both. The love of your children resides in your heart, but the mind may take over with anxieties and phobias; or you may see them as objects to parade and to reflect your glory, which comes from the mind. The same is true of love of your partner for whom you may feel love, but you may still see them as a trophy (which is from the mind). Love of God may well reflect a genuine spiritual/heartfelt feeling, and yet you may wish to impress others with your religious fervour (which is from the mind). Love of food can be deeply experienced and evoke ancient memories, but the desire and the addiction for food; of an appetite that cannot be sated, is from the mind. (And specifically not from the body which may well already be physically sated.)

In Chinese culture

In a conference paper, Jungian Analyst Professor Heyong Shen in China, tells us: "in the original Chinese form, the character for language, culture and civilisation was constructed with heart as the core" (2022 pp. 308). He goes on to inform us:

> The meaning of the heart is the core of Chinese culture, as well as for Chinese philosophy and psychology. Most of the basic psychological terms in Chinese characters are formed originally with the images of the

heart … . The Chinese name for psychology … looks like 'Heart-ology', reading from left to right. If someone reads it from right to left … its meaning is 'learning the truth (reason) of the heart' (ibid.).

I touch on Chinese culture further in chapter ten when looking at the *I Ching* which is deeply concerned with the heart and is often consulted in affairs of the heart.

Heart as metaphor

The heart – as a metaphor – is a sensitive organ which needs to be protected and cherished or it can go hard and rigid. Then it becomes difficult to access which leaves us resorting to our minds and all that entails. We become brittle and uncommunicative. In the extreme we can become like automatons who are ruled by duty, the clock, by rules. You get the picture.

When I refer to the metaphoric heart, this is usually synonymous with the soul (discussed in Chapter eleven). This includes intuition which is what we often mean when we talk of following our heart.

Intuition

Nathalie Pilard (contemporary independent scholar) has made a study of Jung and intuition (2015) in which she sets out the following table which I think usefully divides the multiple facets of intuition which helps us tease apart the different dimensions of the term (Fig. 4.2).

Taking time to reflect on this table to grasp the scope of the term may be useful. I certainly found it so. Pilard breaks down intuition to rightly include everything from psychic sensitivity, to gut instinct and everything in between. Parts (1) and (2) of the table are addressed in chapter eleven so here we are more concerned with parts (2) and (3) which relates to pure intuition and telepathy. I see the different divisions as being on a continuum although that raises the argument as to whether the mediumship end of the spectrum is a higher sensitivity, or contact with departed beings, ghosts or spirits. You will have your own beliefs about such questions.

Following your heart/soul or your intuition is not something that comes easy to everyone. But it is something that can be developed. It is a feeling in your 'bones', and the more you tune in to your intuition, the more reliable it becomes. At least you become more able to pick up on its whisperings. A useful exercise can be to write down what you believe is an intuition and check back to see if this was correct. It is subtle and quiet. Intuition will not insist, and you can easily choose whether to override its message. Intuition is usually perceived in the mind's eye although it does not necessarily arrive fully formed (or visibly) so that one is often not sure where the idea comes from. This probably helps avoid inflationary thinking that one is a prophet! Feet need to be anchored to the ground even while the mind soars.

Occult phenomenon	Intuitive gift at stake

Intuitive Gifts and the various occult phenomena for which they are required.
Source: Jung, CW A, pars.112-134.

Occult phenomenon	Intuitive gift at stake
(1) Past made present: Materialisation of souls (spirits) Telekenesis:	Mediumship
• Hypnotism	Sensitiveness to the rapport (the link to the hypnotist)
• Dopplegänger (ghostly haunting double)	Sensitive to (link with) the dead person
(2) Higher present: Telepathy:	
• Clairvoyance	Faculty of seeing/hearing things which are outside the reach of the five senses
Clairvoyance (strict term: access to "ultimate realities") Second sight	The highest level of mediumship
(3) Future made present: Premonitions Prophetic dreams Prophecies	Pure intuition and temporal annihilation of all functions modifying its cognition (access to Kant's noumenon)

Figure 4.2 Intuitive Gifts and the various occult phenomena for which they are required. Source: Jung, CW A, pars. 112–134. Used with permission, Pilard (2015).

Source: (Pilard 2015 pp. 62).

Bhutan's Gross National Happiness Index

The heart is where happiness lives and where it can be nurtured and increased. In a rather counter-intuitive move (at least from a Western materialist perspective), in nineteen seventy-two the Fourth King of Bhutan, King Jigme Singye Wangchuck, declared Gross National Happiness is more important than Gross Domestic Product. This simple, paradoxically obvious idea is radical and went against the grain of every other country's measures. Ever since, the idea of Gross National Happiness (GNH) has influenced Bhutan's economic and social policy, and also captured the imagination of others far beyond its borders. The GNH Index includes traditional areas of socio-economic concern such as living standards, health and education and less traditional aspects of culture and psychological wellbeing. It is a holistic reflection of the general wellbeing of the Bhutanese population rather than a subjective psychological ranking of 'happiness' alone.

The level of GNH for an individual and for Bhutan as a country are determined by measuring:

1 Psychological wellbeing
2 Health
3 Education
4 Time use
5 Cultural diversity and resilience
6 Good governance
7 Community vitality
8 Ecological diversity and resilience
9 Living standards

The analysis explores the happiness people enjoy already, then focuses on how policies can increase happiness and sufficiency among the unhappy and narrowly happy people. What a far cry this is from the morally bankrupt systems focussed on acquisition of financial wealth under which many of us [in the West] live.

In 2011, the United Nations (UN) unanimously adopted a General Assembly resolution, introduced by Bhutan with support from sixty-eight member states, calling for a "holistic approach to development" aimed at promoting sustainable happiness and wellbeing. This was followed in April 2012 by a UN High-Level Meeting on "Happiness and Wellbeing: Defining a New Economic Paradigm" designed to bring world leaders, experts and civil society and spiritual leaders together to develop a new economic paradigm based on sustainability and wellbeing. This builds on the Government of Bhutan's pioneering work to develop the GNH Index.

The goal is that all government projects and policies collaborate to maximise GNH.

(See the research of the Oxford Policy & Human Development Initiative at https://ophi.org.uk/policy/national-policy/gross-national-happiness-index/ accessed 11 October 2020).

Love

Talking of the heart can easily become sentimental. And yet it is what has preoccupied poets forever.

There are a number of facets to love which resides in the heart. Love is an archetypal experience which comes in many forms: mother-love, brotherly *philia,* fellow feeling with friends, passion with a lover, commitment in a marriage. For some, love of God; love of one's vocation or career. Charity (from 'caritas') means giving or selflessness. Love of a sport or favourite team even. In some languages there are many words for love to differentiate the particular form. Ancient Greek distinguishes as follows:

- Agape denotes the highest form of unconditional love associated with charity and love of God as well as God's love of man.
- Eros relates to passionate/sexual love; the realm of intimate relationships.
- Philia is used for affection as between equals.
- Storge is another variant on affectionate fellow-feeling most often used as between parents and their children.

Platonic love relates to a deep bond between partners but without sexual intimacy or desire.

Love is an essential component of a fulfilled existence. Without it, life becomes meaningless, hollow and empty. Its archetypal nature means we are deeply preoccupied with love (although not necessarily in a conscious way). We all want to be in love and need to be loved. It is a fundamental, existential or archetypal need. A spiritual or religious perspective might see that love is our essence as human beings (Williams 2019 pp. 50). This is something to be cherished and protected. It can so easily be bruised or even damaged, sometimes beyond repair.

Heart chakra

I will come to chakras in chapter eleven, but it is worth touching on the heart chakra here as it is a useful way of conceptualising some of the ways we get blocked in life. Chakras are an ancient energy system. If the word 'chakra' is alienating, perhaps just think about the metaphorical heart area. We have probably all experienced an ache in that part of the body when we have been emotionally hurt. And equally may have experienced a hardening of the body in that area when we get defensive or angry. These are the energies I am referring to. Having that framework in mind can help to soften the body and transform the feeling being held in that area of the body. The body is giving you vital information with these sensations which is an invaluable non-verbal form of wisdom.

I find these ideas of great use clinically too. There are times when I will explore where feelings are held in the body and this not only helps bring them into awareness, but helps us understand how and where the body is holding these feelings or emotions which has great psychological significance. If energy is stuck in the throat, there is often something unsaid. If it is held in the chest, breathing will be shallow and this indicates a blockage from a free flow of energy through all the deeper energy centres in the body preventing a person from experiencing a feeling more fully. If there is a blockage of energy in the heart area this will inform you of the nature of the issue more precisely. This clinical approach often unblocks an impasse and frees a person up to engage with a feeling more fully and experience greater access to their whole range of emotional affects.

There are some who would regard talk of the heart as belonging to 'the feminine' which I emphatically want to avoid. I see no need to limit us to such thinking, even though 'the feminine' can be conceptualised as being available to all genders. The heart energies I am referring to are accessible equally by all. Although culturally it has been more acceptable for women and girls to be in touch with their emotions, thank goodness the dial has shifted and it is becoming increasingly ordinary for all members of society to reveal vulnerability. We do not have to be ashamed of having a heart!

The heart is a tender organ which needs regular care and protection. If it gets clogged up with brooding hatred or venom or holds grudges, it can make life very uncomfortable and unpleasant. Alongside a psychological approach, heightening attention to these energetic blockages can clear the way for greater joy and love and peace.

I want to express my hesitation in writing that last sentence as it makes me feel quite vulnerable and I fear being regarded as soppy, naïve, a hippie or unserious! It is interesting, I find, that articulating these sentiments seems less acceptable than talking about, say, hatred and envy and anger. Is there something culturally *verboten* about opening our soft hearts to these senti-ments, and do we thereby create a less loving society? Do we also thereby rob ourselves of embracing more love and joy in our lives? Perhaps – when we close down the channel to this source of knowledge – we also deprive ourselves of the wisdom our heart can impart to us.

References

Pilard, N. (2015) *Jung and Intuition: On the Centrality and Variety of Forms of Intuition in Jung and Post-Jungians.* London: Karnac Books.

Rumi, J. M. (1999) *Whispers of the Beloved.* (Trans. M. Mafi and A.M. Kolin). London: Thorsens.

Saint-Exupéry, A. (1943) (Trans. R. Howard) *The Little Prince.* London: Egmont, (2005).

Shen, H. (2022) "Civilization within the Heart: the Image and Meaning of 'Civilisation' and 'Culture' in Chinese Characters" in *Journal of Analytical Psychology* 67(1): 306–316.

Williams, R. (2019) *Jung: The Basics.* London and New York: Routledge.

Chapter 5

What is the goal of life? What is the point?

My chapter title is deliberately on the depressive side. These are questions most people will ask themselves at some point during their lives and a meaning does need to be found if we are to experience life as having purpose; if we are to find some sense of our place in the scheme of things, and to experience life as fulfilling and worthwhile.

Let us begin by laying out some of the goals people tend to aspire to:

- Having children/creating a family
- Finding love
- Personal/career ambition
- Duty
- Acquisition of wealth and power
- Political change
- Sporting or artistic endeavour

For some, the purpose is to get through this life to what they see as 'a better place'.

For Jung, religion plays a central role in the psyche. He was interested in life in the broadest possible terms incorporating ideas from science, philosophy, mythology, alchemy, mysticism, Gnosticism, religion as well as psychology. His take on psyche encompassed the deepest realms including soul and spirit. He saw religion as an archetypal impulse.

Religious perspectives

In Hinduism there are four Purusharthas (goals or objects of human pursuit):

- Artha (prosperity)
- Kama (pleasure, love)
- Dharma (righteousness, or moral values), and
- Moksha (liberation/spiritual values)

DOI: 10.4324/9781003284550-8

Buddhists believe that human life is a cycle of suffering and rebirth, and if one achieves a state of enlightenment (nirvana), it is possible to escape this cycle. In Buddhism there are four universal noble truths, which may be considered more as guiding principles than goals:

1   All beings experience pain and misery (dukkha) during their lifetime: *"Birth is pain, old age is pain, sickness is pain, death is pain; sorrow, grief and anxiety is pain. Contact with the unpleasant is pain. Separating from the pleasant is pain. Not getting what one wants is pain. In short, the five assemblies of mind and matter that are subject to attachment are pain".*
2   The origin (samudaya) of pain and misery is due to a specific cause: *"It is the desire that leads to rebirth, accompanied by pleasure and passion, seeking pleasure here and there; that is, the desire for pleasures, the desire for existence, the desire for non-existence".*
3   The cessation (nirodha) of pain and misery can be achieved as follows: *"With the complete non-passion and cessation of this very desire, with its abandonment and renunciation, with its liberation and detachment from it."*
4   The method we must follow to stop pain and misery is that of the Noble Eightfold Path.

The Noble Eightfold Path enables us to overcome our egocentricity, feel greater harmony with the world around us and eventually eliminate the pain we often experience. In this path, the Wheel, symbol of Dhamma, is presented with eight rays depicting the following eight principles:

1   Right View
2   Right Thought
3   Right Speech
4   Right Action
5   Right Livelihood
6   Right Effort
7   Right Mindfulness
8   Right Concentration

(See: https://www.theravada.gr/en/about-buddhism/the-four-noble-truths/ and https://www.theravada.gr/en/about-buddhism/the-noble-eightfold-path/ accessed 18th April 2022.)

In Islam, the purpose of creation for all men and women is to know and worship God.

For Muslims, 'purpose' in life is seen as a test to identify those that accomplish those two goals. Muslims believe that God's guidance was revealed to many prophets across time (Abraham, Moses and Jesus) and it reached its apotheosis with the 'last Messenger', Mohammad. Islam teaches there is life after death. We will all then be judged by God on how well a person worshipped and obeyed God, and how well the guidance God gave to Mohammad was followed.

Judaism dates back four thousand years making it the oldest monotheism. The goal of Orthodox Jewish life is to embody Torah (the scrolls which contain the first five books of the Hebrew Bible, or the Five Books of Moses). Jews believe there is nothing a human being can do for God, as God – being infinite – has no needs; God is the provider of all. Judaism is matrilineal, meaning it runs through the maternal line. (Although the Reform school – non-Orthodox- allows for patrilineal descent and considers people Jewish even if only the father is Jewish.) One of the highest values in Judaism is pleasure and the ultimate is seen as being pleasure in the connection to God. An important tenet in Judaism is *Tikkun Olam*, which (in Hebrew) means healing/repairing the world.

All of these have validity. Let us dig down though.

Goals

When I refer to goals in life, I am including purpose. What was the purpose of you being incarnated into life, at this time, in this body, in this place, in this family? Might your individual incarnation be for some evolutionary purpose in the development of your soul or the world? Was it to rush around like a blue arsed fly getting to appointments and becoming frazzled? Was it to please people, or meet deadlines? I don't think so!

The most universal goal of existence is having children and passing on our genes. Leaving children in the world when we die can feel like a form of immortality in that we know something of our make-up continues after we die. For others that sense of continuity may be found in leaving a business behind, or project, legacy or book, for instance. In modern times we have been able to name stars after our loved ones which will remain shining for all eternity (at least as long as the universe survives!)

Is this enough? Some people content themselves with less than others. (I will leave aside social/political/class aspects to that notion in this context although clearly these factors are significant.) We all have varying capacities, potentials and different tasks to fulfil in life. Your goal may be experienced as an urgent need, a background beat, or perhaps not at all. We need to discover meaning to life in our own ways; to hear the call of our souls. This is the path of individuation, as Jung put it, discovering our own purpose in this life; the manifesting of each person's unique 'genius'. Some believe we arrive on earth with a purpose already coded into our being. I do not mean such tasks are pre-ordained (although I do believe Karma has a role here). We have different stories to live out. Although if you think about prodigies, for instance, there is a sense that their destiny was inevitable. That said, their potential has to be encouraged, nurtured and be enacted. If Mr Mozart had sent his son down the mines, we may never have known about little Amadeus. At least, would we? A question to contemplate.

One example which might flesh out the idea that we have tasks in life we must deal with, is that trauma often passes down through the generations when it has not been possible for a trauma to be faced by the original 'victim'. The task is therefore left to subsequent generations to deal with. (It is debateable whether that might be seen as a task in the sense I am intending, or whether this is a problem being kicked down the line to be dealt with by subsequent generations. This is a distinction which needs to be borne in mind.) I am most familiar with Holocaust trauma which is currently in the fourth generation. Some people have been able to process that trauma more fully than others; some not at all. I have a dear family friend who has made it her purpose in life to educate children in schools about the reality of the Shoah from her first-hand accounts and that has partly been her way of coping with the trauma in an attempt to avoid unconsciously bequeathing the story – the patterns of behaviour, the corporeal experience held in the body and mind – to her descendants. Primo Levi (1919–1987) famously survived Auschwitz only to commit suicide in later life (probably). Events such as he and all the survivors endured leave life-long scars.

Murray Stein reflects on some of these questions:

> Initiations by the spirit introduce and induce people into a new kind of consciousness that answers questions related to a sense of identity and consequently lead to meaningful action. In contrast to initiations that are sponsored by and dedicated to the social world – baptisms, bar mitzvahs, weddings etc – which answer questions about who one is with respect to one's community and one's social location, initiations into the spiritual world tell of why one was born and of a destiny for one's unique life. The questions answered here are not "Who am I?" or "What is my name", or "Where do I stand in relation to other people?". They are rather: "What is the meaning of my life from the perspective of Divinity?" "What is my destiny?" The result of receiving an initiation in the spiritual vertex is a sense of transcendence and "gnosis", which is a type of knowledge that is rooted in the archetypal world. This is not rational knowledge. It is noetic (from the Greek *nous*), which means that it is derived from what Aristotle called "something within ... that is divine" and that therefore partakes of eternity.
>
> (2014 pp. 79)

We can all see when someone was born for a purpose, when they have a special gift. It brings about a wry smile. It is joyful to witness someone living out their destiny. Their talents or gifts shine out.

In contrast, when someone is floundering to find a real purpose, their life can seem quite empty. They might intuit something is not right, but feel helpless to know how to resolve this dis-ease. Loss of meaning, having no spiritual or soulful connection to deeper levels within, can lead to a sense of disenchantment or even depression. These are matters where therapy and analysis can help if the person is open to the possibility of change and able to do the emotional and spiritual graft. No one has an easy ride in life and it is often a battle to fulfil our potential and achieve the goals we need to reach in life. Embracing life means both wanted and unwanted aspects which not everyone can face. The twists and turns constantly force us to test our commitment, our resilience in the face of obstacles and to find the strength to go forward towards our aims. This is an archetypal quest.

Cupid and Psyche

The story of Cupid and Psyche comes to mind in which, after Psyche loses her beloved Cupid following an act of disobedience or failure of trust, Psyche must go through a series of trials before she is able to reunite with Cupid for all eternity. Psyche had been forced to only meet with her husband at night when his apparently 'ugly' face was obscured by darkness. Convinced by her envious sisters that he was a monster who would murder her, Psyche takes a knife in one hand and an oil lamp in the other to kill him. The lamp reveals her husband to be beautiful but, no sooner has she seen his face, then he is awakened by oil from her lamp dripping on his face. He flees telling her she has betrayed his trust. After searching high and low for Cupid, Psyche begs Aphrodite (Cupid's mother) to see Cupid who had been imprisoned in Aphrodite's Palace. Aphrodite sets Psyche four impossible tasks to prove her love. She had to sort grain from seeds; gather some fleece and collect water from the River Styx (with each of which task she was magically helped). These initial tasks done, Psyche was sent to Hades to bring back a box with the elixir of beauty for Aphrodite, who ordered Psyche not to open the box. Instead of the elixir, there was Morpheus (the god of sleep and dreams) hiding in the box and, since Psyche could not resist opening the box, she fell into a slumber. Upon discovering what had happened Cupid ran away from the Palace and begged Zeus to save Psyche. Touched by their plight, Zeus made Psyche immortal so that the two lovers could remain together in all eternity. (The story is contained in the second century Roman novel, *The Golden Ass* by Lucius Apuleius Madaura (1995).

Stacey Shelby, a Canadian Jungian psychotherapist who is on the faculty at Pacifica Graduate Institute in California which specialises in mythological approaches to depth psychology, writes about this myth and has devised various imaginative exercises to play with the idea of the tasks Psyche is set (2022 pp. 61, 87, 159, 180). These could be reflected upon alone, through journaling, or with others in dialogue if you are reading together in a book group. (I would encourage you to read the text in full to more deeply engage with the myth rather than skipping to the exercises as you will gain more from this.) This might help you identify the purposive nature of such tasks, or challenges.

The myth of Cupid and Psyche is a story about the growth and development of soul as Psyche grapples with the vagaries of life. Shelby sees this as the foundational myth of the human experience and most particularly for the field of psychology (the study of the soul) (ibid.). I think it is a tale many of us can relate to as we encounter life's many challenges.

Clinical vignette

The danger of not finding your own purpose in life may be seen from a clinical account. It is a contemporary story with affects and ramifications of archetypal proportions. This is the tale of a sister who was so consumed with envy and hatred of her sibling that she devoured the sibling with catastrophic consequences for all concerned, including herself. I will call the sisters Raquel and Stella. Raquel was the older sister and really never got over the fact that Stella was born. In early life this manifested in relatively innocuous ways, but in adulthood it became increasingly toxic and – swept along by a malignant narcissistic personality disorder – took on very damaging characteristics. Stella managed, through graft, commitment and enormous determination, to carve out a good life and found a true vocation. This could not be borne by Raquel who tried to follow in her younger sibling's footsteps to join the same profession (acting upon her uncontainable envy). But, because it was not Raquel's true path in life, her life soured and she could not manifest the same success and sense of satisfaction that she was trying to emulate. She simply was not following her own star. How very different life would have been for all concerned if Raquel had been able to find her own path. She became increasingly embittered and hateful and acted this out in seriously destructive ways for all those around her, including her children. When the true gifts we all possess are not found in life, they wither and become a curse. We are constantly chasing our tail knowing that our authentic purpose has not been found; frustrated in not finding what makes us tick; what truly makes life feel right. This is most often quite unconscious but nevertheless has a profound impact on our lives and those of others around us. Nothing is ever quite right. This can easily become projected out onto others rather than looking in the mirror and seeing what is amiss.

This example perhaps illustrates the futility of comparing oneself with others or feeling envious and competitive of other people's achievements. Our focus is better spent aligning to our own purpose and fostering our own potential. It is by doing this that we stand a chance of walking in our own shoes and finding the fulfilment in life we all need, more aligned to our own personal path or destiny.

Accepting the inevitability of the finitude of life and making sure we live as good a life (however defined) as possible, before we reach the exit we must pass through where death escorts us as we leave this life, is crucial to living a full and satisfying life while we are here. If we do not show up for life while we have this precious chance, what a sad and empty ending it may be. No one wants to arrive at their death bed feeling the opportunity to live more fully had been missed. Courage and determined effort are needed to incarnate our potential. We have this opportunity. Let's not mistake the empty fripperies this world holds out to us as anything more than they are. We need to take the opportunity life is offering for greater fulfilment and wholeness with both hands if we are to live our fullest potential and ensure our life has meaning and purpose; if we are to live from love and not fear or anxiety; or hatred and envy as in the case mentioned above. We all have the potential to do more than that. Our souls are guiding us and helping us reach that potential if we can only tune in to that call.

References

Apuleius Madaura, L. (1995) *The Golden Ass.* Oxford and New York: Oxford University Press.

Shelby, S. (2022) *Love and Soul-Making: Searching the Depths of Romantic Love.* Asheville, North Carolina: Chiron Publications.

Stein, M. (2014) *Minding the Self: Jungian Meditations on Contemporary Spirituality.* London and New York: Routledge.

Chapter 6

Ethics and integrity

Ethics and integrity often sit alongside morality with which I am not concerned here. Morality judges rightness and wrongness in personal values. It is concerned with virtue and purity or sanctity. Although morals are often applied collectively to groups, as in a religious context, they concern a person's inner mores. Law is different again from morality in that it has explicit written rules with penalties.

Ethics relate to codes of practice or behaviour, being concerned with matters of principle where there might be a view about sexual mores, professional practice and financial probity.

A distinction between morals and ethics might be goodness (morals) v. rightness (ethics). As a non-philosopher I am not qualified to delve too deeply into the intricate origins of each and that is in any case beyond the scope of this study.

This chapter is about living with personal integrity, albeit this might be in relation to external factors. Integrity is a key quality in living a life based on spiritual foundations (see also Young-Eisendrath and Miller 2000). It is related to aligning to our authentic path, about personal individuation, about having a clear conscience and so living at ease with ourselves, our 'God', and others.

It is important to avoid simple platitudes, as if there were some equivalence between 'behaving with ethics and integrity' and things going well in life. Life is more complicated than that and there are no prizes for good behaviour! When justice seems to evade us, perhaps a new paradigm needs to be found as karma is not always instantly apparent. It can take long periods for things to turn 'right', if they do at all within our limited perspective and even within our life span. We do not always know why things happen and why someone benefits when they seem so apparently undeserving. But clinging to a righteous outcome can make a person bitter. Byron Katie (whose work I do not in general admire) has a snappy aphorism: "There is 'my business', 'your business', and 'God's business'" (Mitchell 2022) and pondering on this can be useful at a time when you are wondering why someone is not being punished for a misdeed. Not our business!

DOI: 10.4324/9781003284550-9

Bad things happen to 'good' people. People maim and hurt each other; unethical people profit; criminals get away with it. But who are we to judge the outcome of events which are beyond our ken? A spiritual path has no notion of sin. There is no moral imperative; no punishment. Heaven and hell exist right here on earth.

We simply have to mind 'our business', do our best and strive to live with a clear conscience if we want to live at ease and in tune with universal, spiritual values.

We are often tested on these boundaries when temptation knocks on the door. Am I going to kiss someone's boyfriend/girlfriend; or have an affair? (Even if no one would ever find out?!) The temptation can be overwhelming and the internal dialogue convincing. Or, when we are given too much money in change in a shop. Do you give it back? (I've noticed how, when I am happy and breezy, I will automatically hand the money back. But, if I'm feeling grumpy and hard done by, will I be as scrupulous?) If a footballer knows the referee is not looking, can s/he get away with a foul? If you scrape someone's car, do you leave a note? (In London the answer to that last point is generally no!)

We know in our bones when something is honest or appropriate. These are the ways in which our moral and ethical compass can be read. Every child has an innate key into integrity. They know the difference between right and wrong. I always remember when I was perhaps four years old, I was playing with a little girl who lived nearby, and I stole a small monkey made of pipe cleaners which belonged to her. It was a random, spontaneous act which I got away with. I never heard anything more about it. The little girl may never even have noticed. But I always remembered what it felt like to steal and it was not good. It left me with a sense of guilt and shame which was uncomfortable and which I have never forgotten. Our inner compass informs us when we are acting with integrity, or not.

Another central learning for me about integrity was when I was perhaps ten years old. My father had discovered a man he knew had been dishonest in business, perhaps even criminal, and when my father confronted him about it, my father was offered advancement to keep it quiet. I felt such pride and admiration that he chose to walk away from the situation and sacrificed material gain he could probably have really used rather than collude with the misdeed. He did not want to be tainted by the other man's dishonesty or become complicit in it. That taught me what integrity means.

There is a link between integrity and shame. In the UK we are currently being ruled by a government which has no moral compass. (Other countries have their own examples (see Lee 2017)). Its leader (at the time of writing) is renowned for his lack of integrity and his indifference to blatant, pathological lying both in public and in private. (His philandering is public knowledge.) In the example about the monkey I stole as a child, I automatically felt ashamed. But I would suggest that linkage is broken in the case of narcissistic individuals who believe in their own arrogant exceptionalism. There is no shame, and therefore no problem in lying or perpetrating dishonest acts. This can feel quite disturbing to the onlooker. Robert Lifton in the United States, writing about the Trump phenomenon, called this atmosphere "malignant normality" (2017 pp. xv).

Acting with a lack of integrity or ethics could be construed as being possessed by what Jung called the Shadow which is "the thing a person has no wish to be" (1946 par.470). And yet we so easily slip into or become unconsciously caught by such a dynamic. It is the human plight to have to grapple with these ethical dilemmas.

John Beebe, in his virtuoso *Integrity in Depth* (1922), suggests it is important to embrace shame when we are at fault since this links integrity to Shadow. He posits there are stages of integrity, advancing the relation to the Shadow. This begins with denial, moving to acceptance of Shadow, with a final stage where there is: "a sense of restored wholeness once the "full disclosure" of the shadow has been integrated" (1992 pp. 61). He goes on: "We are still in the process of learning that integrity is achieved by an openness to the impure on the one hand and a participation in the pure on the other and that we cannot afford to leave out either pole" (ibid. pp. 69). There needs to be a dialectical flow between erring and repairing to restore a sense of integrity. Taking responsibility for our failings, for our Shadow, is an act of integrity.

Secrets bring up these considerations. In general, I am averse to having secrets as they are a form of deceit I prefer to avoid. This is in stark contrast to discretion or confidentiality with which I have no problem. But by their very nature secrets are hidden and intended to deceive another. They are intrinsically dishonest. Only something devious or unwanted needs to be hidden, on the whole. They may be intended to protect another, I realise. But is this not deferring the wound or harm which will result when the secret becomes known, as they almost always do? Secrets are generally kept if it is obvious it will hurt the person from whom it is hidden. A 'white lie' is usually seen as a kindness. A pleasant surprise is something different again.

Ethical dilemmas in analysis

Ethics and integrity are the everyday fare of psychotherapy and analysis. I relish these conundrums when they arise as they make you reflect deeply and explore unexpected pockets which may mean scrutinising your conscience or own sense of integrity and ethical boundaries.

The issue of integrity in analytic work often arises around money. The subject of money is there from the very outset when a fee is agreed. I deliberately do not display my fee publicly on my website because, for me, it is part of an analytic conversation where we will agree a fee that is fair to both parties. This will likely touch on deeply personal matters needing sensitivity to potential feelings of shame which can arise in discussing money and thus requires integrity on both sides.

Recently I had an instance of a patient telling me I had under-charged two sessions. This communication contained a plethora of messages: about the good esteem between us, that he wanted to ensure I was not underpaid, that he was a person of integrity who did not want to 'get away' with under-paying on account of my mistake. It felt good that he was honest.

Ethical questions arise around titles and qualifications. I recently came to know of a case where a therapist was behaving unscrupulously, but he was not a member of any professional body where he could be held to account. (In the UK there is currently no statutory regulation of psychotherapy and psychoanalysis although the majority of practitioners belong to accrediting bodies who have rigorous standards and manage complaints.)

The field of training of therapists and analysts is rife with dilemmas in-volving integrity and ethical considerations, not least of all in the decision whether someone qualifies. I have been involved in the training of therapists in a wide range of organisations and a problem which has arisen in every one of them is the difficulty of pulling the plug on someone's training and the right moment when this may be done. In a number of cases the decision has been kicked down the track in the hope that something will change, and then the person is so far into the course that it becomes ever more difficult to challenge their suitability. This is a genuine problem but one which it is vital to face. The fact is that some people get through trainings who are not suitable or ready to qualify. This is a failure of integrity on the part of the trainings. The courage to challenge suitability is an absolute necessity and it does the trainee no favours to allow them to progress into a profession for which they are not suited or ready.

I will not expand further on professional concerns with ethics and in-tegrity – a vast field – because my focus here is on these areas in a more general sense.

In personal relationships

Integrity arises in personal relationships all the time. At one end of the spectrum it might be a matter of parity in undertaking household chores; at the other, marital fidelity. How we navigate these issues is the test of any relationship. Do we keep our promises? Are we transparent about our spending? Do we want to be together? If someone catches our eye at a party, do we hold their gaze and flirt (when you know your partner is not watching)? Do you pretend to be asleep? Do you always answer the phone? Were you really apologising, or holding something back you thought you could get away with? Did your apology come from a sense of true regret? Did it come from your depths? These dilemmas arise constantly, requiring us to exercise ethical judgements, to have scruples, and to check our sense of integrity.

Scrutinising ourselves for integrity and honesty is a spiritual act. If our relationships are to have depth and meaning, they need to contain a spiritual or soulful component. These elements bind us at deep levels which can make for rich and satisfying connections in which mistakes and flaws can be managed.

References

Beebe, J. (1992) *Integrity in Depth*. College Station: Texas A&M University Press.

Jung, C.G. (1946) *The Psychology of the Transference* in CW16.

Lee, B. (Ed.) (2017) *The Dangerous Case of Donald Trump*. New York: St Martin's Press.

Lifton, R. (2017) "Foreword: Our Witness to Malignant Normality" in *The Dangerous Case of Donald Trump* (Ed.Lee). New York: St Martin's Press.

Mitchell, B.K. (2022) *Loving What Is: Four Questions That Can Change Your Life*. London: Rider.

Young-Eisendrath, P. and Miller, M. (2000) *The Psychology of Mature Spirituality: Integrity, Wisdom, Transcendence*. London and New York: Routledge.

Chapter 7

Peace, clarity, joy and kindness. A clear conscience

We now move on to clear a space for peace, clarity, joy and kindness. Let's take a moment to just sit with that idea. [Seriously, pause.] It's like drinking a cool glass of iced water on a hot day. This is the stuff that can sometimes feel so unreachable. Other priorities so often take precedence. And yet, what could be more important? (The rebuttal that maybe jumped into your mind immediately when I asked that, is I guess the thing(s) that keeps you from feeling the good stuff!)

> **Question:** When did you last feel peace, clarity, joy or kindness?
> If you're reading this in a book group, try sharing your replies.
> If not, perhaps jot down your answers.

According to the *I Ching,* (of which more in chapter ten):

> In the sphere of human affairs, the condition of harmony assures good fortune, that of disharmony predicates misfortune.
>
> (Wilhelm 1951 pp. 283)

Joy

Joy, peace, clarity and kindness are all essential components of a harmonious existence and create the conditions for greater wellbeing on the levels of mind, body, soul and spirit.

Joy, like peace, cannot be created. It needs to be discovered as they (or their potential) both reside within us already. They bloom when you are able to experience them. Not when the right man or woman comes along, or the coffers are brimming. But when the heart is full. It is difficult not to sound cheesy when talking about these subjects and 'sophisticated' people

DOI: 10.4324/9781003284550-10

tend to denigrate such feelings as simple. But, to me, simple is a treasure to be tended.

Our nature is to be in joy, in peace, kindness and clarity. If you look at a baby (who has been well cared for and whose physical needs are being met) it shines out brightly. This is partly why we love babies and are attracted to them. We love that simple, pure joy they exude.

In adulthood we often only feel these tender emotions in intimate play or when we are surrounded by those with whom we feel most safe. We don't want to look foolish or naïve! Only children feel joy with abandon, surely! We learn to create a carapace to protect ourselves from the embarrassment or shame of these feelings, and the tragedy is that it blocks the connection with these feelings, making them more difficult to acknowledge even within our own minds. Cynicism is seen as more realistic and mature; even 'cool' and urbane.

For some joy is accessed through music or dance, both great ways to tap into the experience. Or singing; perhaps especially singing with others. Or through ecstatic sex. Intimacy is certainly an important ingredient. Sport is an everyday experience which has a joyful, spiritual potential. If you look at a crowd watching sport, it is clear there is a dimension to it which can be ecstatic. Just as you might feel at a rock gig. There is a surrender of the personal ego to the collective ecstasy of the moment. Or you might experience joy all alone in a garden smelling a flower. In the Coronavirus pandemic my first outing back into the world was a trip to the sea which brought joyful tears to my eyes. The simple pleasure of feeling the salty water on my bare feet and seeing a wide expanse of horizon before my eyes was absolutely joyous after having been cooped up in lockdown.

Of course, experiencing joy – as simple as that may sound – is certainly not so easily attainable. A patient who comes to mind frequently had a rather dour exterior. She struggled with enormous darkness and was troubled in relationships with envy (in both directions) and hatred. Yet, when she practiced her art, joy bubbled to the surface in passionate surges revealing a deep, joyful heart. (This is an example of someone's light being their Shadow.)

In their *Book of Joy* (Lama, Tutu *et al* 2016) which recounts the story of a week-long series of dialogues on joy between the Dalai Lama and Archbishop Desmond Tutu, two great men, which took place in Dharamsala in India (the Dalai Lama's home), they identify eight pillars of joy:

- Perspective
- Humility
- Humour
- Acceptance

- Forgiveness
- Gratitude
- Compassion
- Generosity

Some of these I have already touched on in previous chapters as vital components of a spiritual approach. Some we may see as aspirational; others more readily accessible. Each of these pillars contribute to a harmonious existence if we can truly experience them. And that is sometimes hard work. In the face of the vicissitudes of life, it is not always easy to gravitate towards such noble sentiments. And the writers do not sidestep the obstacles that prevent us from experiencing joy. Facing adversities is an inescapable part of life. Compassion, for instance, is not simple kindness or do-gooding; its meaning is actually to suffer alongside another. These are deep concepts. You may find it useful to spend time meditating on each of them, or even one of them, to expand on their meaning for you. This could take the form of writing, dialoguing or using art materials. (This does not require any artistic skills! The idea is not to produce an aesthetic object, but rather to express and examine something for yourself.) This exploration might draw out how you relate to these both as an individual as well as in your family or relationships. You might even find it useful to dialogue with your family or those you are in relationships with by drawing together. If you take a piece of paper and put marks on it in turn, it can be interesting to see how you relate to each other on the page. Does it become competitive? Is it a struggle? Is there a flow between the shapes on the page and a fluidity in the interaction? Does it feel like play, or battle? This can draw out the dynamic between the parties cooperating together (or not!) in such an exercise.

The *Book of Joy* ends with a section called "Joy Practices" which sets out a whole series of exercises or experiments to help us cultivate a relationship with joy. It recommends morning intention setting, looking at how to overcome the obstacles to joy, and meditations on the eight pillars of joy set out above (2016 pp. 307–348).

"Ultimately", they tell us, "joy is not something to learn, it is something to live. And our greatest joy is lived in deep, loving, and generous relationships with others" (Lama *et al* 2016 pp. 348).

Peace, clarity and kindness

Of course, much of what I am saying here can be applied equally to the other notions included in the title of this chapter: Peace, clarity and kindness. The experience of each of these tenderises our hearts, making it a soft, open and alive organ (which of course I mean metaphorically although it would be an interesting piece of research to explore how the softness of the metaphorical heart corresponds to the physical organ. Surely there must be a correlation between mental and physical health in such ways).

Peace might sound like an old-fashioned hippy idea. And yet, do we not all need to feel peace in life, as well as clarity and kindness? These are simple ideas, which are each of such profound necessity to a life lived well and in which we can foster good relationships with others. Without them, we are restless and cannot function harmoniously. Without clarity we do not know; we live in a fog and cannot see our way in life. Without clarity we are confused which steals our peace. Clarity is like being awake; acting consciously which tends to mean doing less harm. Clearing the mind of intrusive thoughts is something we all need to do at times during the day to focus on what is important. It helps us think straight and therefore to act with greater integrity; with more intention and care. I think of a newly washed glass. If you run your finger around the rim of a newly washed glass it creates a vibration, a ringing tone like a Himalayan singing bowl; something akin to the vibrant clarity we can experience when we feel attuned to our own inner integrity which you might experience as a sharpness of mind or being centred. In Chinese philosophy this would be seen as being in *Tao*.

Peace is not only an idea which links to notions of living harmoniously with others externally. I am not focussing here on the absence of war or conflict. My concern here though is rather on inner peace. About achieving a level of tranquillity within, even when there is outer – or inner – turmoil. If we were to wait for world peace, we might sadly never find ourselves achieving inner harmony. Problems will never go away. Therefore, we need to find a way of living well alongside difficulties and challenges. They cannot be an insurmountable block to peace. Global Peace Ambassador, Prem Rawat, states: "My commitment is to peace. ... Peace is a real thing. Peace resides in the heart of every human being" (See https://www.wopg.org/about/ accessed online 4th September 2020). Rawat runs a Peace Education Programme in over 70 countries where modules (available for free) look at peace, appreciation, inner strength, self-awareness, clarity, understanding, dignity, choice, hope, and contentment.

In nineteen eighty-one an International Day of Peace was established by the United Nations General Assembly and which is marked on 21st September each year. Two decades later, in two thousand and one, the UN General Assembly declared this as an annual day devoted to strengthening the ideals of peace, through observing twenty-four hours of non-violence and cease-fire around the globe.

Kindness

I am writing this during the Coronavirus pandemic (where the act of breathing itself has been so challenged). One thing I have noticed is that, amongst many other ghastly things, these events seem to be eliciting kindness in some of us. Facing crises and tragedy can sometimes put us in touch with our tenderness which is where kindness lives. This is such a seemingly mundane quality, and yet it can also be healing and affecting in the most profound ways. It's a paradox, isn't it, that kindness (like love) is one of those things that you can give to your utmost, and still be full of it.

There is even evidence which suggests helping others – being kind – can promote physiological changes in the brain linked with happiness (Post 2014 2:1–53). Kindness and other facets of happiness are deeply connected to the achievement of good mental health.

Plato is reported to have said: "*Be kind, for everyone you meet is fighting a hard battle*". Not a bad adage to hold in mind.

Even when it seems mad … .

There was a point in life when I was suffering under enormous duress from a psychic attack. I tried everything and naturally the more I engaged with it, it simply fed the energy of the problem which made it more intransigent and unbearable. Then one day as I was idly looking at my computer, I came upon a talk by William Bloom who is a leading figure in Glastonbury. (See https://www.youtube.com/watch?v=j8HxnRi6EpU accessed 3rd September 2020.) I began listening and for the most part it was all fairly familiar fare about psychic protection. But then a particular phrase jumped out at me where he talked about someone being in a situation just like my own. My ears pricked up. What he suggested was that, when you are in a situation that seems completely intractable, try taking responsibility (even if you are not the party responsible for the injury). You are the person who is able on a universal level to take responsibility; you are the one who is suffering. "It's my responsibility", you might reflect. You might wonder if something deep within your soul has attracted this circumstance or person towards you. Give up your sorrow to the universe. There is no shame; no guilt. Ask for forgiveness, he suggested. You are experiencing this situation as there is a lesson for you to learn. Send the person love! Unconditional love. Yeh, right, you might think! This sounds utterly bonkers and counter-intuitive. But I did try this. I went and lay down quietly and genuinely – with all my heart – I sent love to the person who was doing me harm. And, honestly, I can say it was quite transformative. This is a sort of Buddhist practice. Obviously, these things only work if they are approached with genuine sincerity. But work they can do. (William Bloom has many lectures available on YouTube and has written a number of books on spirituality and psychic protection.)

Kindness cannot be hidden behind or it can become a form of denial. There are some who believe you can meditate your way out of 'bad' feelings. Others tend to the view that feelings need to be authentically expressed in order to clear them out of the system in order to move on. I had an example of this dilemma recently when someone wrote to me on a public discussion group online accusing me of something terrible which was completely untrue. I knew that she was elderly and must have been confused, but was so horrified at my reputation being traduced, so I responded initially in a way that felt a little harsh asking her to withdraw her accusation. Overnight this was playing on my mind and I was not sure what to do. Rousing from a brief nap the next day, my mind was clear and I simply knew I needed to contact her. So, I wrote to her privately asking how she was, saying no harm had been done and wishing her well. I had re-found my kindness and was able to communicate from the heart. And happily this dissolved the matter which I believe left us both feeling relieved. This little anecdote demonstrates how none of us are saints, but with a soft heart which is amenable to change, our spiritual nature can guide us.

Conscience

In 2019 the United Nations General Assembly declared 5th April the International Day of Conscience. The preamble to the UN's Universal Declaration of Human Rights states that:

> disregard and contempt for human rights have resulted in barbarous acts which have outraged the conscience of humankind, and the advent of a world in which human beings shall enjoy freedom of speech and belief and freedom from fear and want has been proclaimed as the highest aspiration of the common people.

Article one of the Declaration states that "all human beings are born free and equal in dignity and rights and are endowed with reason and conscience and should act towards one another in a spirit of brotherhood" (see https://www.un.org/en/observances/conscience-day accessed online 4th September 2020).

In announcing this International Day of Conscience, Dr Hong, Tao-Tze, President of the Federation of World Peace and Love, stated:

> Conscience is the wellspring of love; it is essential to awaken world citizens' conscience to promote love, tolerance, acceptance, and care among people, thus enhancing friendships, family bonds, and international relationships, which facilitates a united world, where all people work together for the common good.
>
> (See http://www.fowpal.org/Endorse/doidoc_endorse/index.php
> Accessed online 4th September 2020)

Conscience on a personal level is something we each have to grapple with each day. Some things pray on the mind over many years. A guilty or shameful act can leave a trail of unprocessed feelings over decades and the ramifications can even travel through the generations.

Conscience is partly connected to the notions of forgiveness and atonement making it difficult to talk about one without the other. Atonement is a precious but rare occurrence in my experience. If you have acted in bad faith, consciously or unconsciously, atoning is the way to clear your conscience. It is then for the person you have harmed to offer forgiveness, or not.

Repentance (being contrite and feeling regretful) is a necessary first step in the process of having a conscience, of atonement and the establishment of penitence. Only when this has occurred can reconciliation (an attitude of concern for the person who has been harmed) take place. The atonement then recognises the wound, creating scope for potential transformation. It requires facing what one has done, making it right, perhaps getting forgiveness. But what has been done can never not have been done.

Jung discusses conscience in a wonderfully evocative dream about a man with 'dirty hands' (1958 para. 826). The man's dirty hands in the dream point to an unconscious attitude about a moral dilemma regarding a dodgy business deal. Jung deduced from the dream that the man's 'bad conscience' is missing. Jung contrasts his own formulation with Freud's concept of the superego (which in Freudian language is the part of the psyche which judges and makes moral evaluations). He suggests that, because the dreamer did not recognise the dubious nature of the dilemma 'and therefore lacked any motive for repression' (ibid.: para 828), the idea of conscious repression could not apply. Atonement is a conscious humbling rather than a moral superego flagellation from 'on high'.

We know when we have done something 'wrong'. Our conscience tells us. There is a niggling discomfort in the back or the front of our minds until the situation is either pushed back into the unconscious, or the situation is put right. It might be an unduly strong word used, or outright criminal behaviour. Having no conscience is the sign of a sociopath or narcissist. I will restrain myself from naming any examples although I suspect we can all think of some!

There have been eras where atonement was common within cultures. For example, Marie-Louise von Franz (1915–1998) (leading contemporary of Jung who collaborated with Jung on his alchemical opus, and expert on fairy tales) informs us in ancient China synchronicity was routinely considered to aid understanding by for instance interpreting natural phenomena such as earthquakes as auguring well or ill. She tells us the emperor was responsible for harmony in nature and in society:

> If [the emperor] or his government deviated from Tao, heaven expressed its anger in the form of unusual phenomena. These were appropriately interpreted, and the ruler then had to atone for his past behaviour and change his ways.

(1993 p. 192)

Yom Kippur

Yom Kippur – the Day of Atonement – is the most sacred and solemn day in the Jewish calendar, ten days after Jewish New Year. This ten-day period is known as The Days of Repentance or Days of Awe. Yom Kippur is marked by fasting, abstaining from work, sex, washing, wearing of perfume and leather shoes (much like the Christian period of Lent). Yom Kippur is spent in continuous prayer for forgiveness. To truly engage with such a process has a transformative effect, although, as with all religious dogma, it can simply be treated as a ritualistic act.

An extract from a letter elucidates a modern/progressive interpretation of the Jewish Day of Atonement which is all about conscience:

> In the Jewish tradition, we say that the "book of life" is open ... till the end of Yom Kippur ... In that book of life our fate for the next year gets written and then at the end of Yom Kippur it is sealed. In *Tikkun* [a spiritual progressive community], we've transformed that imagery into a deep spiritual truth: we are taking a ten day period to examine what changes are needed in our lives, and how seriously we will take the (full year) process of making those changes. By condensing the period of heightened attention to ten days, we are making sure that we have a time when these issues are totally "front burner" in our consciousness. If we haven't been able to make any progress in self-awareness and steps toward change in those ten days, then in a certain sense our fate is sealed: we will continue to receive the karmic consequences of being the way that we are at the current moment, and to the extent that we want that to change, this ten day period becomes a spiritual retreat and intensive short-term psychotherapy to work out what we need to be.
>
> (letter from Rabbi Michael Lerner, Founding Editor of *Tikkun* magazine, sent 29th September 2006 via email)

Honesty

Without wishing to get into philosophical arguments about the nature of truth, I would raise the vexed matter of telling the truth. Of course there are times when it is kind to be 'economical' with the truth and protect people by being tactful. But doesn't it feel good to be honest and truthful? Only a naïve person would never lie. But there is a simplicity to living an honest life which keeps the conscience crystal clear.

References

Jung, C.G. (1958) "A Psychological View of Conscience" in CW10.

Lama, D., Tutu, D. (with Abrams, D.) (2016) *The Boy of Joy*. London: Hutchinson.

Post, S. (2014) "It's Good To Be Good: 2014 Biennial Scientific Report on Health, Happiness, Longevity, and Helping Others" *International Journal of Person Centred Medicine*.

Von Franz, M-L. (1993) *Projection and Re-collection in Jungian psychology: Reflections of the Soul*. La Salle & London: Open Court.

Wilhelm, R. (Trans) (1951) *The I Ching or Book of Changes*, (rendered into English by C.F. Baynes). London: Routledge & Kegan Paul.

Chapter 8

Suicide and depression

This chapter is in no way intended to be an exhaustive account of depression and suicide. These may seem like paradoxical topics to be covering in a book on spirituality, but do these matters not take us directly to some of the most urgent and profound questions about life we ever face? When swept up in depression or suicidal thoughts, we face philosophical and spiritual dilemmas as at no other time. In some ways I want to normalise these subjects as matters most people encounter at some juncture in life; when life itself loses meaning, or when there does not seem to be anyone to turn to. The road can seem to run out. Or things happen (possibly trauma, abuse or neglect) which just cannot be metabolised. These are the everyday fare of therapy and analysis. Talking about what can seem like taboo topics can be a help, and incorporating these understandings – perhaps alongside another human being - can enable one to embrace life more fully and authentically.

As Albert Camus put it in his masterful *Myth of Sisyphus,* "There is but one truly serious philosophical problem and that is suicide" (1942).

My first personal encounter with suicide – or at least an attempt – was when I was fifteen. A girl who had joined my school and with whom I had immediately become fast friends in the way teenagers can do, took an overdose and it was me she asked the hospital to contact. We had only been friends a short time so I was deeply shocked although honoured that she would turn to me in such a moment. This gave me a kind of responsibility that I was barely able to grasp at that age but perhaps inevitably led me to think deeply about how a person could be overwhelmed by life which became my soul's path.

James Hillman discusses the analyst's responsibilities when dealing with suicide and how it is important to fight the urge to stop the act at the expense of teasing out the meaning for the individual. (This is clearly no easy task when the analyst has to cope with her own anxieties about what may transpire, while constantly assessing the likelihood of the suicidal ideation becoming concretised.) The analyst must be vigilant to her own despair in the work with such a patient which may well mirror the patient's despair. These are the most difficult and fretful times in the work, in my experience.

DOI: 10.4324/9781003284550-11

Collegial support becomes vital, as will any other forms of support one can draw on.

A fine example of how the urge towards suicide was cut off at the pass by an act of grace in the form of a synchronicity (see Chapter thirteen) is in a work by Roderick Main (Professor of Analytical Psychology at the University of Essex and a world authority on synchronicity):

> An analyst on vacation suddenly had a strong visual impression of one of her patients she knew to be suicidal. Unable to account for the impression as having arisen by any normal chain of mental associations, she immediately sent a telegram telling the patient not to do anything foolish. Two days later she learned that, just before the telegram arrived, the patient had gone into the kitchen and turned on the gas valve with the intention of killing herself. Startled by the postman ringing the doorbell, she turned the valve off; and even more struck by the content of the telegram he delivered, she did not resume her attempt.
>
> (summarised from von Franz 1992: 24–25 quoted in Main 2007: 1–2)

It is impossible to explain such matters rationally. We can only be thankful that they occur. These occurrences often elicit a sense that there is a spiritual dimension to life and provide a sense of meaning. It might be the nugget of gold buried in the despair.

For some life is a gift; others a burden. Hope seems to be a decisive factor in being able to imagine a future worth living. Not banal positivity, or putting on a smiley face. But genuine faith that life may be worth living. Hope is such a common-or-garden idea, and yet without it, life becomes bleak. Mintz (quoted in Rosen) suggests that hope may provide suicide antibodies (Rosen 2002 pp. 43).

Making the choice to end your life is a momentous decision. It might be a way of taking agency when faced with a terminal illness; or indeed a way of protecting family members from the consequences of such a diagnosis. This could turn the event into a potentially loving action, although no one would want to simplify such a choice. Equally it can be an act of impotent rage to extract punishment on those who are to be left behind. I wonder how often there is a fantasy of "I'll show her/him/them!", as if there was a chance of witnessing the distress of the person finding the body, when of course the very act ends the possibility of fulfilling that desire? Having suicidal thoughts can both be distressing to experience and difficult to discuss as shame may be involved; or a sense of failure to be able to carry on. It can be frightening, not knowing if the impulse to act might overwhelm. Driving across a bridge or flyover can evoke fantasies, 'if I just turned the wheel … .'. This brings up the question of who is in charge, which can be difficult to ascertain in such an overwhelming state of mind and perhaps it is even harder to regain a sense of equilibrium, to calm down the nervous system and reassess when gripped by such powerful affects.

There are cases which are described as "suicide by cop" where – particularly in the United States where police and civilians are so heavily armed – people deliberately carry out an act to provoke a police officer into shooting them. This can be deeply traumatising for the shooter. It is similarly distressing for train drivers having to cope with people who jump onto the rails. These acts bring us face to face in the most horrific manner with grisly realities.

There are some who would suggest we do not have the right to end our own lives and this is 'God's business'. The same arguments are used at the other end of the spectrum when considering abortion and a woman's right to choose. These are complicated emotional and philosophical decisions about which we all need to come to our own conclusions.

Caroline Flack

In the UK there was a tragic tale in the news (15th February 2020) where a beautiful young woman who had found fame presenting so-called 'reality' shows on the television, committed suicide. Her position meant she was subjected to tremendous public scrutiny and lived out her ordinary domestic problems in the glare of the spotlight. Caroline Flack was her name and she was but forty years old. She – apparently - had everything in life that could be desired. But she – understandably - could not stand the shame of being publicly humiliated when she was up in court for allegedly assaulting her boyfriend. Shortly before she took her life (in December 2019) she had published an Instagram post which was widely publicised and which I found poignant and inspirational. She said:

In a world where you can be anything, be *kind* (emphasis added).

It is an irony, isn't it, that she took her life the day after Valentine's Day when there is such a frenzy of idealisation and the pressure to be in the 'perfect' relationship. I find this so sad. (For more on kindness, see chapter seven.)

In a note Flack wrote shortly before her suicide, she said:

For a lot of people, being arrested for common assault is an extreme way to have some sort of spiritual awakening ... I was arrested for common assault on my boyfriend ... Within 24 hours my whole world and future was swept from under my feet and all the walls that I had taken so long to build around me, collapsed. I've been having some sort of emotional breakdown for a very long time. But I am NOT a domestic abuser. We had an argument and an accident happened. An accident. The blood that someone SOLD to a newspaper was MY blood and that was something very sad and very personal ... . I'm so sorry to my family for what I have brought upon them and for what my friends have had to go through … . I'm not thinking about 'how I'm going to get my career back.' I'm thinking about how I'm going to get mine and my family's life back. I can't say any more than that.

(Eastern Daily Press 19th February 2020. See: https://www.edp24.co.uk/ news/caroline-flack-unpublished-instagram-post-she-wrote-before- death-1–6520870 accessed 13th October 2020)

It's terrible to imagine what must have been going through her mind to lead her to taking the ultimate step. It is the very cliff edge of despair and loss of hope in a potential future.

In a touching tribute to Flack, comedian Russell Brand (who has an interest in spirituality) has talked of having collated suicide notes from a number of souls who had made that choice for a monologue he performed entitled 'Verbatim Piece'. (This formed part of a series of monologues he curated for The Old Vic Theatre in London which explored mental health and addiction.) He said the writing of his monologue:

provided a blurred portal into the mind of the person that would go on to take their own life. I sensed a familiar resonance throughout these varied pieces, a common tune in the expression of these distinct people; it was 'ordinariness'. The ordinariness of the thoughts, feelings and events that led them to make the ultimate act of self sacrifice. … Normal feelings … I suspect we all feel at times. The line then that separates people who kill themselves and people that don't is vague and uncertain, it is a line within each of us, not between us.

(See: https://www.russellbrand.com/caroline-flack/ accessed 9th May 2022)

He went on: "I am angry and sad that Caroline Flack found herself in that place. I am sad because she was a lovely little person … and the idea that she had been so drained of hope by her circumstances chokes me. … I have resigned from fame because it brought out the worst in me, vanity, insecurity, jealousy, competitiveness. Most people I've spoken to have comparable experiences, it's hard to endure what celebrity does to your mental health without a robust constitution or strong counter measures to ground and protect you" (ibid.).

Brand then goes on to make the broader points:

While we are unique and different, beautiful in our vast and distinct identities – and all identities can be honoured, we are all capable of kindness, we are all capable of redemption, we are all worthy of love. Whenever we speak and act and relate we emanate intent through the invisible threads that connect us. … Caroline was surrounded by friends and families that loved her, that love her still through a shattered lens of anguish, and that love could not incubate her or protect her from the pain and shame that ended her life. We have the power to hurt one another and the power to heal one another, perhaps that's the only power we have (ibid.).

There is much to absorb and ponder on in what Brand writes which emanates deep empathy and understanding.

A place needs to be made for suffering. In the Introduction to this volume I mentioned the 'Wounded Healer' and how our damage can become the source of healing. We need to encounter suffering in life not only because it is inevitable, but also because it makes us richer and more three-dimensional human beings able to empathise. Suffering marinates the soul and creates resilience. How full of hubris we might be without suffering.

Alistair Campbell

In his new book, Alistair Campbell (2020) (who used to be Tony Blair's right hand man) speaks of his struggles with depression and suicidal ideation. Because of the necessity to protect patient material, Campbell's story provides a useful vantage point into an authentic personal account which sidesteps professional ethical dilemmas about publishing clinical material. I am citing this work with deep respect for Campbell's candour and unflinching honesty. He talks of using a 1–10 scale each morning to assess where he feels which I know from others people find helpful. 'One' is unalloyed joy; 'ten' is actively suicidal. (Most people will experience neither extreme.) Campbell talks about a recent visit to Australia (where he had been appointed as 'Australians for Mental Health' global ambassador). A road transport official told him the official suicide statistics saying the real figures were totally underestimated "because so many road traffic deaths, which are classed as accidents, are actually almost certainly suicides" (Campbell 2020 pp. 49). This is such an interesting finding which I think may well disguise the real statistics. I am going to quote a long extract from Campbell about his experience of suicidal depression because it is a powerful evocation that may resonate and be helpful to those who have known these depths of despair:

It usually … starts as I wake. … .[M]y head feels a little heavier than usual, and I have a desire to go back to sleep, but can't. … I lie on my back, stare at the ceiling, and to my left, about six to eight feet away, I have a sense of a dark grey cloud, oval, about five times the size of a rugby ball, which fills me with dread. It has a colour, a texture, and it has a feel, a kind of really unpleasant sort of jelly feel. I might talk to it: "Please, no, go away. Just fuck off." … [I]n my mind's eye there is now a smile on this oval cloud, and it is moving in ... and I am trying to push it away, but I can't. Its smile is growing because the cloud knows I am about to give up the struggle and let it in. Reluctantly, I say: 'come on then, let's get it over with,' and then it is inside me, and it feels like a heavy liquid is being poured through my veins, and my body starts to join my mind in feeling heavy. The cloud has evaporated, but its smile is still there, and it is saying, 'Gotcha ... again ... you thought you were rid of me ... no chance ... I'm back, and this time I'm never going away.'

(2020 pp. 54)

This gives such a visceral sense of Campbell's suffering. He goes on:

The dynamo I normally feel 24/7 whirring inside me ... is switched off. Literally, you feel as if there is a power cut ... . Energy gone. Power gone. Desire gone. Motivation gone. The ability to feel anything other than the numbing pain the cloud has brought about – gone. Everything gone, gone, all gone ...

It hurts everywhere, uniformly, outside and, especially, inside. My voice weakens and I have a mild but unpleasant metallic taste in my mouth. As to what I am feeling emotionally, yes, I am sad, but it is much worse than that. It is despair. Hopelessness. Hopelessness in both meanings of the word ... I feel devoid of hope that my life will ever be good, and I feel pathetic, worthless, useless, that I have so much going for me and yet, yet again, this fucking cloud has come in, taken me over, beaten me.

(ibid. pp. 55–56)

Campbell's account is real. The depression is taking grip. He continues:

Whatever is going on around me, things that I would normally be interested in, I'm not. There is an existential feeling – 'I just don't want to be here.' I don't want to be with these people, right here, right now. And I just don't want to be here. Full stop. Now the depression is in full control ... . I can literally see no point, in the moment or in the future ... Dead and alive at the same time ... I keep coming back to that as the best description. That is when, these days at least, I will vacate ... [D]isappear. Out to the car, drive aimlessly ... walk aimlessly ... anywhere I can be alone, and not have to speak. Here is where it is hard for partners. I want Fiona to be nearby, but I don't want her in my face. It is hard for me, and hard for her. ... Sleep can help. Exercise can help. Music can help. Above all, getting on well in my key relationships helps.

(ibid. pp. 56–57)

I am grateful to Campbell for this account. The courage to articulate these sentiments so vividly is truly impressive. And he also lays out such helpful resources in the closing lines: sleep, exercise, music and relationships are all of tremendous help in maintaining mental health and coping with such low points.

Prospective perspective

Suicide can be conceptualised as an urge towards transformation – something has to break the impasse that is being experienced. In that fateful moment, it may appear to be the only option left.

There are those, such as my Jungian colleague Ann Baring (whom I mentioned for her work on alchemy in chapter one) who see suicidal thoughts through a prospective lens, as a preparation for a new orientation in life; even as the call of the buried spirit (Baring 2013 pp. 480). Of course, it takes enormous strength and resilience to be able to discern such meaning at a time of utter despair and it may be that others (such as analyst or family) must hold on to that perspective at times for the individual who is struggling to envisage a future.

For David Rosen (contemporary Jungian Analyst and psychiatrist in the United States), his approach is to think in terms of what he calls 'egocide' and transformation. By this he means that the ego (the 'I' or 'me' with which you consciously identify) must die in service to the Self (capitalised as Jung sometimes does to indicate a 'self' that is greater than personal ie a 'true' self which feels genuine and grounded in the body). The ego must surrender to the Self – the central core of our being - for mature transformation to occur. This means a symbolic death of the ego may obviate the need to kill oneself as it is not the being *in toto* which is suffering (although it may feel that way). It is the ego which is wounded by what may be experienced as apparent failures in life which can lead to suicidal thoughts. We are, though, much more than our problems and our egos. And allowing the dissolution of that destructive aspect, may lead to a transformational rebirth into an existence less wounded by the supposed failure (or whatever it may be).

Rosen's approach includes deep engagement with creativity (which requires no artistic prowess) but which can be a healing way to engage with emotional dilemmas and destructive thoughts. The very act of creativity becomes a way of processing; sifting, putting things into a new perspective, potentially reaching a catharsis and breaking what may feel like an impasse. Indeed, this is exactly how Jung processed his own machinations of the soul which led to his *The Red Book* (Shamdasani 2009) where he created his own personal mythology using art images and narrative.

Collective suicidal urges

All the above has been about individual acts or impulses towards suicide. I want also to mention how unconsciously we seem to live in a way which might be described as suicidal in a collective sense. By this I mean how difficult it is to remain aware of the global destruction of the planet we are perpetrating by our unsustainable ways of living which is killing off the planet on which we are dependant for survival. Add to this the human drive towards war which has even (in the case of countries such as the United Kingdom and France and Belgium) led to colonising other countries historically which leaves its traces long after the 'colony' has been repatriated. Or the macho brinksmanship which characterises many global negotiations. (You might think of examples such as the Cuban missile crisis in 1962, or the Brexit talks which may well break up the United Kingdom and cause untold damage in so many ways). Or the collective greed which has led to umpteen wars in the Middle East, for instance, to gain control of the natural resources in the region. Or our addiction to travelling by air even in the face of mounting evidence that it is simply no longer viable to carry on living as if our actions had no consequences. This implacable blindness; this relentless insistence on having what we want, when we want it (like a stroppy child), has run its course. And yet – even when so many of us were calling out for no return to 'normal' during the Coronavirus pandemic – it is been utterly depressing and demoralising to see the weight of governments around the world refuse to embrace the change we so desperately need if the planet is to be allowed to breathe again. It is difficult to see these as anything but collectively suicidal. Or indeed ecosidal (as I set out in Chapter three.) (Rosen comes to somewhat similar conclusions about what he calls omnicide (2002 pp. 218–220).

References

Baring, A. (2013). The Dream of the Cosmos: A Quest for the Soul. Dorset: Archive Publishing.

Campbell, A. (2020) *Living Better: How I Learned to Survive Depression*. London: John Murray.

Camus, A. (1942) *The Myth of Sisyphus*. Harmondsworth: Penguin.

Main, R. (2007) *Revelations of Chance: Synchronicity as Spiritual Experience*. New York: SUNY Press.

Rosen, D. (2002) *Transforming Depression: Healing the Soul through Creativity*. York Beach, ME: Nicolas-Hays Inc.

Shamdasani, S. (Ed.) (2009). *C.G. Jung's The Red Book: Liber Lovus*. London: W.W. Norton & Company.

Part 3

Puzzles

We will now look at the question of destiny, whether it exists, whether it has a role in life and how it may be at the heart of mantic practices.

DOI: 10.4324/9781003284550-12

Part 3

Puzzles

Chapter 9

Predestination. Why do things go 'wrong'? Destiny or fate?

> Obstacles do not block the path, they are the path.
>
> —Zen Proverb

> When you don't follow your nature there is a hole in the universe where you were supposed to be.
>
> Dane Rudhyar

Will, intention and choice

In different ways, this chapter is about will, intention and choice. That is, how much do these factors guide our path in life, or are our actions and 'choices' guided by a pre-ordained destiny, by chance, by the will of our personal ego? A combination of these factors? Or, is there something else going on?

Many writers have explored this question, not least of all the Pulitzer prize-winning American playwright Thornton Wilder (1897–1975) in his short story entitled *The Bridge of San Luis Rey* (2000). When the bridge over a gorge in Peru collapses, five people plunge to their deaths and the narrator explores why those particular individuals might have met their fate.

Of course, there are many actual events in real life which leave us open-mouthed at the apparent coincidence of events which surely must have had some meaning. Don't they? I cite some real corkers (great examples) in the next chapter when looking at synchronicity.

This is not to say that asserting our will is not valuable and important. We must do so at times to feel a sense of agency and empowerment that we are fulfilling a wish/desire/intention. But sometimes life just seems to have other plans which may be experienced for good or ill. There is that wonderful saying: if you want to make God laugh, tell him/her your plans!

DOI: 10.4324/9781003284550-13

> **Discussion**
>
> If you are reading this in a reading group, I suspect you may all have examples to share where it felt as if a meeting or event was fated or brought about by something more than chance or personal intention.

Predestination?

I will always remember when I was about seven years old I asked my mother what predestination meant, and her reply was quite concrete and fatalistic, as if we were victims to what was laid out for us. So, if you never get out of bed, I mused, your life would still pan out along its pre-destined lines? I instinctively knew that she did not understand the notion. Passive fatalism can leave you bitter at the injustice of your lot. You have to engage with life, to contribute your effort towards your goal (be it modest or grand). We could go off here on a little excursus about whether the energy required to engage is a gift to take you in a certain direction. Many of us recognise there is sometimes a helping hand at play. Perhaps that is an idea you might play with or discuss in your book group if this is how you are reading. Whatever you come up with, it does at times feel as if some things do appear to be 'meant'; as if some things are inescapable.

Sometimes fiction is the best teacher. In Philip Pullman's *His Dark Materials* trilogy - which includes *Northern Lights* (1995), *The Subtle Knife* (1997) and *The Amber* Spyglass (2000) - he created a universe where we all have daimons who are spirit guides in animal form. In children they are constantly transmuting from one animal to another depending upon mood and reflecting the affect in the environment surrounding the child until, in adulthood, the daimon settles in to become a constant creature perfectly tailored to your character and nature and which becomes your personal companion (soul mate) and guide. I will not go into how this brilliantly encapsulates Jung's thoughts on the Self as I have done so elsewhere (Williams 2020). I have no idea whether Pullman was aware of or had read the works of James Hillman, but Pullman's creation un-cannily mirrors Hillman. James Hillman (1926–2011) (a most brilliant man who founded the field of Archetypal Psychology which is an offshoot of Jung's Analytical Psychology) sees us all as having a daimon which holds our 'calling', an idea Hillman in turn retrieves from Plato. Hillman puts it thus:

> The soul of each of us is given a unique daimon before we are born, and it has selected an image or pattern that we live on earth. This

soul-companion, the daimon, guides us here; in the process of arrival, however, we forget all that took place and believe we come empty into this world.

(1996 pp. 8)

Hillman suggests it is the daimon who recalls our journey and therefore our destiny. (Remember how this very story came up in chapter one in Jewish lore and in the founding myths of the Yanomami community in the Brazilian Amazon?) Going back to Hillman: "The daimon remembers what is in your image and belongs to your pattern, and therefore your daimon *is the carrier of your destiny*" (ibid.) (emphasis added).

Hillman goes on to lay out the notion set out by Plotinus (205–270 AD) (the major Hellenistic philosopher) that we choose our parents:

we elected the body, the parents, the place, and the circumstances that suited the soul ... . This suggests that the circumstances, including my body and my parents whom I may curse, are my soul's own choice – and I do not understand this because I have forgotten.

(ibid.)

Discuss! Imagine how – if we truly believed this - it could affect our relationships with both our families and our bodies which sometimes – perhaps often – become so toxic and redolent with shame.

This separation from our 'home' or our source can produce a deep loneliness which Hillman encapsulates in his usual achingly poetic way:

Loneliness presents the emotions of exile; the soul has not been able to fully grow down, and is wanting to return. To where? We do not know, for that place the myths and cosmologies say is gone from memory. But the imaginative yearning and the sadness attest to exile from what the soul cannot express except as loneliness. All it can recall is a nostalgia of feeling and an imagination of yearning. And a condition of want beyond personal needs.

(1996 pp. 56–7)

This philosophical motif relating to inheritance also appears in the belief system of the Dagara tribe. Contemporary writer Malidoma Somé, writing about his initiation as an African shaman, tells us that the Dagara believe:

Before you were born, your family learned who you were and what your purpose is. You chose to be born within a particular family because that made your purpose easier to fulfil. ... When you do not know who you are, you follow the knowledge of the wind.

(1994 pp. 253)

I think "following the knowledge of the wind" describes well how lost people can become when they are not in tune with their purpose. For many, finding meaning and purpose in life is a lifetime's journey. Others – not just prodigies and those with an exceptional talent - know their purpose, or their destiny, from a very early age. Perhaps some of our struggles in life are not just to find our purpose, but also fighting *against* what we are being led towards. Our ego may have another agenda and struggle to take on the challenges which are our destiny. Timing is all and sometimes we are just not ready to enter into a situation or relationship which we 'want'. Dreams can help to guide us in the right direction. It is also true that we can become quite twisted away from our nature by events, traumas, family patterns and neuroses. I think here of the patient (mentioned below) whose mother lied to her at a young age about her educational potential which warped the entire path of her life until she discovered the lie and was able to get her life back onto its proper track. These are the sorts of matters that can be addressed so well in Jungian analysis and psychotherapy.

Gerhard Adler (1904–1988) (one of the editors of Jung's *Collected Works* and founder of my own training society) reports an interesting example of what we might call fate in a rather personal chapter he wrote. Growing up he was best buddies with two other six year old boys with whom he was inseparable. About nine months after meeting, Adler's family moved to a distant part of Berlin away from where he had known the little boys. Some decades later, after Adler had become a Jungian analyst, he happened upon one of the boys who, it transpired, had also become a Jungian analyst, and the other brother had had a Jungian analysis and become steeped in Jungian ideas. This must be pretty unusual at the least (Adler 1978 pp. 88). Adler wonders if this was some kind of pre-destined fate.

I imagine many of us will have experienced situations where it seems beyond chance that events have panned out the way they have. I know for myself there is one friendship which was absolutely fated. I received a clinical referral from him via another colleague many years ago when he had asked the colleague to track someone down with a particular psychotherapy specialism. I then kept coming across the man's name, even though I had never heard of him previously. There must have been about four or five instances of his name turning up in different ways. It happened that I was at that time looking for a new clinical supervisor and I thought I would approach him as I was so intrigued by this series of events. I found his number in the telephone directory (which dates this anecdote back to the Ark!) And, when I rang, he picked up the phone on the first ring (which was most unusual). I said I was wondering about whether we might supervise together, and he said "oh, I was just writing to my society to say I have a space for a supervisee! Oh, well I won't write then". We met and have had a close association for the many years since. This situation would be characterised as a synchronicity but I would also say it was also fated which brings together some of the factors that I am attempting to draw together in this work. Things are not purely random. There is a guiding force behind the scenes which we can think about through the prism of whichever belief system or philosophy fits for each of us. In the words of Shinoda Bolen: "Synchronicity can pave the way for people coming together. By unravelling the circumstances through which two people meet to enter a significant relationship, the delicate, unseen hand of fate, destiny, synchronicity, or underlying *Tao* – by whatever name the matchmaker is called – can be discerned" (quoted in Cousineau 1997 pp. 84).

There is another instance I can cite which is of much more recent origin. A patient recently mentioned the name of a friend who had written a book and I thought I recognised the name (which was a very unusual one) but I put it to the back of my mind so as to be present in the session. About a week later I was looking for something on my bookshelf when I happened upon the book the patient had mentioned. "Oh, that's the name!" I thought to myself. When I somewhat idly browsed through the book which I remembered as being very enjoyable, I noticed it contained the name of someone I needed to contact! Synchronicity/fate? Surely. Returning to the words of Gerhard Adler as I can put it no better, he calls these happenings: "the profound experience of the miracle and enigma of the psyche, in the face of which awe and reverence are the only possible responses" (1978 pp. 101).

Why do things go 'wrong'?

Sometimes things have to go 'wrong' in order for them to go right. What I have found many times in life is that, if things had gone according to plan, the result would have been much less satisfying and enriching than it ultimately turned out. There are two examples I have alluded to in this book. The first was the friend I mentioned in the introduction who became a hermit living in the woods. The second is a very similar story referred to in Appendix B in the transcript of the interview with Dr Palmer, who also found himself in similar circumstances, living without a home, and in both cases this was a key turning point. You could say they had hit rock bottom, in the language of Twelve Step programmes, or see it as an enantiodromia in Jungian language, meaning that things had reached the end of the line so that the situation began to reverse. Sometimes things have to hit rock bottom before we are willing or able to make a move to instigate change. But why the course of life apparently goes wrong is really a mystery sometimes, as well as being a matter of perspective. Think back to the images of the planets I evoked in chapter two. There are also times when things go 'wrong' because the course of a life has been interfered with. For instance:

The wounded child inside many males is a boy who, when he first spoke his truths, was silenced by paternal sadism, by a patriarchal world that did not want him to claim his true feelings. The wounded child inside many females is a girl who was taught from early childhood that she must become something other than herself, deny her true feelings, in order to attract and please others. When men and women punish each other for truth telling, we reinforce the notion that lies are better. To be loving we willingly hear the other's truth, and most important, we affirm the value of truth telling. Lies may make people feel better, but they do not help them to know love.

(hooks 2001 pp. 49)

Let me give you an example of what I mean from clinical practice:

Clinical vignette

Sandra had been in therapy with me for many years before, at the age of forty-nine, she discovered a family secret that changed the course of her life overnight. It took tremendous psychological and emotional work to capitalise on the shift needed to forge the new way forward, and determination to make things different. During the Christmas holidays Sandra went to visit her cousin in another country which she had never done before. One evening as the two cousins sat talking after dinner, the cousin (Liesl) said to Sandra: "your mother told me once how guilty she felt about your education". Sandra did not know what Liesl was referring to. It transpired that some years ago Sandra's mother had confided in Liesl that she felt guilty because, when Sandra was eleven years old and about to change schools, she had lied to Sandra about her academic achievements because the mother did not want Sandra's sister to know that Sandra was brighter than her older sister. The result of this was that Sandra was sent to a terrible school which warped the entire course of her life to that point. This piece of news was shattering for Sandra to hear and the more she thought about it, the more sense it made of her apparent failures. She had puzzled throughout life why she had not been able to manifest her potential. She had always known she was clever, but had left school with barely any qualifications so that her options were limited. Being sent to the school her sister attended to shield the sister from her own envious and competitive feelings with Sandra had the most negative effect on all concerned and their relationships. The result of this piece of news coming to light was that, when Sandra returned to the UK, she applied to university and went on to gain a Masters degree with distinction which finally recognised her inherent abilities. Although she had managed to claw her way into a good job before university, the degree and the freedom she felt by things being put back on the right track was utterly liberating and enabled Sandra to go on to achieve at a high level.

The corollary to this story is that, if things had not 'gone wrong', the path Sandra would have taken would have been to become an interpreter in

Brussels or Strasbourg, she thought. But in fact her ultimate destination in life was to be far more deeply satisfying than the path she would have taken.

To add a further layer of complexity to this story, the result of the lie also gave her sister a false sense of her own abilities which led to her becoming a Malignant Narcissist to the detriment of all around her. Her sense of importance became utterly distorted and inflated by the lie with very negative consequences for all. Malignant Narcissism is one of the most toxic types of personality disorder which combines elements of narcissism and antisocial behaviour, often accompanied by sadism. Psychoanalyst Otto Kernberg first discussed Malignant Narcissism in depth in the 1960s following on the heals of the work of Erich Fromm (see Kernberg 1989).

The dark story that unfolded could be seen under the heading of intergenerational trauma but I am somewhat loathe to categorise it in that way as my sense was that, although the situation may have been exacerbated by the transmission of intergenerational trauma, it did not need to be passed on in the way in which it had been. The missing piece of the picture was the older sister's inability to deal with her own problems which had been distorted by the lie. There never was a good turn to this story and the family rift became immutable when the older sister prevented Sandra from even attending her mother's funeral, and then stole Sandra's inheritance on the death of her parents. The sister's belief that she was *entitled* can be traced directly back to this sad story of the lie which I suggest had inflated her ego. There was no happy ending, except – importantly - that Sandra found a different relationship to the grisly events and went on to thrive, albeit without her family of origin.

I have gone into this story in some detail because I think it demonstrates well that events like these *could* have led to a very different outcome. It is easy to imagine that Sandra might have taken her own life. She might never have found fulfilment at all if it were not for that fateful trip over Christmas, if the cousin had not spoken out and so forth. In the midst of such terrible circumstances, the stars aligned to change the course of Sandra's life. I would emphasise again that this was only possible because Sandra picked up on the nudges life was giving her and was able to do the psychological and emotional graft required to turn things around. Changing one's destiny is no easy task.

The soul's calling

James Hillman (mentioned above) cites the examples of a great many well-known people whose fate was surely set at birth. For instance, he tells us Picasso left school at age ten, unable to learn the alphabet and stubbornly refused to do anything but paint (1996 pp. 104). Hillman writes at length about the story of Judy Garland whose sister says Judy already knew at age two that she was destined to sing and dance (1996 pp. 49). There are many other examples. Of course we are not all exceptionals such as these but perhaps in our own ways we may have a purpose to fulfil and the yearning we all feel at times may be the forward thrust we need to better align to that purpose. And 'our own ways' is the key. It is our own destiny we need to fulfil. Not slavishly following society's values, nor mimicking celebrities, nor conforming to family aspirations. I do not mean this to imply a self-centred indifference to others, but rather that the call of the individual soul needs to be answered.

Destiny or fate in myth

Some situations do simply seem to be unavoidable. Mythologically the story of Oedipus would be a case in point. The story – which is seen by psychoanalysts as being central to the human psyche - runs as follows.

In Greek mythology, Oedipus was the son of Laius and Jocasta who were the King and Queen of Thebes in Central Greece. Laius had consulted the Oracle at Delphi when they were trying to conceive and was told not to have a child because it was ordained that any child of the marriage would murder his father and marry his mother. To side-step this fate, Oedipus was given to a servant with instructions to kill the child but the servant could not bring himself to do so and left the baby to die in the mountains. Baby Oedipus was found and adopted by King Polybus and Queen Merope of Corinth whom he grew up believing to be his biological parents. When later in life Oedipus discovered the curse on him, that he would murder his father and wed his mother, he ran away from his adopted parents to ensure this could not occur in an effort to derail his fate. But Oedipus met Laius, his birth father, at a crossroads one day. They got into an argument and Oedipus killed him. Fate could not be avoided. On his wanderings Oedipus found himself in Thebes where he encountered the sphinx who was guarding the gates to the city. The riddle set by the sphinx as a password to gain entry to the city and which no one had been able to fathom ran as follows:

> What walks on four feet in the morning, two in the afternoon, and three at night?" Oedipus answered: "Man - man crawls on all fours as a baby, on two legs as an adult, and then with a walking stick in old age.

As a reward for rescuing the city from the sphinx, Oedipus was offered the throne of Thebes and the hand in marriage of the ex-king's widow who, it later transpired, was his very own birth mother. Jocasta bore Oedipus four children before a belated investigation into the death of Laius led Oedipus to discover the dreadful truth of his marriage. Upon realising what had occurred, Jocasta hanged herself, and Oedipus gouged out his eyes with two pins snatched from her robe. Again, fate could not be avoided.

Destiny or fate?

There are some who believe we are born as a *tabula rasa*, meaning we are a blank slate and will be shaped purely by people and circumstances we en-counter as we go through life. No soul choosing to be born; no attraction to parents who might have the lessons we need; no innate nature. This seems to be a rather sterile philosophy, devoid of mystery and depth. (Of course, I am somewhat partial as I do not believe this is our born state.)

The situation is complicated further if you believe in the notion that we are reborn and make choices in former lives which affect our current si-tuation; that our previous actions may lead to challenges in subsequent incarnations. I imagine we have all had the feeling at times that a problem is so intractable and so repetitious that surely there must be a lesson there somewhere. Alan Leo (1860–1917), a leading figure in astrology who was mentored by Madame Blavatsky, the famous Russian occultist who co-founded the Theosophical Society in 1875, asserted that: "astrology 'has no permanent value' without incorporating the reality of former lives" (Greene 2018 pp. 120). Leo is credited with being the first 'psychological' astrologer because he transformed astrology from being a predictive or divinatory method to one for reading character in the service of human spiritual de-velopment. Retired Jungian analyst Liz Greene is the preeminent exponent of psychological astrology in the twentieth and twenty-first centuries.

Jung dedicated a whole chapter of his autobiography to the subject of life after death (Jaffé 1963 pp. 330–358). He recounts a scene which he describes as a hint rather than proof. He was lying in bed one night after having been to the funeral of a friend the previous day when he felt a presence at the foot of his bed. He said it did not feel like an apparition but was inviting Jung to follow him. He saw it as an inner image. The figure led Jung to the bedroom door, out of the house, into the garden and to the house of the man who had died who lived just nearby. The figure led Jung into the man's study, climbed a stool and pointed to the second of five books with red bindings on the second shelf from the top. The next day Jung could not help himself from visiting the widow and asked if he might look something up in the library, whereupon he discovered a stool at the bookshelf. He stood on the stool to discover five books with red bindings. The title of the second volume which the figure had indicated was entitled "The Legacy of the Dead" (ibid. pp. 343–4.) This is but one of many tales Jung recounts of such a nature. His autiobiography (which was written in collaboration with Aniela Jaffé) is a treasure trove of fascinating dreams, visions and experiences throughout a lifetime steeped in the mysterious aspects of life. In it, Jung explores whether souls return to live again, speculating that:

> if a karma still remains to be disposed of, then the soul relapses again into desires and returns to life once more, perhaps even doing so out of the

realisation that something remains to be completed./In my case it must have been primarily a passionate urge towards understanding which brought about my birth. For that is the strongest element in my nature.

(ibid. pp. 354)

So, in this context we might say that it was Jung's destiny to explore understanding, which he certainly did.

> Perhaps that leads us to think about our own destinies. Do you feel you have a distinct purpose in life? Do you feel pulled to fulfil some purpose? Perhaps that might be to reunite with a soul partner? To right an injustice? To fulfil an aspect of your being? Or to live a longed-for dream. You might find it interesting to discuss these points with others or to note them for yourself.

Liz Greene, (whose work I discuss in chapter ten) states:

> Jung also equated fate with the Self, the goal of the individuation process, 'because it is the most complete expression of that fateful combination we call individuality'. What happens to any individual ... is therefore a reflection of the mysterious inner process, which can only be transformed (although neither avoided nor eradicated) through consciousness. 'If we do not see a thing', Jung commented in one of his ETH lectures, 'Fate does it to us' (2018 pp. 123).
>
> (The Jung quote is from Welsh & Hannah (Eds.) 1959–60)

Greene (2018) tells us that Jung adopted some of his ideas about fate from the Stoics who were a school of Hellenistic philosophy founded in the third century BC. Dramatist as well as philosopher, Seneca (c. 4 BC – AD 65), and Marcus Aurelius (Roman emperor from 161 to 180) were both noted Stoic philosophers. (This is where the word stoicism comes from.) Of particular significance is the fact that Jung used:

> the concept of *Heimarmene*, which he described as 'the compulsion of the stars'. He also defined *Heimarmene* as 'the dependence of character and destiny on certain moments in time'. The term 'destiny' is subtly different from the idea of fate as either karmic retribution or pathological compulsion, and suggests something more akin to Neopolatonic ideas of the teleological nature of the personal daimon ... the broad outline of the path or personal myth an individual must follow in life in order to fulfil the requirements of the soul and, ultimately, the intelligent design of ... the universal deity of Stoic philosophy.
>
> (Greene 2018 pp. 123)

Heimarmene is the Ancient Greek goddess of destiny and fate, generally referring to the fate of the universe rather than personal fate.

Greene concludes:

> Fate, time, and the movements of the heavens are inextricably bound up with Jung's concept of individuation. Freedom from fate, in late antique approaches, involved a form of gnosis or inner realisation that could break the compulsions of the planetary daimons.
>
> (ibid. pp. 142)

Greene's stellar scholarship helps us to understand the enormous scope of Jung's cosmology which incorporates Orphic, Neoplatonic, Hermetic, and Gnostic thought which are all mustered in the service of elaborating his unique vision of a psychology, at the centre of which is the process of individuation whereby we are each able to incarnate our potential; to work towards fulfilling our fate. This is a continually unfolding/evolving process throughout life.

Greene conceives of the balance between will and fate thus:

> One analogy I have always liked for astrological patterns, and also for the process of 'individuation' as I understand it, is the 16th-century Italian *Commedia dell' arte*. The stock characters – the mischievous servants like Arlecchino and Pulcinello, the crabby, miserly old men like Pantalone and il Dottore, the enchanted young lovers like Flavio and Isabella, the pompous but well-meaning public authorities like il Capitano – are always recognisable to the audience by their stylised costumes and masks, and their exaggerated gestures and movements. In effect, they are archetypes. Every production is both scripted and improvised. The exits and entrances of the characters are scripted, and certain crises and resolutions must take place. But how the characters get to these scripted nodal points is up to the actors, who, if they attune themselves well as both individuals and representations of mythic types, perform in ways that entertain and also strike deep resonances in the audience. Every performance is entirely different, but every performance follows the same pattern ... [the] paradox of free will and fate is being enacted.
>
> (Liz Greene letter to International Association of Jungian Studies Discussion List 10 August 2020 (accessed 10 August 2020))

In fiction

There are two cracking novels which take a look at whether destiny and fate can be averted which are both light summer reads. The first is Ben Elton's *Time and Time Again* (2014). The premise of the novel is that the protagonist, a retired British army captain and adventurer, had been invited back to the Cambridge college where he had once studied by his former professor, now the Master of Trinity. She asks him: "If you could change *one* thing in history … .." (2014 pp. 34). The professor pushes him not to choose a personal moment. The reason she is asking him is because, when Sir Isaac Newton (who had revolutionised our understanding of the physical universe) had studied at Trinity, he had written a letter. This letter had been handed down – unopened - from Master to Master for three hundred years, to be opened on New Year's Day 2024. It referred the reader to a wooden box containing a package of papers revealing Newton's unpublished – and of course untested - discovery of how to bend time and light, to go back in time! After much debate, the Master and the adventurer decided the most significant point in history which changed the course of the world was 28th June 1914 when Archduke Ferdinand was assassinated and which led to the outbreak of the First World War. The adventurer, Hugh Stanton, was sent back in time, using Newton's formula, to assassinate the man who was about to assassinate Archduke Ferdinand. That, they believed, would prevent the killing of so many millions – and the world would be a better place. Well, of course things never work out as planned! And the book explores the unexpected ramifications of attempting to 'change destiny'.

The Stephen King novel, 11.22.63, runs along precisely the same lines but takes the reader back to the assassination of John F. Kennedy. Both are brilliant novels. Stephen King's novel was in fact published before Elton's and Elton had seemingly been inspired by it.

Reflections

Again and again in these stories and accounts we have to consider if life is unfolding in a fatalistic, pre-destined way, or whether we have any agency in the way our lives pan out. Our perspective on these questions has profound ramifications for how our life will unfold, whether we will be able to align to an authentic and meaningful path, or feel like a cork bobbing along on a choppy sea accepting the scraps which happen to fall into our laps. Although trying to control life is hopelessly ego-centric and futile, what I am trying to point towards is the benefit of surrendering the ego and embracing a wiser, deeper and a spiritual direction to guide us and to enter into our lives. Although the fragile ego often struggles to maintain supremacy, you will likely discover that the gifts far outweigh the sacrifices as the path we can be led to contains far greater riches than we ordinarily seek or even imagine. Our earthly desires are often limited to the superficial fripperies which the mind can conjure, rather than the numinous blessings that are available to us all.

I will now return to more esoteric matters in chapter ten which touches on deep mysteries.

References

Adler, G. (1978) "Reflections on "Chance" and "Fate"" in *The Shaman from Elko: Papers in Honour of Joseph L. Henderson*. Boston, Massachusetts: Sigo Press.

Cousineau, P. (1997) *Soul Moments: Marvelous Stories of Synchronicity – Meaningful Coincidences from a Seemingly Random World*. Berkeley, California: Conari Press.

Elton, B. (2014) *Time and Time Again*. London: Transworld Publishers.

Greene, L. (2018) *Jung's Studies in Astrology: Prophecy, Magic and the Qualities of Time*. London and New York: Routledge.

Hillman, J. (1996) *The Soul's Code: In Search of Character and Calling*. New York: Warner Books.

hooks, b. (2001) *All About Love*. New York: Harper Perennial.

Jaffé, A. (1963) *Memories, Dreams, Reflections*. London: Fontana, 1995.

Kernberg, O. F. (1989). "The narcissistic personality disorder and the differential diagnosis of antisocial behavior" in *Psychiatric Clinics of North America*, *12*(3), 553–570.

King, S. (2011) *11.22.63*. London: Hodder & Stoughton.

Pullman, P. (1995). *Northern Lights*. London: Scholastic Children's Books.

Pullman, P. (1997) *The Subtle Knife*. London: Scholastic Children's Books.

Pullman, P. (2000) *The Amber Spyglass*. London: Scholastic Children's Books.

Somé, M.P., (1994) *Of Water and the Spirit: Ritual, Magic and Initiation in the Life of an African Shaman*. New York: Penguin Books.

Welsh, E. & Hannah, B. (1959–60) (Trans and Eds) *Modern Psychology: Notes on Lectures Given at the Eidgenössische Technische Hochschule, Zurich by Prof. Dr C.G. Jung, October 1933–July 1941*. 3 volumes. Zurich: K Schippert.

Wilder, T. (2000) *The Bridge of San Luis Rey*. London: Penguin.

Williams, R. (2020) "Our Connection with Animals and the Universe: Psychology, Symbols, Spirituality and the New Physics" in *Depth Psychology and Climate Change: The Green Book* (Ed.Mathers). London and New York: Routledge.

Chapter 10

Mantic practices – Tarot, I Ching, Astrology – and synchronicity

Mantic practices are as old as time. The word 'mantic' stems from the Classical Greek word 'mantikos' from which *mantis*, meaning prophet, seer or soothsayer, is derived. It refers to the power of divining or prophesising. If you look further into the etymology of mantic, you will find links to *mania*. Divinatory practices are often seen as a kind of madness as they are non-rational. (Note, I'm not saying *irr*ational.) The name of the curious insect, the praying mantis, is derived from the same root because it looks as if its limbs are in prayer.

People often play with mantic practices in a light-hearted, perhaps casual way, in order to see if what comes up is meaningful. This is like an experiment to assess whether the uncanny really 'knows'; a way of testing faith and playing with the idea of whether there is something more than the strictly material operating behind the scenes in life. It can be a way of pushing the limits of our secret desires and wishes when we articulate them, even when we do so within the privacy of our own minds.

The systems I am looking at in this chapter are more than superficial, superstitious games though. They all have deep and ancient roots. You might see them as random, like pulling the petals off a daisy and saying "he loves me, he loves me not". But let's take a look.

Synchronicity

You might be surprised to learn that Jung – a medical doctor of gravitas and learning – took mantic practices deadly serious. He linked them to his ideas of synchronicity. Indeed, in some of his research on synchronicity he used astrology as a method to explore its value and utility.

Synchronicity is different to serendipity, happenstance or coincidence. Synchronicities often feel compelling and even weirdly uncanny which is perhaps not surprising when we consider that the root of 'weird' is 'wyrd', the Anglo-Saxon word for fate. They feel intended; a unique, tailored gift in that

DOI: 10.4324/9781003284550-14

moment. You may experience synchronicity as a communication from God, or destiny, the angels or the universe, according to your own philosophical system. You may see synchronicities as an act of grace (see chapter thirteen) which I suggest is likewise the underlying principle governing each of the mantic practices I discuss below.

Jung called synchronicity an 'a-causal connecting principle' meaning two factors are joined but not in such a way that one *caused* the other. An example might be one like the following from my clinical practice. In a session one day many years ago, someone brought a dream about five coins. When I went out to lunch directly after the session, I found five coins outside my front door. I had and have no explanation for this and unfortunately I did not have an opportunity to explore this with the person bringing the dream. But it gave me a sense of something significant being in the air which has remained with me over many years.

Jung suggested that the intensity of the relationship between analyst and analysand might even lead to what he called parapsychological – or synchronistic – events (Jaffé 1963 pp. 159). It is an interesting idea which I think anecdotally has validity. There are copious examples in the literature.

Jung conceived of the unconscious as containing a dimension he called the psychoid which is where he saw there being no distinction between matter and psyche (which is how mind and body are inextricably connected and psychological issues can manifest in the body) so that time and place do not hold sway as in everyday mundane reality. He saw the psychoid as possessing parapsychological qualities which he associates with synchronicity. Mystery cannot be theorised away, but this is how he explained it in his psychological model. This also accounts for phenomena such as telepathy where one mind is not (on this level) distinct from another and people can tune in to one another.

Jung first began to develop his ideas around synchronicity in discussions he had with Albert Einstein in the years 1909–1913 when they met for a series of dinners. Einstein was then formulating his own theories about relativity which sparked Jung to think about the relationship between space and time for himself. It is the pliability of these factors which is at play in synchronicity where apparently unconnected matters seem to cross space and time and manifest in inexplicable ways. There is a wonderful book by Phil Cousineau which contains copious enthraling tales of synchronicities such as the following:

On December 5, 1664, the first date in the greatest series of coincidences in history occurred. On this date, a ship in the Menai Strait, off north Wales, sank with 81 passengers on board. There was one survivor – a man named Hugh Williams. On the same date in 1785, a ship sank with 60 passengers aboard. There was one survivor – a man named Hugh Williams. On the very same date in 1860, a ship sank with 25 passengers on board. There was one survivor – a man named Hugh Williams.

(1997 pp. 13)

What can we make of that?

Staying with the sea-faring theme, there is another story picked up by the novelist Arthur Koestler (1905–1983) who noticed in the 1898 novel, *Futility*, by Morgan Robertson, that it foresaw the sinking of the Titanic:

In the book, a ship called the Titan collides on its maiden voyage with an iceberg in a fateful place in the Atlantic near the spot the *Titanic* sunk fourteen years later. Pushing the coincidence one step further, Koestler reprinted a letter from a ship's captain describing a moment in 1939 when he was sailing through the same waters where the *Titanic* sunk. On a sudden hunch, he stopped the ship just in time to avoid a fatal collision with an iceberg. The name on the side of the ship? The Titan.

(ibid. pp. 14)

Writing itself can be a tremendous encounter with synchronicities. I find, when I sit down to write, the right books come my way, as do the people I need to progress the ideas I'm thinking about. I would guess that many writers and artists experience this although they may not use that terminology. The flow that opens up when you surrender to the creative process is humbling and delightful (on a good day!) Obviously, it is tremendously hard work too for us mere mortals, but the joy of feeling supported by the universe is a wonderful thing.

If you wish to explore synchronicity in greater depth, I can recommend the various books I have set out in a bibliography at the end of this chapter.

Tarot

The Tarot is believed to have originated from a deck of cards invented in Italy in the fourteenth century. It is thought the Romany people probably started to use this deck for cartomancy (fortune telling) about a century later. There are a wide variety of decks available. The artwork on each card is made up of symbolism from astrology, numerology and Kabbalah. The cards represent a certain energy which may be interpreted. The standard deck which some see as definitive is the Rider-Waite seventy-eight card Tarot deck dating from 1910 which was designed by the artist and occultist Pamela Colman Smith (1878–1951) under the direction of Arthur Edward Waite (1857–1942). Waite was a leading scholar of the occult and member the Victorian era Hermetic Order of the Golden Dawn, a secret society devoted to the study and practice of the occult, metaphysics, and paranormal activities during the late nineteenth and early twentieth centuries. Rider refers to the name of the publishing house.

There are four suits in a Tarot deck: Wands, Cups, Swords and Pentacles (referred to as the Minor Arcana). (A pentacle is a star-shaped talisman that is used in magical evocation.) Then there are twenty-two cards containing archetypal characters or themes (the Major Arcana). Each card represents a specific energy and different Tarot decks interpret this energy in their own unique styles.

The name Tarot of Marseilles indicates not a single deck of cards but rather a series of iconographic models. At the end of the 1600's, this type of deck spread all over Europe. Within a century, the iconography of Marseilles was the most ubiquitous and the use of these decks became synonymous with quality.

There are now innumerable different designs as artists put their own stamp on the cards. One set is by the rather dark figure of Aleister Crowley (1875–1947), once called the wickedest man in the world. There are many beautiful contemporary decks by for instance Juliet Sharman-Burke (with artwork by Giovanni Caselli) which was co-authored with Liz Greene whose work I discuss below in relation to astrology and in chapter 9 on destiny and fate. Robert Wang has also created a Jungian Tarot deck (2017).

Tarot is read by laying cards out in different 'spreads' (layouts) which I will not go into here. Alternatively, they can be used individually so that I will sometimes simply pull one card from the pack to 'take the temperature' of a mood or situation. I have to say that they are *always* spot on. But of course, it is not simply a matter of the card conveying something, but rather the state of mind of the person pulling the card. These practices need to be approached with a humble heart, without desiring to control the result, and with an open mind. What makes the cards fall in a particular order? What draws me to a particular card in that instant? I scatter the cards face down and choose one at random.

Just before embarking on writing this book, for instance, I picked out a single card: (Fig. 10.1)

Two of Wands

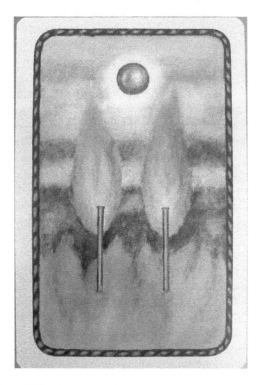

Figure 10.1 Two of Wands tarot card.

Invention

Rashness. Creative inventiveness. Idea that is absolutely brilliant and original, product of a completely free, intelligent and independent mind. Inventor has little support as no precedent exists for his work.

Now, I'm too modest to say this was a prediction! But at the least I found it an encouragement to go ahead with the ideas that were in my mind.

A great deal of time could be spent looking at each card in turn as they are archetypal images which contain dense symbolic information which can take you down through rich layers of meanings and associations.

I will take one card as an example. *The Fool* is a character who has been represented in every era and culture which is what makes him archetypal.

He is a tricky character to deal with, but he's no fool! He is not an idiot, which is different. An 'idiot' is stupid, whereas a Fool is a great Trickster character who fools you into thinking he is stupid. He is in reality pretty smart and wise although his nature may be seen as naïve. The Fool in Shakespeare is always the character who can deliver unpalatable truths 'in jest', in ways which are acceptable as he is not taken seriously, or you are not certain if he means it. Or he can be kicked away as an annoying knave. He is depicted in Tarot as standing on the edge of a cliff as if about to take a next step. This could indicate spontaneity/a leap of faith, or (if the card is drawn upside down) folly. He carries but a little sack on his stick/magic wand (like Dick Whittington), so he is quite unencumbered by cares. He has a dog at his side representing his instincts. In the Tarot deck the Fool is numbered 0 which symbolises infinite potential.

My colleague, Dr Carola Mathers, has kindly shared with me some un-published notes on The Fool from which I cite a few pertinent extracts here:

> In the Tarot, the Fool is outside time, in between birth and death. He lacks qualities of foresight, awareness of his limitations, and of his shadow. He thinks he can do anything: walk off a cliff and not get hurt. In his inflatedness he is like the Trickster and the *puer*. This is like the analysand who begins therapy expecting to have an easy ride, not expecting danger or difficulty. The Fool needs to work to develop psychological maturity and self-awareness, and so he enters time, travelling through the Major Arcana on a path of self-knowledge, to wholeness, to individuation. ... Foolishness is an antidote or corrective to pompousness, self-importance and inflation. ... The Fool also relates to beginnings. Here he is linked to embarrassment and shame, and thus to the Shadow. A beginner may often feel foolish
>
> (Mathers, unpublished notes sent in personal communication
> 21st August 2020)

In 1933 (aged 58) when Jung was giving his series of *Visions Seminars* in his native Zurich (the notes of which were originally kept under wraps only for the eyes of those who were present in person), he went into some detail about how he regarded Tarot:

> They are psychological images, symbols with which one plays ... For example, the symbol of the sun, or the symbol of the man hung up by the feet, or the tower struck by lightning, or the wheel of fortune, and so on. Those are sort of archetypal ideas, of a differentiated nature, which mingle with the ordinary constituents of the unconscious. The Tarot in itself is an attempt at representing the constituents of the flow of the unconscious, and therefore it is applicable for an intuitive method that has the purpose of understanding the flow of life, possibly even predicting future events, at all

events lending itself to the reading of the conditions of the present moment. It is in that way analogous to the *I Ching*, the Chinese divination method that allows at least a reading of the present condition.

(1998, pp. 923)

Marie-Louise von Franz (1915–1998) who collaborated with Jung in his work on alchemy and is known for her studies on fairy tales, numerology and more, reports in her *Psyche & Matter* (1988) that, towards the end of his life, Jung would suggest that, in cases where they thought the archetypal layer of the unconscious was present, they could use various divinatory methods such as the *I Ching*, Tarot and astrology, in order to see if those methods bore out his hypothesis according to his own method. About a year before he died, Jung wrote about the disappointing end to his grand experiment:

> Under certain conditions it is possible to experiment with archetypes, as my "astrological experiment" has shown. As a matter of fact we had begun such experiments at the C. G. Jung Institute in Zurich, using the historically known intuitive, i.e., synchronistic methods (astrology, geomancy, Tarot cards, and the *I Ching*). … Paranormal psychic phenomena have interested me all my life.
>
> (Letter to Mr A.D. Cornell dated
> 9th February 1960)

I Ching

The *I Ching,* or *Book of Changes,* which might be described as an ancient classical Chinese shamanic document, was made available to a Western audience thanks to sinologist Richard Wilhelm (1873–1930) who lived in China for twenty-fives years, was steeped in its culture and learnt to speak and write Chinese fluently. His eminent teacher who introduced him to the *I Ching* was related to Confucius. Both branches of Chinese philosophy – Confucianism and Taoism – are rooted in the *I Ching*. The guiding principles of the Tao (sometimes written as Dao) (meaning 'the way' or 'the path') stem from Lao Tzu (an older contemporary of Confucius (551–479 BC)) whose masterpiece is the fourth century BC, *Tao Te Ching* (1963). Living in *Tao* is living in harmony and the *I Ching* is constantly looking for such balance:

> The dark begets the light and the light begets the dark in ceaseless alternation, but that which begets this alternation, that to which all life owes its existence, is tao with its law of change.
>
> (Wilhelm 1951 pp. 299–300)

Wilhelm calls the *I Ching* one of the most important books in world literature. The language is archaic and can be impenetrable.

The *I Ching* has been called a Book of Oracles. When Jung was asked to write a foreword by Richard Wilhelm for his translation of the *I Ching*, Jung consulted the *I Ching* about the project of bringing this work to the attention of an English speaking audience as an experiment. Hexagram 50, The Cauldron, arose. "Thus", Jung tells us "it describes itself as a ... ritual vessel containing cooked food. Here the food is to be understood as spiritual nourishment" (1950 par, 977) which, following the Wilhelm Commentary on the Hexagram, Jung sees as revealing the will of God. (See also Main 2007 pp. 186) and which Jung thus saw as a fortuitous signal to proceed.

The *I Ching* is made up of a series of sixty-four hexagrams, that is patterns of lines, either broken (seen as yin, signifying 'no', or negative, or feminine) or unbroken (seen as yang, signifying 'yes', or positive, or male). In Fig. 10.2 I set out the major characteristics associated with the broken and unbroken lines:

Unbroken Line	Broken line
Yang	Yin
Yes	No
Positive	Negative
Creative	Receptive
Male	Feminine
Active	Passive
Firm/Strong	Yielding
Movement	Rest
Light	Dark
Day	Night
Sun	Moon

Figure 10.2 Broken and unbroken *I Ching* lines.

I realise that it may sound very programmatic (and some of the attributes of male and female do not resonate well to modern ears), but in fact there is enormous subtlety to the system. For instance, yin/the dark and yang/the light denote respectively the shadowed and light side of a mountain or river. Yang represents the south side of the mountain, because this side receives the sunlight, but it connotes the north side of the river, because the light of the river is reflected to that side (1951 pp.297). It is this flow of one turning into the other (and importantly containing a seed of the other represented by the dot of opposite colour in each side) that led to the creation of the now familiar yin/yang symbol (shown in Fig. 10.3):

Figure 10.3 Yin/Yang symbol.

Each *I Ching* hexagram is made up of six lines which may be individually read as positive or negative; the odd numbered ones are seen as superior, and the even numbered ones as inferior. The lines are read from bottom to top, with each line being numbered since the place in the hexagram where each line is located is seen as significant. Each of the lines is capable of change (ie from broken to unbroken, or the reverse) so that a second hexagram incorporating the changed lines would then come into play which adds layers of complexity to the interpretation.

The lines are obtained by throwing either forty-nine yarrow stalks (a type of plant stem) or three coins. Using coins is the usual way nowadays as it is easier to find coins than yarrow stalks! As with other divinatory practices, the yarrow stalks or coins need to be thrown in the right frame of mind. Much as I have spoken of approaching spiritual practices with a humble heart, Wilhelm tells us:

> All individuals are not equally fitted to consult the oracle. It requires a clear and tranquil mind, receptive to the cosmic influences hidden in the humble divining stalks.
>
> (1951 pp. liv)

The person consulting the oracle is cautioned not to ask the same question over again until you get the answer you want! It has to be approached with respect.

Once you have worked out the value of the lines you have thrown (with each line being 6, 7, 8 or 9 according to how the coins fall), you refer to the

table (shown in Fig. 10.4). The first three lines you have thrown are represented on the vertical axis; the top three on the horizontal axis, and the
point on the table where the two meet is the number of the hexagram to
consult. You follow the same system if any of the lines are 'changing' lines.

TRIGRAMS UPPER ▶ LOWER▼	Ch'ien ⚌	Chên ☳	K'an ☵	Kên ☶	K'un ☷	Sun ☴	Li ☲	Tui ☱
Ch'ien ☰	I	34	5	26	11	9	14	43
Chên ☳	25	51	3	27	24	42	21	17
K'an ☵	6	40	29	4	7	59	64	47
Kên ☶	33	62	39	52	15	53	56	31
K'un ☷	12	16	8	23	2	20	35	45
Sun ☴	44	32	48	18	46	57	50	28
Li ☲	13	55	63	22	36	37	30	49
Tui ☱	10	54	60	41	19	61	38	58

Key for Identifying the Hexagrams

Figure 10.4 Key to identifying I Ching hexagrams.

Once you have established which hexagram(s) you have thrown, you refer
to the body of the work which contains a text laying out the meaning of the
hexagram as a whole as well as each individual line. Only the moving lines
are relevant. A commentary on each of these texts has also been added to
help the person consulting the oracle to understand the complex meanings of
each hexagram which refer to seasons (eg timing), to family relationships, to
love, to work and all of human existence.

The I Ching sets out in great detail the significance of all the nuances of
line position and relationships between lines. Roderick Main also provides a
very clear exposition of the system which you might find more accessible
(2007 pp. 153–160). In this volume Main is the first to really interrogate the
connection, which interests me here, between synchronicity and spirituality,
ie that there is something more at play than mere coincidence in the

throwing of the coins (or choosing of the Tarot card) and it is this which is what has proved so attractive to readers over the centuries since the system was devised. We are drawn to the mysterious and numinous. As I suggested above, some would regard the factor at play in the throw of the dice or the cards or the sticks, as the intervention of grace.

I realise this may all sound rather enigmatic and beyond belief; even like magic. All I can say is that, when you use these methods, the results can be quite uncannily accurate, even in the face of the causalistic thinking which dominates Western society. Roderick Main posits something which I think is spot on:

> part of the contemporary appeal of the *I Ching* in the West may derive from it serving as a symbol for the integration of scientific, magical, and spiritual thinking.
>
> (1999 pp. 263)

Jung saw the throwing of the yarrow stalks or coins leading to a particular hexagram as an example of synchronicity in action. The stalks or coins fall quite randomly, and yet have meaning which can be quite detailed and precise. That said, the meanings can be very hard to discern as the language of the text is rather opaque leaving it open to ambiguity. There are occasions, though, when it is quite direct. In Jung's autobiography he relates the following story of using the *I Ching* with a patient:

> I remember, for example, the case of a young man with a strong mother complex. He wanted to marry, and had made the acquaintance of a seemingly suitable girl. However, he felt uncertain, fearing that under the influence of his complex he might once more find himself in the power of an overwhelming mother. I conducted the experiment with him. The text of his hexagram read: "The maiden is powerful. One should not marry such a maiden".
>
> (Jaffé 1963 pp. 408 quoted in Main 1999 pp. 264–5).

There is a second case cited in Main (2007) where Main touches on the case of Gerhard Adler (who was in analysis with Jung at the time, who went on to co-edit the *Collected Works* and founded the analytical society of which I am a member). Adler draws the same hexagram, having consulted the *I Ching* with precisely the same question, about whether to marry, as in the previously cited case. Adler's story runs as follows:

> The context of [Adler's] inquiry was the following "rather long-standing problem." He was in love with a girl who was very attractive and intelligent and whose background fitted his own; he would have considered marriage but was inhibited by the fact that she was also highly neurotic and "plagued by constant psychosomatic symptoms."

His question, accordingly, was "Shall I marry her or not?" The *I Ching* responded with the configuration of lines in … Hexagram 44, Kou/ Coming to Meet; there were no moving lines, so just this one hexagram was to be considered. The principal text to the hexagram, the Judgment, seemed to give Adler an explicit and unequivocal answer to his question: "Coming to meet. The maiden is powerful. One should not marry such a maiden.

(Main 2007 pp. 149).

I have spoken to Roderick Main who does not think these are the same cases, although it seems extraordinary that they should be so similar. Main has taken his reference to the Adler anecdote from *The Shaman of Elko* (Ed. Hill 1978) and says: "Adler was prompted to experiment with the *I Ching* by Toni Sussmann, a pupil of Jung's working in Berlin. It isn't clear whether he asked his question in her presence or not, but it doesn't seem to have been in Jung's presence, though Adler was in analysis with him at the time" (Main personal communication 21st August 2020). I have tried to obtain further verification of whether these cases are the same. I spoke to Dr Martin Stone who has a family connection to Adler and he told me:

I did know the reference in 'Chance and Synchronicity' (Joe Henderson's festschrift, *The Shaman of Elko*), and I recollect Gerhard mentioning the case. … What I hadn't remembered was the case quoted in MDR, but they are indeed strikingly similar. What we do know is that Adler was in analysis with Jung at that time; that he was later in analysis with Aniela Jaffé; that she effectively wrote MDR from Jung's notes and dictation; and that Jaffé was joint editor of Jung's letters with Adler./The connections are all there. We all know how stories get slightly changed, either to conflate, or for convenience, or to make a beurre story, or through lapses of memory, so Jaffé/Jung might have said the incident took place in Jung's presence, when in fact it was told him by Adler in analysis (and Adler might also not have wanted his name to be quoted in MDR in this context). I suspect we'll never know the answer to this as all the key players are dead.

(Stone personal communication
22nd August 2020)

I further contacted Professor Sonu Shamdasani to see if he could shed any light on this mystery. He replied: "it obviously looks the same case to me. I think in the Memories context he wouldn't have mentioned the name as it was not relevant, and he usually gave anecdotes like this without revealing identities." (Personal communication 12th September 2022).

I find this story fascinating whichever way it falls. It may be that I have discovered the case Jung quotes is Adler, or it may be a double synchronicity if two cases with the same problem, arrived at the same hexagram in such similar circumstances.

Jung viewed the *I Ching* as the Eastern equivalent of Western astrology. He was using the *I Ching* from about 1920 onwards and enthusiastically agreed to write the Foreword to the Wilhelm-Baynes translation. Jung had become friends with Wilhelm and they had a mutually beneficial cross-fertilisation of ideas.

What I want to emphasise is not that the words in the text of the *I Ching* or the astrological chart are a magical formula, but that it is the combination of the interaction of the person consulting it, and the attitude they bring to it as they throw the yarrow stalks or coins, that creates a meaningful result which amounts to a synchronistic event. As Ritsema and Karcher put it (quoted in Main 2007 pp. 162), in a divinatory system like the *I Ching*: "a procedure using chance provides a gap through which … spirit expresses itself by picking out one of the available symbols" (1994 pp. 11). There is always an 'x' factor at play, as in all of life: "This ultimate meaning of tao is the spirit, the divine, the unfathomable in it, that which must be revered in silence" (Wilhelm 1951 pp. 301). This links the notion of what Jung called synchronicity with the divine itself and perhaps accounts for the numinous feeling which is always associated with a genuine synchronicity. I would add to this that the authors of the oracle would have known that the act of throwing the stalks or the coins would have had a meaningful significance in producing the specific hexagram as it was intended as a divinatory oracle: "The conscious process stops with the formulation of the question. The unconscious process begins with the division of the yarrow stalks, and when we compare the result of this division with the text of the book, we obtain the oracle" (Wilhelm 1951 pp. 314). You might say that the turn to the oracle is akin to a prayer, asking for divine guidance and the resulting 'throw' is the reply.

Ritsema and Karcher were directors of an *I Ching* Project (which ran from 1988–94) at the Eranos Centre in Ascona, Switzerland. The Centre was established by Olga-Fröbe Kapteyn (1881–1962) (who was once an analysand of Jung) in 1933 and is situated on the banks of Lake Maggiore. Over the years it has hosted interdisciplinary conferences whose specific purpose is to foster dialogue among a select group of scholars from diverse disciplines, as well as running their Eranos-Jung Lectures, a cycle of monthly lectures named in memory of the important role that Jung played during his twenty-year-long participation in the Eranos activities. Flowing from their *In Ching* Project, Ritsema and Karcher went on to produce their own original translation of the *I Ching* which aims to highlight not only the divinatory function of the volume, but the psychological dimension of it too.

Astrology

When I first tried to calculate astrological charts as a teenager it all had to be done manually using mathematics which was way too complicated for me. This is before computers! I therefore gave up on the mathematical calculating quite quickly but never lost the interest in divinatory methods.

Astrology has become so incorporated into ordinary life that there are columns in daily newspapers and on websites which people turn to quite casually without probably thinking about their deeper esoteric roots. We scan them like checking the weather forecast. Perhaps there is a sense that, because they are not personalised, they can only apply in a very general sense. But even such columns can be spookily accurate.

There are different methods of calculating horoscopes. In the West we use a method based on the sun sign. In the Indian subcontinent they use a Hindu method otherwise known as the Vedic method which is purported to be the oldest form of Astrology known, being 5,000–7,000 years old. The Vedic method uses the moon sign as the basis for predictions. That method also uses the date, place and time of birth just as the Western sun sign predictions. I've had charts drawn up using both methods at different points in life and they were both very accurate in completely different styles.

Jung saw astronomy as the corner-stone of all truth which he saw as: "a mother to all the other arts" (1954a par.390). In a letter to Freud in 1911 Jung wrote:

> My evenings are taken up very largely with astrology. I make horoscopic calculations in order to find a clue to the core of psychological truth … It appears that the signs of the zodiac are character pictures, in other words libido symbols which depict the typical qualities of the libido at a given moment.
>
> ("Letter Jung to Freud,
> 12th June 1911", pp. 427)

Later in another letter Jung went on to say:

> Several "layers of meaning" should be taken into account in interpreting the Houses … So far as I can judge, it would seem to me advantageous for astrology to take the existence of psychology into account, above all the psychology of the personality and of the unconscious. I am almost sure that something could be learnt from its symbolic method of interpretation; for that has to do with the interpretation of the archetypes (the gods) and their mutual relations, the common concern of both arts.
>
> (Letter to André Barbault, 26th May 1954b, in Jung Letters,
> Vol. 2, pp. 175–76)

In discussing Jung and Plotinus in her scholarly study of Jung and astrology, Liz Greene (who is the preeminent exponent of psychological astrology in the world), states that Plotinus: "dismissed the idea that the planets 'produce' effects in a material manner. They 'signify' rather than cause events; they are 'letters perpetually being inscribed on the heavens'" (2018 pp. 92). In other words, for both Jung and Plotinus they are symbols. (The quote from Plotinus is from his Ennead II.3.7.).

Greene describes Alan Leo (1860–1917) as "a unique figure in the esoteric world of fin-de-siècle Britain because, virtually single-handed, he brought astrology into the modern era as a tool for insight into character rather than a method of prediction" (2018 pp. 39). He was mentored by Madame Blavatsky, the famous Russian occultist who co-founded the Theosophical Society in 1875. Greene tells us that Leo:

> insisted that astrology 'has no permanent value' without incorporating the reality of former lives.
>
> (2018 pp. 120)

(The Leo quote comes from *Esoteric Astrology* (London: Modern Astrology Office, 1913), p.vii). Leo believed character is destiny.

I do not know the basis on which he makes such an assertion. Obviously, astrology is based on the very moment of one's birth into this incarnation. To speculate on how that might relate to former lives goes rather too far away from the scope of the current work but it would, I am sure, be a very interesting topic to explore.

It is interesting to note that, just as Jung at times consulted the *I Ching* with patients, he did the same with astrology:

> In cases of difficult psychological diagnosis I usually get a horoscope in order to have a further point of view from an entirely different angle. I must say that I very often found that the astrological data elucidated certain points which I otherwise would have been unable to understand–
> Letter to B. V. Raman, 6 September 1947, pp. 475

It would be very unusual to find a therapist doing that these days, although I think it does sometimes happen.

Jung was not just interested in astrology as a mantic practice though. He was interested in it for its connections to alchemy (with its solar and lunar imagery for instance). Indeed, Jung saw them as inextricably bound together:

> Alchemy is inconceivable without the influence of her elder sister astrology, and the statements of these ... disciplines must be taken into account in any psychological evaluation of the luminaries.
>
> (1963 par. 222)

He used the images associated with planets as archetypal imagery that plays out across cultures too. This was particularly taken up by the likes of James Hillman who founded the field of Archetypal Psychology. Hillman is the most poetic of writers whom it is well worth exploring and he has written prolifically. His *Re-Visioning Psychology* (1975) was nominated for the Pulitzer Prize.

Hillman's son, Laurence, in fact became an astrologer. In an interview with Laurence Hillman I discovered online, I learnt:

> What I encountered was a brilliant astrologer with keen psychological insight into the subtleties of his craft. Surprisingly, he mentioned that he'd never actually read any of his father's books from cover to cover (a way to differentiate his own developing ideas, perhaps?). Yet, he went on to explain how growing up around psychologists—especially Jungians—caused him to be virtually "marinated in the archetypes" from an early age.
>
> (Grasse 2020. See: https://www.astrologyuniversity.com/laurence-hillman-interview/ accessed 25th August 2020)

Laurence Hillman tells us how he came to find his vocation:

> Well, I was a bored teenager living in Zürich, Switzerland, and my mother was very interested in astrology. Just so I'd have something to do, she suggested I study astrology with a family friend I'd known all my life, who was a professional astrologer. When I went to him, he said, "So, you're here to study astrology?" I said, "I guess." Then, just ten minutes into my first lesson, I had a clear vision that this is what I wanted to do for the rest of my life. My next thought after that was: I'm going to do this full-time when I turn 40, because there are a lot of other things I've got to do first. And that's pretty much what happened. I started full-time when I was 38, though by then I'd been practicing astrology for two decades already.
>
> (Grasse 2020)

These are the moments in life to treasure.

Interestingly Laurence Hillman goes on to say:

> "Later still, theater provided me with a similar metaphor for describing what I imagined to be unfolding inside of us: We have an inner stage —the psyche—where our personal play unfolds. The ten planets are like characters interacting on the stage of that inner drama" (Grasse 2020) which resonates very much with how many Jungians would approach working with dreams.
>
> (see Williams 2019)

Laurence Hillman elaborates in that interview on how he uses astrology in theatre workshops in a way that sounds very interesting and creative:

> I begin … with the image of the horoscope being a circular stage where the planets are acting out a play, a drama, and each one of them is an archetypal character playing a role. It's as though the heavenly bodies dropped onto that inner stage at the moment of one's birth, and we've taken a snapshot of it from the rigging above, freezing that moment in time. The aspects tell us who is arguing with whom, who is kissing whom, and so forth.
>
> (Grasse 2020)

The apple does not fall so far from the tree!

Astrology is not all about prediction. It is also about character and how our character is cast at the moment of birth. These need not be fixed in stone though and, paying attention to your astrological chart can open out the potential to ameliorate difficult features, to learn how to dance around or manage tricky character traits.

☯

In some ways it is horses for courses. You choose the method of divination that most resonates with you. They all operate along the same lines, manifesting synchronistic results which can then be reflected on at length and be used as a guide.

Since I am not an expert in any of these practices, I am appending a bibliography to point you in the direction of specialists in these areas and further literature to explore. I have included these practices here as they are of such significance and interest in the overall scope of the connections to spirituality which I have tried to delineate and I hope to have at least whetted your appetite to consider if there is more to these practices than meets the eye.

References

Cousineau, P. (1997) *Soul Moments: Marvellous Stories of Synchronicity – Meaningful Coincidences from a Seemingly Random World.* Berkeley, California: Conari Press.

Grasse, R. (2020) "All the World's a Play – A Conversation with Laurence Hillman". Online interview at: https://www.astrologyuniversity.com/laurence-hillman-interview/ accessed 25th August 2020.

Greene, L. (2018) *Jung's Studies in Astrology: Prophecy, Magic and the Qualities of Time.* London and New York: Routledge.

Hill, G. (1978) (Ed.) *The Shaman from Elko: Papers in Honour of Joseph L Henderson.* Boston, Massachusetts: Sigo Press.

Hillman, J. (1975) *Re-visioning Psychology.* New York: Harper Perennial, 1992.

Jung, C.G. (1911) "Letter Jung to Freud 12 June 1911". *The Freud/Jung Letters.* (Ed. Maguire) (Trans. Manheim and Hull). London: The Hogarth Press and Routledge & Kegan Paul, 1974.

Jaffé, A. (1963) *Memories, Dreams, Reflections*. London: Fontana, 1995.

Jung, C.G. (1947) "Letter to B. V. Raman, 6 September 1947". *C.G. Jung Letters*, Vol. 1, p. 475. (Selected and edited by G. Adler in collaboration with A. Jaffé). (Trans. R.F.C. Hull). London: Routledge & Kegan Paul.

Jung, C.G. (1954a) "On the Nature of the Psyche" in CW8.

Jung, C.G. (1954b) Letter to André Barbault, 26th May 1954, in Jung Letters, Vol. 2, pp. 175–176.

Jung, C.G. (1963) *Mysterium Coniunctionis*. CW14. London: Routledge & Kegan Paul.

Jung, C.G. (1950) "Foreword to the *I Ching*" in CW11.

Jung. C.G. (1998) *Visions: Notes of the Seminar given in 1930–1934 by C. G. Jung. Volume 2.* (Ed. Douglas). London: Routledge.

Jung, C.G. (1960) "Letter to A.D. Cornell dated 9th February 1960" in *C.G. Jung Letters in two volumes. Volume 2. 1951–1961.* (Selected and edited by G. Adler in collaboration with A. Jaffé) (Trans. R.F.C. Hull). London: Routledge & Kegan Paul.

Main, R. (1999) "Magic and Science in the Modern Western Tradition of the I Ching" in *Journal of Contemporary Religion* 14(2).

Main, R. (2007) *Revelations of Chance: Synchronicity as Spiritual Experience*. New York: SUNY.

Mathers, C. (2020) Unpublished notes sent in personal communication 21st August 2020.

Ritsema, R. and Karcher, S. (1994) *I Ching: The Classic Chinese Oracle of Change*. Shaftesbury, UK: Element.

Tzu, L. (1963) *Tao Te Ching*. (Trans. D.C. Lau). Harmondsworth: Penguin Books.

von Franz, M-L (1988) *Psyche & Matter*. Boston and London: Shambhala Books.

Wang, R. (2017) *Jungian Tarot Deck*. US Games.

Wilhelm, R. (Trans) (1951) *The I Ching or Book of Changes*, (rendered into English by C.F. Baynes). London: Routledge & Kegan Paul.

Williams, R. (2019) *Jung: The Basics*. London and New York: Routledge.

Bibliography

On synchronicity

Jung, C.G. (1985) *Synchronicity: An Acausal Connecting Principle*. London and New York: Routledge.

Main, R. (2004) *The Rupture of Time: Synchronicity and Jung's Critique of Modern Western Culture*. London and New York: Routledge.

Von Franz, M-L. (1980) *On Divination and Synchronicity: The Psychology of Meaningful Chance*. (Trans. Dykes). Toronto: Inner City Books.

On I Ching

Wilhelm, H. (1960) *Change: Eight Lectures on the I Ching*. Princeton: Princeton University Press, 2019.

On astrology

Cornelius, G. (2003) The *Moment of Astrology: Origins in Divination.* Bournemouth: Wessex Astrologer Ltd.

Greene, J. (1986) *The Astrology of Fate.* Newburyport, MA: Red Wheel/Weiser.

Hall, J. (2000) *Patterns of the Past: The Birthchart, Karma and Reincarnation.* Bournemouth: The Wessex Astrologer.

Hand, R. (1997) *Horoscope Symbols.* Atglen, PA: Schiffer Publishing.

Hyde, M. (1992) *Jung and Astrology.* Wellingorough: Aquarian Press.

Resources

The Advisory Panel on Astrological Education https://apae.org.uk/
The Centre for Psychological Astrology https://www.cpalondon.com/
The Company of Astrologers http://www.companyofastrologers.com/
Astrology University https://www.astrologyuniversity.com/

Part 4

The ineffable

In this final section, we look at some of the most challenging matters we may ever face: questions of the limits of existence, phantoms, the transcendent, the sacred and the deeply mysterious. We begin with a piece of qualitative research to ground the ineffable in the day-to-day experience of contemporary practitioners.

DOI: 10.4324/9781003284550-15

Part 1

the tangible

Chapter 11

Soul and spirit in analysis

Soul

Listening to the call of our soul and spirit is our quintessential task in life. Learning to distinguish between the different calls on our attention is not easy and that is the challenge we are constantly set. Is this intuition, or fear, or anxiety or paranoia? Is this the call of my soul? Individuation is about aligning with your soul; searching to find your purpose. Addictive thinking, obsessions or desires to conform or please can be compelling and convince you that you are following the right path. Hormones exert great influence. Responsibilities abound. Families make demands. All of these and more make listening to the sometimes quiet insistence of the soul's beckoning quite a challenge. We might attune to this beat through dreams or synchronicities. Dreams are for some the only connection to a life beyond the diurnal realm which makes that connection so vital and meaningful. A synchronicity can land like a thud that is impossible to ignore and brings a sense of what is meant; a sense of being guided. The trick is to pick up the track and follow it. And the more aligned with your heart and soul you are; the more rooted in your body and instincts you are; the lighter your step, the easier it becomes to follow the call.

Of course, following your own star is never and can never be easy. Mythologist and storyteller Michael Meade recounts a wonderful tale of Eisik being called by a dream three times which tells him to travel to a distant city where he will find great treasure at the foot of a bridge. Finally, after the third dream, he can resist the call no longer but feels foolish and inhibited from digging for the treasure as there are guards on the bridge. After days of pacing up and down one of the guards approaches Eisik and asks if he is alright. Eisik swallows his vulnerability in feeling quite foolish about taking a dream seriously and tells the guard why he is there. The guard agrees it is silly to listen to a dream and tells Eisik that he himself had had a dream the previous night where a man called Eisik is told to return home and look behind the loose bricks of his hearth where he will discover a great quantity of gold (2012 pp. 151–176 and 200–201)!

DOI: 10.4324/9781003284550-16

(After writing this, I came across another version of this story which purports to originate in Germany where a man finds a copper strong box full of gold coins under a tree (Allix 2021 pp. 158–9).)

Soul is at the very heart of depth encounters in life. We may not use that language, but we sure recognise that depth when we experience it:

> *We all experience 'soul moments' in life - when we see a magnificent sunrise, hear the call of the loon, see the wrinkles in our mother's hands, or smell the sweetness of a baby. During these moments, our body, as well as our brain, resonates as we experience the glory of being a human being.*
>
> (italics in original) (Woodman 1995 pp. 32)

Most of us long for a "soul mate", although that term has become somewhat clichéd. The company of those with whom we feel such a close affinity is beyond measure and makes life feel fully lived and valuable. We feel understood and recognised when we resonate with each other's souls. In classical antiquity souls are seen as already connected in the World Soul or *Anima Mundi* so perhaps it is no wonder we feel something move when we meet a fellow traveller whose soul touches ours.

Writing in 1964, James Hillman noted that "soul": "is not a scientific term, and it appears very rarely in psychology today, and then usually with inverted commas as if to keep it from infecting its scientifically sterile surround" (2020 pp. 37). I am not sure that much has changed in straight psychology in the decades since Hillman wrote those words. But in Analytical Psychology (Jungian psychology) soul is at the forefront of our explorations and this chapter seeks to draw that out.

Hillman – the preeminent writer in this field on the subject of soul – goes on to play with the idea that, alongside a case history, analysts might take a soul history when first meeting with a patient:

> Case history reports on the achievements and failures of life with the world of facts. But the soul has neither achieved nor failed in the same way ... . Its material is experience and its realizations are accomplished not just by efforts of will. The soul imagines and plays ... Taking a soul history means capturing emotions, fantasies, and images by entering into the game and dreaming the myth along with the patient. *Taking a soul history means becoming a part of the other person's fate ... .* [Soul's] facts are symbols and paradoxes.
>
> (emphasis in original) (2020 pp. 64)

Psyche and soul are used interchangeably in Jungian discourse. Soul, for Jung, was "the very essence of relationship" (1946 par. 504) and a good deal of his mature work is concerned with soul.

'Psychotherapist' means 'healer of souls', which is in stark contrast to the current political moves based on financial expediency to turn State provided therapy (by the National Health Service in Britain) into a manualised practice, sometimes even excluding the presence of an individual altogether and using a computer programme! Nothing could be further from the actual origins of what true psychotherapy is about when two individuals meet together in a room. This very morning there was a radio report that the British Medical Association has published research showing the results of working with a computerised 'therapist' and a cognitive based 'human' therapist were indistinguishable! (Weary sigh!) This – alas – is the class apartheid that has been created whereby those with few financial resources are left to take this scrap from the table, while the middle classes who can afford it are able to access 'proper' therapy from a practitioner and a modality of their choosing. Again, nothing could be further from the origins of the meeting of two individual souls in the service of healing. This is not a good situation and is damaging to the soul.

Both soul and spirit transverse sexuality. They may both be experienced as an aspect of sexuality as well as more broadly as the deepest layers of our being. When our souls or spirits meet in sexual congress, the greatest depths (or heights) are encountered. Soul might be experienced like a bass note; spirit like a high ethereal tone. The arc of the journey of the soul is slow and is discernible over years; whereas the spirit can move like lightening. Not always, but can.

Soul is connected to earth and water which links us, or roots us, to the earth (creating a channel to receive the healing energy which comes up from Gaia). Soul connects us through our bodies to the chthonic levels.

Spirit is connected to fire and air. It metaphorically takes us up; our spirit rises, transcending the diurnal realm.

You might say that soul is like a membrane that links the physical world to the spirit. It gives us access on the physical plane to spiritual experience.

Spirit

For Jung – as for me – 'spirit' is not a concept, but rather an empirical phenomenon which may be experienced by anyone and everyone. When I refer to spirit I am referring to the spiritual aspect of ourselves; I am re-ferring to the transcendent dimension of existence rather than paranormal 'spirits' which is the subject of the next chapter.

Spirit is also seen as the energising element in creativity whereby you might feel as if the words are writing themselves, or the painting is painting itself. The *numen* or the uplifting nature of a work of art may be experienced as spiritual. (Jung wrote a whole volume on *The Spirit in Man, Art and Literature* (1966)) which includes essays on Picasso and James Joyce's Ulysses.) This is not to say simply these works were inspired by spirit, as much as animated by spirit. An example of this might be that, when I am writing, I will sometimes wake with words going through my mind which I dash to catch as they are often nuggets of gold which were not in my conscious awareness any more than a dream image I might awaken to remember. These moments are precious and fleeting. In *Jung: The Basics* I cite various examples of artworks and scientific findings having been dreamt, such as Paul McCartney 'dreaming' his song, *Yesterday*. (McCartney calls this magic.) There are copious examples of inspiration having arrived via a dream which feels as if it is a gift from God or from 'the other side'. (You will interpret this through the lens of your own belief system and may have other ideas about the source.) However you conceptualise such experiences, they leave an indelible impression and are experienced as precious.

It is to spirit that we aim our prayers. And perhaps how we experience our prayers being answered. Although that may of course not be directly in the way we wished! Spirit has the greater wisdom beyond our perspective as to what we might need.

For those interested in looking into Jung's perspective on spirit academically, a journal article has appeared by a Danish practitioner which looks at the development of Jung's use of the term across his lifetime which incorporates a broad spectrum of views (Gitz-Johansen 2020 pp. 653). Gitz-Johansen discusses Jung's "spirit of the times" and "spirit of the depths" which Jung describes in *The Red Book* (2009) but these may be seen as complexes which lead Jung – or connect him – to the world of soul. Jung used this way of referring to the 'spirit of the times' and of 'the depths' to elaborate his own thinking about the world of soul and spirit as he experienced it. They certainly have a numinous quality and operate at a deep level, but may be distinct from what I refer to as the spiritual dimension of life which is seen as the divine spark of life which animates us all and which some call God. (N.B. I am not referring to a supernatural 'God' who resides somewhere "up" or "out there", but to an energy which is omnipresent, meaning both out and most specifically inside of each of us; a level at which frankly "inside" and "outside" have no meaning.) This is what the alchemists referred to as *quinta essentia* (the quintessence of our very nature). *What* Jung refers to as 'the spirit of the times' and 'the spirit of the depths' might be thought of as 'god' images, or images of 'the gods' in a metaphorical or mythological sense.

Another way of looking at this may be that archetypes (which have complexes at their core) may carry the message of spirit in the sense that the right people may appear at the right time; or archetypal characters in myth and fairy tale carrying the salient message which is needed in order to get on the right path may arrive, for instance. These might better be described as sprites rather than spirits as such. I realise this may sound like dancing on the head of a pin, but these are fine points of difference I am trying to distinguish.

Jung saw spirit along these lines when he characterised spirit as fragments of the psyche. However, they do not need to remain split-off and can be married within the overarching psyche. This is the ultimate work which culminated in Jung's mature opus on alchemy. These facets of life need to be incorporated in order for us to become more whole and connected to our fullest potential as humans. Not just for ourselves as individuals but for the healing of the world too. We can all witness the consequences of narcissistic self-absorption in the world around us if soul and spirit are left out of the equation.

Chakras

If you think in chakras, soul relates to the Root or Base Chakra known as Mulhadhara in Sanskrit. It is located around the perineum and is associated with the colour red. While the Crown Chakra (Sahasrara in Sanskrit, associated with the colours violet/white) is the door to the spirit, the divine light which is seen as the source. Spirit is accessed through the Brow chakra (associated with indigo), also known as Ajna in Sanskrit, or the third eye.

Chakras are energy centres which connect our physical bodies with the spiritual realm via an aura (like the membrane I mentioned earlier). There are seven basic Chakras (although some systems break them down into more), each associated with different parts of the mind and body. In this table, I set out the seven chakras alongside the aspects with which they are associated: (Fig. 11.1)

I've listed them top to bottom to mirror the physical locality to which they are linked, although they are usually displayed the other way up in line with the flow of energy which rises up from the Root chakra. (This energy is known in India as *prana* and in China as *chi*.) This flow of energy is represented *par excellence* in Kundalini where the energy of the snake is seen as rising up through the body from the Root chakra and climaxes in rising through the Crown up to the spiritual heights and awakening. Each Chakra

	Chakra	Represents	Element	Animal	Colour
7	Crown	Spirituality		Butterfly	Violet
6	Brow	Awareness		Eagle	Indigo
5	Throat	Communication		White elephant	Blue
4	Heart	Love	Air	Antelope	Green
3	Solar Plexus	Wisdom	Fire	Ram	Yellow
2	Sacral	Sexuality/creativity	Water	Crocodile	Orange
1	Root	Basic trust/security	Earth	Elephant	Red

Figure 11.1 Table of chakras.

is linked to an endocrine organ. Attuning to Chakras can be helpful to locate the *locus* of a physical or emotional issue or discomfort which can then
be attended to either through a self-practice or with/by a healer. The system
of acupuncture (as well as other 'alternative' methods) is based partly on
chakra energy centres.

In a Taoist practice the chakras are also described as the trunk of Tao. In
this model the sexual centre is also seen as the spiritual centre which reveres
sexuality as sacred. In a recent book translated from Japanese, Chiga reports
on his deep study of the *Tao Te Ching* (Tzu 1963) (an ancient sacred treatise
written by an older contemporary of Confucius) and his travels in China
where he met a holy man named Mr M. Chiga discovered that in fact the
Tao Te Ching is written in a code using what are called *Shakuji* which are
letters replacing the original letter used because they have the same sound
but a different meaning. Translation revealed a deeply sacred sexual
meaning to the esoteric text (Chiga 2020). A practice Chiga discovered is
called Yahma which equates to yoga with its links to Kundalini and Tantra
which he describes in an inspiring way. He encountered this practice in a
remote village in China where he experienced what he called a oneness on
earth (ibid. pp. 98). This is the goal (although that is a much too concrete
material word) of all spiritual practice. He recounts a harmony in the vil-
lagers which is all too distant from the lived experience of much of our lives
in 'sophisticated' advanced economies. Chiga describes his wonder at what
he witnessed in the remote village saying:

> Their marital lives were not controlled by laws or government.
> According to the conditions, there seemed to be many patterns of
> marriage, such as one husband with some wives, one woman with
> some men, a night-visitation marriage, and so on, all based on one
> husband with one wife. To my surprise, even though several patterns
> of marriage existed freely, a perfect balance was kept as a whole. The
> whole of the relationship between males and females in this village
> created such a perfect harmony, as if all were united into one
> complicated organic existence ... It was as if all people were lovers
> who understood each other, and no jealousy was felt because of
> physical contact with the opposite sex. It was because they didn't have
> a personal desire to seek for the opposite sex within their psyche,
> where they are satisfied with the great Tao ... It was the same toward
> other living beings. It was impossible to monopolize a fortune, and
> they didn't have a concept of fortune itself ... .. After that experience,
> I came to marvellously understand the mental state in which people
> are so hungry for money or power./*The desire by civilized people for
> tangible things is a compensation for lack of love. We have confused the
> spiritual world and the material world in our psyches.*
>
> (2020 pp. 103–4) (emphasis added)

Research

Anecdotally I have found in my practice that the majority of people seeking Jungian analysis turn to that approach because they are looking for someone who is able to work with soul and spirit, or at least who values soul and spirit. This may not always be obvious because many Jungian practitioners work with soul and spirit without ever mentioning those terms. It can be used in the most subtle of ways as it underpins much Jungian theory. I thought it would be interesting to test my hypothesis in writing this book and so I devised a set of ten questions which I decided to send to a broad span of Jungian analysts across the world. I wondered whether my experience would be universal, as well as whether there would be a cultural or gendered dimension to my questions.

For the purpose of my research project I wrote to the Chairs or Presidents of all 69 Jungian societies of the International Association for Analytical Psychology (IAAP) (which is the overarching membership body for all Jungian analysts worldwide). I asked them to circulate my survey to their members. There are currently roughly 3,500 Jungian analysts across the world. The societies are in Africa, Asia, Australia (covering Australia and New Zealand), Europe, North America and South America. That said, the majority of societies are in Europe and North America with as yet only one society in Africa (in South Africa). In Asia the societies are located in China, Japan, Korea and Taiwan. There are also Developing Groups (which means societies which are working towards becoming full IAAP societies) in Tunisia as well as Beijing, Guangzhou, Hong Kong, India, Macau, Shanghai and Wuhan plus in Central and Eastern Europe and a few in Latin America.

I cannot tell how many of my research questionnaires were actually forwarded to members and language may have been a barrier in this as I am sorry to say I did not think in time about getting the questionnaire translated from English. I do know that the representative in China who replied to me very kindly translated my questionnaire for which I am grateful.

It is therefore difficult to know what percentage of replies I received but I did not intend this to be a numbers game. The numbers involved in this research make it statistically insignificant so I will not be drawing any grand conclusions. By its very nature, the questions I asked were open and looking for narrative answers rather than quantitative findings. I received responses from analysts in Australia, China, Germany, the UK, US, Switzerland, The Netherlands, Ukraine and Uruguay. I have included even very brief responses to give a flavour of replies. Please bear in mind that for many respondents English is not their first language.

You might find it interesting to see how what seems obvious to one person, seems equally obvious in another direction altogether for others.

The questionnaire I sent out read as follows:

The following is a survey of Jungian analysts in several countries which I am doing for the purpose of the book I am currently writing on spirituality. In the book I look at personal experience, clinical narratives and dilemmas including material on destiny/fate, spiritualism and the paranormal.

The book is aimed at all those who are interested in spirituality, mysticism, esoterica, personal search, incarnating their potential and developing spiritual practice, as well as psychotherapists and analysts who may, or may wish to, incorporate such an approach into their practice.

Your replies will be strictly confidential and no identifying information will be included in my write up of the results except for the country of origin.

You are asked to respond to the following questions, please (omitting any you wish to leave blank):

1 Do you find 'soul' and/or 'spirit' spontaneously arise in sessions?
2 If so, how long into the work have such instances arisen (stating as many variations in times as you wish).
3 If soul and spirit arise in sessions, how would you tend to deal with such matters?
4 Do you distinguish between dealing with 'soul' and dealing with 'spirit' in different ways?
5 Are you transparent about your own belief system when these subjects arise?
6 Would you tend you introduce these topics into the work?
7 How do you find people respond to these ideas?
8 Do you notice any perceptible difference in responses along gender, class or cultural lines?
9 Are there any other matters you would wish to raise?
10 In which country do you reside/practice?

I was deliberately opaque about what I meant by 'soul' and 'spirit' as I wanted everyone to respond from their own understanding and that of the people they are working with. I specifically did not layer a religious connotation to their meaning as that is not where I come from, although I realise that some or perhaps even many of the analysts responding may come from a religious tradition which you might discern in some responses.

The replies to the questions are set out in Appendix A. The only changes I have made to the answers is that I have taken out any identifying material so that all the replies are strictly anonymous.

I found it so interesting to read the responses to this survey. There is a wider range of views than I expected. Some responses are wide open and generous; others more cagey. This is perhaps inevitable when dealing with a subject which may be such a private matter. Also, for many I will have been a stranger asking personal questions. In all cases I am deeply grateful to the respondents for taking the time to reply and for sharing their thoughts and experiences so freely which I hope the reader will find to be of value.

It may be unsurprising that most of the respondents who took the time to reply to my questionnaire do engage with spirit and soul (however defined).

I was rather struck that few analysts identified a gender, class or cultural component in whether and how soul and/or spirit feature in analysis. It is a difficult question. I was not thinking that anyone would be more likely to experience soul or spirit than anyone else because they are universal experiences which arise in their many different guises across all cultures and times and genders. It may be that in some cultures it is more or less acceptable to talk about these matters. I think class is a rather unexplored area in the literature and in trainings which perhaps needs greater attention and which might then help us identify whether it is a factor in the work. Certainly it is a factor in accessing analysis.

One of the biggest obstacles in obtaining responses to my survey, I think, was discomfort around what might have been seen as 'introducing' a topic into a session. I would not do that myself as I do not believe it is the analyst's place to set any kind of agenda. But there are times when identifying something as relating to soul and/or spirit can be deeply meaningful and helpful. You can palpably hear an intake of breath at times when soul or spirit are mentioned.

Revealing where we come from spiritually as an analyst is a big question. In some cases it is publicly known through published writings; or we may be surrounded by give away signs in our consulting rooms. These revelations need to be carefully calibrated and analysts will be conscious of what they are revealing. Perhaps it partly depends on where you are on your own spiritual journey, as much as how comfortable you are about being transparent about this aspect of life. As you will see from the replies in Appendix A, some analysts sounded appalled by the idea of being candid about their 'beliefs', while others take it in their stride. Most though treat it as part of the transference relationship and as any other phenomenon that might arise in the work. Others turn these questions to Jung and refer to his position on these matters.

There may be a view that whenever we discuss a dream we are engaging with soul and/or spirit. Many experience dreams as communications not just from the unconscious but from 'God' or spirit or however we might conceptualise that 'higher' (ie more than personal) power. And not surprisingly many folk who fall within this category would be drawn to a Jungian approach for his inclusion of the spiritual realm in his psychology.

When a death enters the consulting room, or a synchronicity, they often evoke a numinous feeling which automatically takes us into the realm of soul and spirit so these matters then become hard to avoid. Depth is present when we touch these topics. Do we soften in our bodies and open to the depth, or become frightened/rigid and defensive? Or perhaps we hide behind a professional persona? It takes courage to allow ourselves to be vulnerable when entering into such unknown territory for both analyst and analysand. This creates new levels of emotional intimacy in the analysing dyad which may need to be managed internally on both sides.

In general terms older people tend to veer towards these topics when contemplating aging, wondering if they have lived well enough; wondering about the meaning of life. Whereas younger folk come at this more often nowadays from eco concerns and thinking about the future viability of our planet. The neoliberal political agendas many of us have suffered in recent decades also tend to make us think more broadly about how we want to live and whether that narrow, ego-centred mentality is fulfilling in the broadest terms.

People seek out therapy and analysis for many different reasons ranging from the ordinary mundane difficulties in day-to-day life we all encounter, to deep spiritual dis-ease and being stuck in patterns which may feel Karmic, intransigent or fixed patterns that need assistance to unpick. The two are not necessarily entirely separate. I am thinking of a patient who was doing office work for many years and felt her soul dying day by day with the daily drudge this work entailed. It took a great many years for her to dig her way out of this deadly grind to manifest her gifts and discover how it was she came to be in such a position. The reasons were deep, partly hidden for many years in family secrets, and extremely challenging to address. But she did break the chains and found a fulfilling career in a field which truly felt like her right path in life. Such work is so moving and transformational. It takes enormous courage to dig so deep, but it is possible.

In Chapter 12 we shift gear to look at spirits, ghosts (both metaphorical and literal) and the paranormal.

References

Allix, S. (2021). *When I was Someone Else: The Incredible True Story of Past Life Connection*. Rochester, Vermont: Park Street Press.

Chiga, K. (2020) *The Code of "Laozi": A Gate for the Great Tao. The Ultimate Principle of Sexuality Hidden in Laozi's Teaching*. (Trans. K. Hirose.) Ashville, North Carolina: Chiron Publications.

Gitz-Johansen, T. (2020) "Jung and the Spirit: A Review of Jung's Discussions of the Phenomenon of Spirit" in *Journal of Analytical Psychology* 65(4):653–671.

Hillman, J. (2020) *Suicide and the Soul*. Thompson, Conn: Spring Publications, 1964).

Jung, C.G. (1946) "Psychology of the Transference" in CW16.

Jung, C.G. (1966) *The Spirit in Man, Art and Literature* in CW15.

Jung, C.G. (2009) *The Red Book* (Ed. Shamdasani). London: W.W. Norton Books.
Meade, M. (2012) *Fate and Destiny: The Two Agreements of the Soul*. Seattle, WA: GreenFire Press.
Tzu, L. (1963) *Tao Te Ching*. (Trans. D.C. Lau.) Harmondsworth: Penguin Books.
Woodman, M. (1995) "Soul Moments" in *Handbook of the Soul*. Boston, New York, Toronto, London: Little Brown.

Chapter 12

Spiritualism, ghosts and the paranormal

From spiritual to spirits we move. This is quite a different turn to what we have been touching on in previous chapters.

Many of us will have encountered ghosts whether literal or metaphorical. Many are certainly fascinated by the idea of being able to see 'through the veil' and experience something more than the mundane reality which is necessarily the stuff of daily life. In this chapter I am going to touch on both the sort of ghost which could be described as supernatural, as well as those which haunt us through intergenerational trauma, and more. My aim is not to convince you that ghosts exist. Rather, to set out some 'out of the ordinary' events. May I ask you, as I did at the beginning, to approach this chapter with an open heart and mind? Perhaps it matters less whether ghosts exist literally, than it does to understand our preoccupations with them and the effect such encounters have on us.

People often search for contact with spirits when they feel bereft, grief-stricken and empty or abandoned. Some religions suggest we will be reunited with loved ones in an afterlife, as if those individual egos continue in another form in a parallel universe. For many this would be hell rather than heaven! Others see our bodies as vehicles to carry our souls and spirits. And many think about our soul and spirit merging with the energy of the universe from whence we came when the last breath leaves our bodies and our stay on earth draws to a close. Our personalities and egos cease to exist. Our bodies are either cremated and scattered on the earth or buried and slowly disintegrate back into the earth. When spirits are channelled through spiritual mediums, might it be that we are not speaking to the individuals who have died themselves from 'the other side', but rather the atoms of energy coalesce to create a vision (whether in image or voice) which we associate with the dead individual in a way that the seeker needs to heal and to find some peace? Perhaps 'the universe' is creating what is required in that moment? Maybe both. We can only speculate. It could of course be plain projection. But are we not helped along the path of life in manifold ways all the time with 'crumbs' leading us to where we need to go, with synchronicities, with

DOI: 10.4324/9781003284550-17

unexpected happenings and meetings, with conversations that set us thinking in new ways?

French journalist, Stephane Allix, raises many interesting questions in his 2017 work about contacting someone across space and time with whom he feels a deep kinship. He asks himself, if we can communicate with the dead, what does that mean for notions of reincarnation, and he grapples with where souls may be located after they have left this realm, amongst other things? Allix sees the dead existing in an eternity outside of time (2017 pp. 197). He questions whether beyond the realm of life and death, there is a universal justice, which takes us into the sphere of karma. Vital questions for us all and that perhaps help us find a sense of acceptance when injustice *appears* to prevail in this life. Allix finally realises that healing the living, heals the dead, which may intuitively be what draws many of us to such quests to get in touch with ancestral stories and resolve the flickering hints we may experience which draw us to the world of spirit. Allix's story, beginning with a vision – or dream – in a shamanic journey, is rather extraordinary and well worth exploring. To think about these matters, we have to free ourselves from binary thinking and allow ourselves to expand our minds beyond the limitations of humdrum reality. You might find it helpful to think along the lines of parallel realities for instance (where multiple universes co-exist). Some who have experienced Near Death Experiences (see below) talk of switching location at the speed of thought (ibid. 198).

Children are fascinated by spooky happenings. I remember in the playground at junior school (around age eight) we would use a Ouija board and do seances. We would also practice levitation where someone would lay on the ground with six of us around the body – two on each side, one at the foot and one at the head. We would each put two fingers underneath the body and recite an incantation led by the person at the head and then lift. The body would be raised to shoulder level and be totally weightless. We would all let go to the immersive experience and – for those moments – become serious and concentrated, until we began to laugh and the 'spell' would be broken. How that happened? No idea! And I was the one leading it and reciting the incantation. I just knew it worked.

The artist Tracey Emin has reported a spectral encounter at a key moment. Emin has talked of having recently recovered from a life-changing episode of cancer which has turned her life upside down and when she just wanted to "go into the cave". She has moved city and entered a new phase of work where she wanted to do black paintings on black. She reports having had a premonition one sunny spring evening when everything went suddenly dark. She reports:

> It was during the first lockdown … . It was light, I was sitting in my living room waiting to look out the window and the TV was on – and suddenly it

went off, the room went completely dark, and this apparition came towards me. I went, 'Oh, fucking hell!.'.
(https://www.theguardian.com/artanddesign/2022/apr/25/tracey-emin-ghost-apparition-new-life-margate-cancer-nudes?CMP=Share_iOSApp_Other accessed 25th April 2022)

These moments are frequently deeply transformative.

Spiritualism

The Spiritualist Movement emerged in the 1840s. Liz Greene, (whose work I discussed in chapter ten) lays out its early formation:

[b]y 1897, at its peak, it had roughly eight million followers across the US and Europe. Attempting to bridge the gap, scientists like Oliver Lodge, Pierre Curie, and William Crookes became involved with spiritualism in an effort to reconcile the two worlds, and the Society for Psychical Research was created in 1882. Even Thomas Edison couldn't resist the pull. His research laboratory at Menlo Park opened in 1876, joined the Theosophical Society in 1878, and in 1920 he announced that he had been working on a machine that would open up lines of communication with the spirit world. Freud became an honorary member of the Society in 1911. Jung joined it in 1917.
(Letter to the IAJS Discussion Seminar 12th August 2020 quoted with permission)

I find it most curious that Freud joined, given his renowned abhorrence of "the black tide of ... occultism" (Jaffé 1963 pp. 173) and his paper, "The 'Uncanny'" (1919) really shows no indication of understanding the truly uncanny at all. He seems to approach it through the familiar lens of some of his existing interests to fit his own theories.

Whereas Jung was concerned with matters of the dead and psychic phenomena for most of his life beginning at a very early age when he perceived his mother as having a two-fold personality which he saw as the daytime mother (pleasant, cheerful, with "hearty animal warmth"), and a night-time mother whom he saw as uncanny. The night-time mother he described as: "like one of those seers who is at the same time a strange animal, like a priestess in a bear's cave" (Jaffé pp. 67).

Jung's thinking

Theoretically, Jung's formulations ranged from thinking spirits could be seen as split-off fragments of the psyche, to seeing them as spirit entities in themselves.

In a talk Jung gave to the Society for Psychic Research in London in 1919 (aged forty-four and during the period when he was just beginning to come into his own professional maturation, firmly distinguishing his own analytic ideas in contradistinction to those of Freud after Freud had terminated their relationship in 1913) he calls parapsychic phenomena "the exteriorized effects of unconscious complexes" (1948 par. 600) and then says he sees no proof whatsoever of the existence of real spirits. However, he later added a footnote qualifying these thoughts although unfortunately the timing of this addition is unclear. This is how he revised his thoughts:

> After collecting psychological experiences from many people and many countries for fifty years, I no longer feel as certain as I did in 1919, when I wrote this sentence. To put it bluntly, I doubt whether an exclusively psychological approach can do justice to the phenomena in question. Not only the findings of parapsychology, but my own theoretical reflections ... have led me to certain postulates which touch on the realm of nuclear physics and the conception of the space-time continuum. This opens up the whole question of the transpsychic reality immediately underlying the psyche.
>
> (1948 par. 600 n.15)

I think this vacillation may well be an example of Jung's personal struggle between wanting to present himself as respectably scientific, particularly to such an audience, and his natural inclination to being of a more mystical bent. The fact is – I believe – he was both.

During Jung's period known as his 'confrontation with the unconscious', he envisaged a relationship with spirit figures in his *Seven Sermons to the Dead* which he originally attributed to the early Christian Gnostic religious teacher Basilides, perhaps as a way of distancing himself from such seemingly cooky matters. It was though the only portion of *The Red Book* (2009) which Jung authorised for public dissemination during his lifetime. *The Seven Sermons* has been described as "a comprehensive psychotheological cosmology" (Shamdasani 2008 pp.19). In it, Philemon (Jung's spirit guide, or alter ego) is teaching the dead about the nature of life and death. Throughout *The Red Book* (2009), the dead guided Jung to understand the unconscious and Jung narrates his ongoing relationship with the figures he converses with in Active Imagination.

Jung talks extensively of many experiences with the dead in his *Memories, Dreams, Reflections* (Jaffé 1963), some of which might be seen as synchronistic happenings (like the crack in the bookcase which famously occurred when he met with Freud); others were visions and Active Imaginations such as those which are set out in Jung's *Red Book* (2009).

One theme Jung draws out in his *Seven Sermons to the Dead* is the idea that not everyone dies in a serene state of having come to a place of peace about life and death and having tied up loose ends in relationships. Indeed, that is a very fortunate individual who does reach such a state. I have personally experienced someone struggle to let go into death because – or so I believe – they were unable to find peace with events around them on their deathbed. The person had a lifelong wish to be cremated and to have her ashes scattered in Israel but the individual responsible for making these arrangements (a daughter) had forced the dying woman to agree to being buried because of the daughter's own fundamentalist religious beliefs. This was utterly repugnant to the dying woman and terrifying as she had had a lifelong fear of being eaten by worms. This meant her soul could not rest and she could not let go into death for considerably longer than the medics predicted was possible. I am afraid that abuses like these are not uncommon in religious communities as elsewhere. So, we come to the notion of restless souls which can be the result of such experiences. This puts into sharp focus the need to find that peace of mind while living and to make a conscious effort to attend to things while we have the chance. We have been given a crack at incarnation and it may be our only shot. This raises the important question as to whether we continue to individuate (that is to develop as beings to fulfil our potential as individual souls) after death. (This could be discussed at great length!) There are arguments for either way (which must necessarily remain conjecture). Stephens sees this question as being the whole exercise of the *Seven Sermons* (2020 pp. 157 n.2). She tells us:

> each sermon is an attempt to explore individuation in terms of each realm of experience; the experience of God as a singular and vast entity, then as it applies to the experiences of plural gods, the community and finally to men.
>
> (ibid. pp. 150)

Stephens raises some fantastically interesting questions:

"Do conversations Jung has with the dead [in the *Seven Sermons*] raise the consciousness of the dead? ...
    What would raising the consciousness of the dead look like?" (ibid.).
    I would add to this list:

- Does that impact upon our relations with our dead?
- Does it help us, the living, to find peace with those we have lost?
- Can we help them? And,
- Can they help us?

(If you are reading this in a book group, I would recommend a substantial period of time could be set aside for these questions. You might need tissues!)

Stephens explores Jung's relationship with the dead at some length (2020). She sees him as vacillating in that, although he had experienced many extraordinary happenings, he saw some of these as falling within the ambit of his theory of archetypes, which may well account for my encounter with the witch which I relate later in this chapter. Jung's Zofingia Lectures (1983) (when he was a medical student of but 21–23 years of age and a member of the Zofingia fraternity) given at Basel University, contain his as yet undeveloped thoughts. (Jung qualified with distinction in 1900.) Jung's dissertation was entitled "On the Psychology and Pathology of So-Called Occult Phenomena" (1902) where he discusses the case of a patient who 'saw' dead people. The identity of the medium is Helène Preiswerk, his cousin, whom he disguises to protect her identity (or to give the impression the medium was totally independent). He actually re-created the seances which formed the substance of the dissertation. It is usual to disguise material so as to protect confidentiality, but in this case Jung appears to have fictionalised his material rather heavily to suit his own purpose. The family had no trouble recognising the account and suffered social stigma as a result (Bair 2003 pp. 62–64). However, this does not detract from the point that Jung did indeed witness and experience many uncanny things.

Near-death experience

There are many accounts of Near Death Experiences which often share similar features such as seeing a tunnel of light. For obvious reasons they can have a great impact on the survivor who truly experiences how precious it is to come through such an experience and return to life often with new vigour. Tony Kofi was 16 when he had a near fatal fall from a height, landing on his head when he was working as a carpentry apprentice in 1981. He describes the slowing down of time as he fell and having a series of images pass through his mind such as the children he would go on to have. To his surprise he saw the image of himself playing a saxophone. He had never played an instrument and had never even seen a saxophone before. This vision drove him to go on to teach himself to play the saxophone and he became an award winning Jazz saxophonist and composer. (See 'The near-death experience that made me a top musician' – BBC News accessed online 22nd December 2021).

Jungian analyst Michael Gellert in the United States recounts an enthralling tale of a Near Death Experience which came in the form of a vision experienced as he underwent brain surgery. Like with Kofi, the experience had a dramatic effect on his life and his philosophical outlook which enriched his marriage which was then on the verge of collapse (2021). The story tracks a shift from sceptical scientific materialism to being forced – by vision and dreams – to face the undeniability to him of something more mysterious or uncanny at play in life.

A most moving account is reported in Walach (2019) where a man visualised himself in his own Near Death Experience encountering a man he had never seen before who looked at him lovingly. Ten years later, at his mother's death bed, she confided to the man that she had had an extramarital affair with a Jewish man who had been killed by the Nazis and she told her son that this man was in fact the son's father. When she showed him a photograph, it was the very same man he had met in his Near Death Experience (pp. 55).

Anita Moorjani, in her personal account of a Near Death Experience, paints a vivid picture of life as she found herself in the liminal space between life and death (Moorjani 2012). She felt peaceful, calm, free of fear and pain. She experienced unconditional love and a feeling of having come home (c.f. the tale from the Kabbalah and the Dagara tribe in chapter one.) She describes being more aware of what was going on around her when she was in a coma than in waking life. She reports:

> The sharpness of my perception was even more intense than if I'd been awake and using my physical senses. I seemed to just know and understand everything – not only what was going on around me, but also what everyone was feeling, as though I were able to see and feel through each person.
>
> (Moorjani 2012 pp. 61)

Later: "I didn't even think it odd that I was aware of my husband and the doctor speaking to each other outside the ICU, some 40 feet down a hallway" (ibid. pp.63). Moorjani had cancerous tumours the size of lemons throughout her lymphatic system and her brain was filled with fluid, as were her lungs. Her skin was covered in lesions leaking toxins. The medics did not believe she would make it through the night (ibid.). She describes fluctuating between being pulled out of the bliss she was experiencing 'on the other side', into the emotional dramas taking place around her hospital bed, and then returning to the heightened state of freedom and unconditional love. She says: "It didn't feel as though I'd *physically* gone somewhere else – it was more as though I'd *awakened*" (ibid. pp.65). She reports encountering relatives and close friends who had died years earlier who said they had been present for her through all the years (ibid. pp.66). I guess some people might call this delirium but bear with me. Even Moorjani describes herself struggling to understand what was happening:

> *Why do I suddenly understand all this?* I wanted to know. *Who's giving me this information? Is it God? Krishna? Buddha? Jesus?* And then I was overwhelmed by the realization that God isn't a *being,* but *a state of being ... and I was now that state of being!*.
>
> (ibid. pp. 68) (emphasis in original)

I think what she means by that last comment is that we each contain that spark of the divine within us. It is not said in an inflated messianic tone, but rather in wonder and awe at the insights being revealed to her which gave her a sense of her place in the universe, with her life like a thread woven into a tapestry, incorporating the good and the bad. She realised she was lovable simply by virtue of existing, not needing to perform, to placate, to please. Not needing to be any particular way, but simply by being. She began to understand that we are all connected – every being, animal, creature, insect, plant, tree:

> I realized that the entire universe is alive and infused with conscious-ness, encompassing all of life and nature. Everything belongs to an infinite Whole. I was intricately, inseparably enmeshed with all of life. We are all facets of that unity – we're *all* One, and each of us has an effect on the collective Whole.
>
> (ibid. pp. 70)

Before moving on from Moorjani, her views on life after death are inter-esting. She felt the idea of reincarnation, with lives running on sequentially, was not borne out by her experience:

> I realized that time doesn't move in a linear fashion unless we're using the filter of our physical bodies and minds. Once we're no longer limited by our earthly senses, every moment exists simultaneously.
>
> (ibid. pp 142)

This chimes with Jung's ideas on the psychoid unconscious and synchronicity (see chapter ten). Also with the notion of parallel universes co-existing.

Near Death Experiences are often reported as having qualities which are similar to (or identical with?) mystical or spiritual experiences which may be deeply transformative (Walach 2019 pp. 50).

If we could truly believe we are enough, we are lovable as we are, we have our place in the universe, I suspect we would all be less driven to consume in the way I described in chapter one. We would all feel greater peace and content-ment in life just as we are. Would our relationships not be better, as well as our connection to ourselves and our environment? It is when we forget how we are connected to each other and the earth that we get into trouble; when we forget we are connected by the same universal love that pumps each breath into our bodies and sustains us in each and every moment.

Parapsychology

For those interested in exploring the topic of parapsychology (the study of psychic phenomena), you might turn to Frederic Myers (1843–1901) (a founder of the Society for Psychical Research) whose classic text, *Human Personality and its Survival of Bodily Death* (1903) explores parapsychology using scientific methodologies. Jungian analyst Joe Cambray (former President of Pacifica Graduate Institute in California who originally trained in hard science as a chemist) informs us that it was Myers who was in fact responsible for introducing Freud's thought to England in 1897 and that Myers' writings were the source of both Joan Riviere's and James Strachey's first contact with Freud's ideas (2004 pp. 224). (Both Riviere and Strachey became important figures in the Freudian world.) This was an era where hypnotism was just being developed, and there were experiments with testing whether thoughts and even tastes could be transmitted to someone in a different room which produced convincing results. Palmer (whom I interview in Appendix B) has tabulated Myers' taste tests and shows us that they were at least 72% successful (2017 pp. 129–131). It was Myers who first coined the term telepathy. He also objected to the term paranormal insisting that everything falls within 'normal'. It is fascinating to note that Myers research appears to have continued in the 'beyond'. Saltmarsh (2004) reports experiments where Myers communicated across the divide and devised experiments to 'prove' life exists after death. There is also a very interesting discussion on YouTube between Jeffrey Mishlove and Dr Terence Palmer (author of *The Science of Spirit Possession*) where Palmer reports that he is in fact in touch with Myers via mediums to this day (see https://www.youtube.com/watch?v=bQ6QIKnZBwM&t=130s accessed 14th August 2020). I was so intrigued by this conversation that I met with Dr Palmer (on 24th August 2020, via Zoom because of the Covid pandemic) and we had a wide-ranging discussion. The story of how Palmer came to open up to the life of the spirit is striking because it precisely mirrored the story of my old friend who, at a crucial juncture in life, ended up living in the woods (mentioned in the Introduction). Palmer told me that in the 1980s his business went bust in the financial crash and he lost everything and ended up homeless and destitute, living like a hermit in a tent. This brought him to the point of reaching out for help and the course of his life was transformed. This account could just as easily have been placed in chapter nine on 'why do things go wrong' where I look at how often it is things have to go wrong in life for them to go right. And 'going right' in this case meant Palmer finding his true vocation as a result of what could be seen as tragic misfortune. It was a psychic experience during this period which changed the course of his life and aligned him with his true purpose. (Dr Palmer has generously given me his permission to publish a transcript of our conversation which appears as Appendix B.)

As a counterpoint to the perhaps light and airy notion of the spiritual as we have been discussing earlier, Palmer is a Spirit Release Therapist who helps people deal with unwanted spirits. He makes the distinction (following Williamson whom he cites) between spirits that exist in the spiritual domain or spirit-world as guides, and spirits of the deceased who remain 'earthbound' for some reason (2017 pp. 8). We might speculate that such 'earthbound' spirits may have unfinished business to work out on this plain before they can be freed from some sort of turmoil. People who die from violence, for instance, may well be utterly discombobulated at the moment of death and may need to find a way to 'understand' what has occurred to achieve some acceptance and peace with what has happened to them.

Palmer also touches on the interesting idea that some diagnoses of Disassociative Identity Disorder (DID, formerly known as Multiple Personality Disorder), may in fact be cases of spiritual possession. Palmer then goes on to tell us that British psychiatrist Arthur Guirdham concluded, after working as a clinician for more than forty years, all forms of mental illness can be caused by spirit interference (Palmer 2017 pp. 22). These would certainly be interesting avenues for further research.

There has been research into psychic capabilities by placing items on top of a wardrobe while a person lies in bed so that it would be impossible to see the items with the naked eye without moving. I am sure there must be many other experiments which have been undertaken to test these capacities in an attempt to garner scientific proof of psychic abilities.

Research psychologist Lawrence LeShan in the United States, who initially saw himself as an arch sceptic, has done research with psychics using rigorous scientifically designed methods (2012). He quotes Italian psychoanalyst Emilio Servadio whom he describes as one of the greatest contemporary experts in psychical research:

> In telepathy, a dualism appears to be temporarily cancelled, and for some moments a 'unity in plurality' re-established.
>
> (quoted in LeShan 2012 pp. 39)

This is how Servadio conceptualises psychic ability to work. The veil that separates us – as we perceive individuals in everyday reality – seems to recede for these moments to enable a true sense to be gained of how we are in reality joined to each other inasmuch as there is no separation in the first place. This chimes with Jung's notion of the psychoid unconscious and the Buddhist notion of 'one mind':

> The statement 'Nor is one's own mind separable from other minds' is another way of expressing the fact of 'all contamination'. Since all distinctions vanish in the unconscious condition, it is only logical that the distinction between separate minds should disappear too.
>
> (Jung 1939[1958] par. 817)

LeShan compares daily reality (which he calls sensory reality) with what he names clairvoyant reality which broadly refers to the more all-encompassing reality wherein it is possible to incorporate notions of synchronicity and the paranormal. LeShan admits these 'realities' are perhaps better seen as a spectrum rather than two distinct entities. He also later added a third dimension which he calls Transpsychic Reality which more or less equates with the numinous. I believe his thinking does elucidate that these mysterious matters are possible and can be conceptualised.

Premonitions

Jung famously had a premonition about the outbreak of World War One which he describes in his memoire (Jaffé 1963). There were many tales of premonitions in the wake of the 11th September 2001 disaster which I refer to elsewhere (Williams 2019 chapter six) where I also discuss a number of precognitive dreams. Jewish journalist, Charlotte Beradt, in Berlin set up a project of clandestinely recording the dreams of her fellow German citizens in the period soon after the Nazis came to power. She amassed a collection of about three hundred dreams which prefigured the totalitarian intentions of the regime:

> A Jewish lawyer dreamed that he was crossing Lapland to reach "the last country on Earth where Jews are still tolerated", but a smiling border official threw his passport into the snow. A green, safe land lay tantalisingly out of reach. It was still 1935.
>
> (Knight 2022)

Beradt was unable to publish her collection, *The Third Reich of Dreams* (1966), until after the war. She wrote:

> these "diaries of the night" seemed "to record seismographically the slightest effects of political events on the psyche". They were raw, untouched by hindsight and possibly prophetic for that reason. "Dream imagery might thus help to describe the structure of a reality that was just on the verge of becoming a nightmare.
>
> (Knight 2022)

In a new book, Sam Knight (award-winning British journalist and staff writer at *The New Yorker*) examines the subject of premonitions. He focuses on John Barker, a 42-year-old psychiatrist at Shelton hospital near Shrewsbury in the UK. Barker was a member of Britain's Society for Psychical Research (mentioned above). Barker visited the site of the Aberfan mining disaster of 1966 where a slag heap (containing waste material from the coal mines disastrously created on a mountain slope above the village adjacent to two schools) was dislodged by driving rain and tragically buried the schools full of children as they answered the morning register. One hundred and forty-four people were killed, a hundred and sixteen of them children, mostly between the ages of seven and ten. I vividly remember being gripped by these images on the news at the time. When Barker talked to witnesses, he noticed there were several incidents connected to the disaster which he felt were "strange and pathetic". He came across accounts of children whose lives had been saved by oversleeping, resting on a wall, delaying for a last cup of tea before leaving home or getting stuck in fog.

Barker found that:

> Bereaved families also spoke of dreams and portents. Weeks after the accident, the mother of an eight-year-old boy named Paul Davies, who died in Pantglas school, found a drawing of massed figures digging in the hillside under the words "the end", which he had made the night before the slide.
>
> (Knight 2022 pp. 25)

A local mother is quoted:

> In Plymouth, the evening before the coal slide, Constance Milder had a vision at a spiritualist meeting. Milder, who was forty-seven, told six witnesses that she saw an old schoolhouse, a Welsh miner, and "an avalanche of coal" rushing down a mountain. "At the bottom of this mountain of hurtling coal was a little boy with a long fringe looking absolutely terrified to death. Then for quite a while I 'saw' rescue operations taking place. I had an impression that the little boy was left behind and saved. He looked so grief-stricken." Milder recognised the boy later on the evening news.
>
> (ibid. pp. 43)

Moved by what he encountered in Aberfan, Baker devised a study where he wanted to gather as many premonitions as possible of such events and to investigate the people reporting them. Out of an initial sixty plausible premonitions, he found evidence that twenty-two were reported before the disaster struck. This convinced Barker that precognition might be as common as left-handedness. He hoped this data could be used to prevent future disasters.

Knight reports:

> Barker used the language of seismology to describe mental processes that might be operating at a deep level within the collective subconscious. He wanted an instrument that was sensitive enough to capture intimations that were otherwise impossible to detect. He envisaged the fully fledged Premonitions Bureau as a "central clearing house to which the public could always write or telephone should they experience any premonitions, particularly those which they felt were related to future catastrophes". Over time, the Premonitions Bureau would become a databank for the nation's dreams and visions – "mass premonitions.".
>
> (ibid. pp. 122)

Personal encounters

I have had a number of encounters with ghosts of different sorts in life. When I was training as a Jungian analyst, which is an intense journey into the depths, I had two experiences which could be described as being 'supernatural' (I am spelling it that way as I do not wish to state categorically that they were supernatural, but they were certainly more than ordinary). One was at a time when I was having a particularly rough time and I asked a friend who is a shaman to do a journey for me which entails the shaman communing with her spirits for guidance. That morning I saw a spirit in the flat where I was attending the training seminars and I later discovered that this was the precise time when the shaman was undertaking the journey with her spirit guide on my behalf.

The second involved what I called a poltergeist. During the same period when I was training, I was brushing my teeth one night when a piece of coral from the back of a bathroom shelf in front of me and above the mirror, came round and hit me on the back of the head. I was quite shaken and searched around to see if anyone was there, knowing that there was not. It really jolted me. (It hadn't fallen as it came from a direction – behind me – which made that impossible.) When I discussed this with my analyst the next day, I remembered I was feeling really angry about something trivial when this occurred and I realised it was as if I needed to have the sense knocked back into me. It also knocked the piece of theory into me about the psyche being capable of being located inside and out of the body as psyche and matter are inextricably linked. Direct experiences like this teach so much more than mere theory. These are the sort of ideas which Jung formulated to explain synchronicity (discussed in chapter ten). We are joined to others, to the earth, to animals and all of the natural world via the networks of energy variously described in chapter three when I talked of how animals know when their owners are ill. It also brought into focus the notion that there are multiple realities. Perhaps it was both a poltergeist and a manifestation of the subjective psyche. This way of thinking helps to hold events and feelings more lightly, with less righteous certainty. For sometimes we simply do not know and many things and feelings can co-exist simultaneously.

A couple of days after the poltergeist incident, I dreamt the 'poltergeist' was tickling my toes as I was half awake and trying to get off to sleep (probably in a dream or perhaps a hypnagogic state). My toe had been sticking out from under the duvet. I pulled it back in. In my mind I surrounded myself with an imaginal crystal pyramid of green light for psychic protection and the poltergeist came round to where my face was turned outward and he knocked on the pyramid as if knocking on a glass door. I had the impression that the presence was a tall, dark man with a large nose. He seemed benign although I was still terrified. He seemed to want me to come out and play!

I was used to all manner of unsettling experiences. While I was writing my Masters dissertation on *The Function and Meaning of 'the Witch' in the Individuation Process of Women* (which was much later published in the Festschrift of my professional association (Bierschenk *et al* 2017), I underwent a series of terrifying dreams night after night which I experienced as visitations from a witch, sometimes in the guise of her animal familiar, a mangy cat. The cat would snap at my feet night after night making it quite difficult to sleep, always ready to pounce. (What is it with feet!) I would often think – in the dream – that I was awake. It was very disorientating and frightening. As I said in chapter one, what you focus your attention on, becomes your experience of life. So, when you focus on a subject intensely as I did during the writing of my dissertation, it takes up a central place in your psyche. The witch became my constant companion for that period. Not a comfortable experience! It had all begun when I felt the witch's presence at my side one day, just out of my sight line, over my shoulder. Then the dreams began.

Growing up in the late 60s/70s there was always plenty of talk of way out subjects like astral travelling and psychedelic experiences. Everyone was into whacky stuff. We would all engage in tarot and palm readings and other similar practices. We all read Hesse's Siddhartha, Kafka, Jean Paul Sartre and such like. The older boys (mostly) would go off and travel overland to India (which is sadly no longer possible). It was a wonderful period. But my engagement was quite superficial as I had not experienced the depths at such a young age.

In my early 20s there was an occasion where I heard my name being called out to me in an empty house. In the same house during that period I was talking with a friend who was asking me if something was OK. I went to answer 'yes' as frankly I was too unassertive then to be honest, when I found the word 'no' coming out of my mouth. It was quite bizarre. I felt my mouth say 'yes', but 'no' came out. It was as if I had been taken over (although I would not wish to suggest this was any more dramatic than it really was). It was utterly without my conscious volition and, although I felt quite discombobulated, I intuitively felt as if I was being taught an important lesson about having the confidence to speak my truth.

There have been instances of items disappearing and then suddenly re-appearing on the table in front of me where they simply were not moments before. You tend to automatically think you must be imagining such things as any alternative seems impossible or implausible.

Then there have been other more trivial instances where I felt a draught blowing against my leg or making the shower curtain billow when there were no windows open and such like. Or paintings being at a tilt without any explanation, a cupboard door being open when you know it was closed. These are I suspect experiences we all have but brush aside as they can so easily be absent-mindedly dismissed.

There was one incident which would strictly be characterised as a dream although it had the feeling of a personal encounter, where I met with Jung. It was at the time when I was about to hand in the manuscript for my first book, *Jung: The Basics.* He looked over the manuscript and gave me his seal of approval! I felt delighted.

Earlier, in my youth, I used to go to the College of Psychic Studies in London to consult a woman who would psychically channel 'the Mandarin'. It was like consulting a medium for guidance, but in this case she would subsume her personal identity and allow the spirit of the Mandarin to take her over. It was a curious experience and I have tape recordings of all the sessions (although unfortunately not in a format that exists any longer. They were on cassette tapes). Her voice would change register and she would 'become' the Mandarin. The insights and thoughts were always very helpful and it was a numinous experience to be present in such company. Perhaps even more uncannily, years later I dreamt that the Mandarin visited me in a dream. (At least, I was not certain if it was a dream as it felt so real.) He simply came to my bedside and knelt down, bowing his head to me which I felt was an intense honour. There were no words. A book has been published about the Mandarin and the deep trance mediumship of Mary Absolum who was the channeller (Rutter 1981).

A haunting

While writing this chapter, I happened to hear on the radio an account of a poltergeist haunting when the author, Kate Summerscale, was inter- viewed on the publication of her new book, *The Haunting of Alma Fielding* (2020). She tells us that at the time of a poltergeist attack on Alma Fielding in 1938 which she describes in the book, there was a huge boom in ghosts and ghost huntings which the author thinks may have been connected to a national jitteriness in the Collective with war in the offing. Naturally people would have been filled with foreboding about those events. Fielding's son was awoken one night to hear a commotion going on in his parents' bedroom. Upon investigation he saw them clinging to each other and screaming while the bed shook and was being moved around the bedroom. The author reports on the investigations of Nandor Fodor (1895–1964), a Hungarian born parapsychologist and researcher, who carried out a battery of tests on Fielding about these events. He concluded that she was subconsciously generating the events in her home. He suggested they were real physical events but generated by her un- conscious mind under pressure of a trauma that had occurred in her childhood (taken from a radio broadcast interview with the author on the BBC Radio 4 *Today* programme, 28th September 2020). This very much accords with my own conclusions about my haunting by the poltergeist and with Jung's ideas about the psyche.

Aboriginal wisdom

David Tacey, writing about his deep connection with the Aboriginal community at Alice Springs where he spent some of his youth, tells us:

> So while for Aboriginal people the active forces are supernatural and external agents, or ghosts of ancestral spirits, for Jung they are deeply *natural*, internal, forgotten agents that are activated by suggestion ... For Jung, the forces are psychological, not in the sense of being 'personal', but in the sense of being transpersonal. The psyche of the modern person has a lineage which goes back to the mists of the past, and unknowingly, we carry that lineage even as we walk in the clear light of the secular present. It is as if an invisible realm of forces and energies surround us, or bathes the psyche in an otherworldly glow.
>
> (emphasis in original) (2009: pp. 49–50)

Tacey, I believe correctly, sees Europeans as egocentric, that is seeing themselves as the centre of the universe but without having a true grasp of the nature of the unitary reality I have been highlighting. He suggests Europeans have seen Aboriginals as 'primitive' on the basis that they are not driven by the consumerist values and materialist ambitions which fuel so many. He goes on:

> Aboriginal people seek to relate to the unseen spirits of the land. They spent an enormous amount of their time in states of attunement and receptivity. They realize that the greater part of reality is invisible, and that human lives are best spent trying to adjust to invisible forces. Aboriginal culture is based on wisdom, whereas European culture is based on knowledge and information. Wisdom seeks to attune itself to spiritual forces, and knowledge seeks to gain mastery and control over the physical world.
>
> (2009 pp. 53–64)

Psilocybin

Psilocybin is gaining increasing currency at the fringes of the therapy world as an adjunct to psychotherapy. Psilocybin (the active ingredient in magic mushrooms) has been used in ritual and in experimentation for centuries. The earliest documented report of its use is in Mexico in 1486 at the coronation of the Aztec emperor (M. Sheldrake 2020 pp. 111). In the modern era it was researched from the 1950s and by the 1960s was on the streets and fairly widely used in the developing drug culture of the 'hippie' movement. It is a psychedelic, mind-altering substance with apparently consciousness expanding properties. Harvard academic and counterculture revolutionary,

Timothy Leary, went to Mexico to experiment with magic mushrooms in 1960 and reports that it was like a "visionary experience". It changed the course of his career and had a huge cultural impact. He believed cultural revolution and spiritual enlightenment could be attained through use of psychedelics (ibid. 130–131).

Whether chemically induced experiences which are believed to be spiritual or mystical are the real McCoy would make an interesting debate. I don't know the answer to that question, but I think it is one worth asking.

Metaphorical ghosts in intergenerational transmission of trauma

For the next section I am switching gear as the sort of ghosts I now turn to are not literal but metaphorical. We know anecdotally that people often feel haunted by their past or their history. And history does transfer from one generation to the next by various means. I wrote about this for an international Congress held in Vienna in 2020 (Williams 2020) and I set out a slightly amended extract from my Congress paper which was written in an academic style for that audience. These are the five different ways I identified in which intergenerational transmission can happen beginning with a piece of personal history:

1   My mother was fourteen when she was sent away from her parents in Vienna as a refugee from the Holocaust on what was called the Kindertransport. Parents sent their children to the UK to live with hosts who had to sponsor them in order for them to be allowed into Britain. This was the same age at which I lost my father so in a different way I was subjected to loss of a parent at the same stage in life as my mother. This is the first level of intergenerational transmission (or perhaps better, repetition) I will mention. What can we call that? Karma … .? In Ayurveda they talk of Samskaras (subtle imprints which form the basis of Karma) to explain how physical, behavioural, mental and emotional traits may be transmitted through generations.

2   Secondly: there are studies such as Verny and Kelly (1981) which show that there is an intrauterine communication between mother and foetus which transmits the mother's feelings. They found that:

when a pregnant woman is tense, stressed, depressed or anxious, her glands secrete an increased amount of neurohormonal substances, such as adrenaline, nor-adrenaline, and serotonin into the blood" which reach the placenta and "create a predisposition to psychological disturbances, such as anxiety and depression.

(quoted in Wardi 1992 p. 58–59)

When things cannot be spoken, they find expression in other ways; the baton is passed to the next generation. Feelings are transmitted to process them, as in the transference we speak of in psychoanalysis, but in intergenerational transmission you don't know you've inherited this role. Feelings, stress and anxiety travel unconsciously from one generation to the next.

This leaves children of Holocaust survivors, in this example, often exploding with the aggression their parents had suppressed which leads to problems of depression and even psychosis. The children (and now grandchildren and great grandchildren) *carry* the trauma.

3   The extraordinary, deaf percussionist Evelyn Glennie (mentioned in chapter two) so beautifully suggests that:

> to truly listen we must use our bodies as resonating chambers (Glennie 2017). But because our bodies *are* resonating chambers, we are always listening, with, or without, cognitive awareness. Intergenerational transmission of traumatic experience tells the story of information flow through our bodies
>
> (Hopenwasser 2017 p. 60)

4   I am not addressing the neuroscience evidence on intergenerational transmission. I will though touch on the work of Rachel Yehuda on how trauma and resilience cross generations. She has studied epigenetics to discover that genes can be turned on and off and be expressed differently through changes in environment and behaviour. Yehuda is a pioneer in understanding how the effects of stress and trauma can transmit biologically, beyond cataclysmic events … . She has studied the children of Holocaust survivors as well as pregnant women who survived the 11th September attacks (Yehuda *et al* 2016 pp. 372–380).

Mark Wimborn (Jungian analyst in Memphis, Tennessee) kindly sent me an extract from his 2016 paper which refers to Yehuda's research stating she provided the:

> first demonstration of an association of pre-conception parental trauma with epigenetic alterations that is evident in both exposed parent and offspring, providing potential insight into how severe psychophysiological trauma can have intergenerational effects.
>
> (Wimborn 2016 p. 372)

Wimborn reports: "This was a genetic study of 32 Jewish men and women who had been in a concentration camp, witnessed or experienced killing or torture, or who were in hiding during WWII. The researchers analysed the genes of their children … and compared the results with Jewish families who were living outside of Europe during the war. The team focussed on one region of a gene associated with the regulation of stress hormones, known to be affected by trauma" (ibid.):

> They found epigenetic tags on the very same part of this gene in both the Holocaust survivors and their offspring.

This was *not* found in any of the control group or their children. The team ruled out that the epigenetic changes were a result of trauma the children had experienced themselves. According to Yehuda *et al*, the gene changes in the children could only be attributed to Holocaust exposure in the parents (Wimborn, personal communication 2nd May 2018).

There are also experiments with mice which show that, when sperm from a stressed mouse is injected into foetal eggs in utero, "the offspring exhibit the same stress behaviours, without any contact with dad" (Gapp *et al* 2014 pp 667–669).

In another study rodents are primed to fear the smell of peppermint. When their offspring are exposed to peppermint, they exhibit the same fear. Note: the fear of the peppermint was established in the memory of the mother *before* pregnancy (Jacek and Sullivan 2014).

The next generation are not simply haunted by the effects being experienced in the family, but are being changed in deep, bodily/chemical ways.

So, the methods of transmission are:

1   Karma,
2   Intrauterine transmission
3   via unconscious affect,
4   bodily affect, and
5   epigenetically

(Williams 2020)

There are notable works on metaphorical ghosts from our histories by British psychoanalyst Stephen Frosh (2013) and Professor of Sociology in California, Avery F. Gordon (1997) which are well worth exploring.

Art

There are many accounts in art and film which explore ghosts and the healing aspects of communing with the dead such as *Truly, Madly, Deeply* (Minghella 1990), the Harry Potter novels (Rowling 1997–2007), or the classic *A Matter of Life and Death* (Powell and Pressburger 1946). Or much of Shakespeare such as *Hamlet* and *Macbeth*. Or in the thirteenth century, Dante's classic *Divine Comedy* trilogy: Inferno (2006), Purgatory (1955), Paradise (1962). Each of these in their own ways puts us in touch with the deeper meanings of life and the eternal issues associated with the passage from life to death and the possibility of a 'beyond'. Of course, this is only a tiny, random selection of artistic works which explore these ideas which are eternally fascinating and appear in much art all over the world and in all historical periods as these concepts are archetypal.

References

Alighieri, D. (1955) (Trans. Kirkpatrick) *The Divine Comedy 2: Purgatory*. London: Penguin Classics.

Alighieri, D. (1962) (Trans. Kirkpatrick) *The Divine Comedy 3: Paradise*. London: Penguin Classics.

Alighieri, D. (2006) (Trans. Kirkpatrick) *The Divine Comedy I: Inferno*. London: Penguin Classics.

Bair, D. (2003) *Jung: A Biography*. New York and London: Little Brown.

Beradt, C. (1966) *The Third Reich of Dreams* (Trans. A. Gottwald). Chicago: Quadrangle Books.

Bierschenk, J., Garrett, S., Heuer, G.M. & Damon, S. (Eds.) (2017) "The Function and Meaning of 'the Witch' in the Individuation Process of Women" in *The Association of Jungian Analysts 40th Anniversary Festschrift*. London: AJA.

Cambray, J. (2004) "Synchronicity as Emergence" in *Analytical Psychology: Contemporary Perspectives in Jungian Analysis*. Hove and New York: Brunner-Routledge.

Freud, S. (1919) "The 'Uncanny'" in *The Standard Edition of the Complete Psychological Works of Sigmund Freud* (Trans. Strachey) Vol. 17. London: The Hogarth Press.

Frosh, S. (2013) *Hauntings: Psychoanalysis and Ghostly Transmissions*. Basingstoke, Hampshire: Palgrave Macmillan.

Gapp, K., Jawaid, A., Sarkies, P., Bohacek, J., Pelczar, P., Prados, J., Farinelli, L., Miska, E. and Mansuy, I.M. (2014) "Implication of sperm RNAs in transgenerational inheritance of the effects of early trauma in mice" in *Nature Neuroscience* volume 17, pp. 667–669.

Gellert, M. (2021) *Far From This Land: A memoir About Evolution, Love, and the Afterlife*. Lake Worth, FL: Nicolas Hays.

Gordon, A. F. (1997) *Ghostly Matters: Haunting and the Sociological Imagination*. Minneapolis & London: University of Minnesota Press.

Hopenwasser, K. (2017) "The Rhythm of Resilience: A Deep Ecology of Entangled Relationality" in *Wounds of History: Repair and Resilience in the Trans-Generational Transmission of Trauma* (Eds. J. Salberg and S. Grand). London & New York: Routledge.

Jacek, D. and Sullivan, R.M. (2014) "Intergenerational transmission of emotional trauma through amygdala-dependent mother-to-infant transfer of specific fear" in *Proceedings of the National Academy of Sciences of the United States of America* 111, 33 (2014): 12222–12227. doi:10.1073/pnas.1316740111.

Jaffé, A. (1963) *Memories, Dreams, Reflections*. London: Fontana, 1995.

Jung, C.G. (1902) "On the Psychology and Pathology of So-Called Occult Phenomena" in CW1.

Jung, C.G. (1939[1958]) "Psychological Commentary on the Tibetan Book of Great Liberation" in CW11.

Jung, C.G. (1948) "The Psychological Foundations of Belief in Spirits" in CW8.

Jung, C.G. (1983) *The Zofingia Lectures*. Supplementary Volume A to the *Collected Works*.

Jung, C.G. (2009) *The Red Book*. (Ed. Shamdasani) (Trans. Kyburz). New York: W.W.Norton.

Knight, S. (2022) *The Premonitions Bureau: A True Story*. London: Faber and Faber.

LeShan, L. (2012) *The Medium, the Mystic and the Physicist: Towards a general theory of the paranormal*. New York: Helios Press.

Minghella, A. (Dir) (1990) *Truly, Madly, Deeply*. BBC and Lionheart.

Moorjani, A. (2012) *Dying To Be Me: My Journey from Cancer, to Near Death to True Healing*. London: Hay House.

Myers, F.W.H. (1903) *Human Personality and its Survival of Bodily Death*. New York: Longmans, Green.

Palmer, T. (2017) *The Science of Spirit Possession* (2nd Edition). Newcastle upon Tyne: Cambridge Scholars Publishing.

Powell, M. & Pressburger, E. (Dirs) (1946) *A Matter of Life and Death*. J. Arthur Rank.

Rowling, J.K. (1997) *Philosopher's Stone*. London: Bloomsbury Publishing.

Rowling, J.K. (1998) *Chamber of Secrets*. London: Bloomsbury Publishing.

Rowling, J.K. (1999) *Prisoner of Azkaban*. London: Bloomsbury Publishing.

Rowling, J.K. (2000) *Goblet of Fire*. London: Bloomsbury Publishing.

Rowling, J.K. (2003) *Order of the Phoenix*. London: Bloomsbury Publishing.

Rowling, J.K. (2005) *Half-Blood Prince*. London: Bloomsbury Publishing.

Rowling, J.K. (2007) *Deathly Hallows*. London: Bloomsbury Publishing.

Rutter, V. (1981). *The Teachings of The Mandarin*. Sittingbourne, Kent: Premier.

Saltmarsh, H.F. (2004) *The Future and Beyond: Evidence for Precognition and the Survival of Death*. Charlottesville, VA: Hampton Roads Publishing.

Shamdasani, S. (2008) "The Boundless Expanse: Jung's Reflections on Death and Life". *Quadrant* 38(1), 9–30.

Sheldrake, M. (2020) *Entangled Life: How Fungi Make Our Worlds, Change Our Minds, and Shape Our Futures*. London: The Bodley Head.

Stephens, S.L. (2020) *C.G. Jung and the Dead: Visions, Active Imagination and the Unconscious Terrain*. London and New York: Routledge.

Summerscale, K (2020) *The Haunting of Alma Fielding: A True Ghost Story*. London: Bloomsbury Circus.

Tacey, D. (2009) *Edge of the Sacred: Jung, Psyche, Earth*. Einsiedeln: Daimon Verlag.

Verny, T., & Kelly, J. (1981) *The Secret Life of the Unborn Child*. London: Sphere Books.

Walach, H. (2019) *Galileo Commission Report: Beyond a Materialist Worldview*. London: Scientific and Medical Network.

Wardi, D. (1992) *Memorial Candles: Children of the Holocaust*. London & New York: Routledge.

Williams, R. (2020) "Intergenerational transmission of trauma in refugee populations: Misdiagnosis as Borderline Personality Disorder?" in the *Proceedings of the Twenty-First Congress of the International Association for Analytical Psychology. Encountering the Other: Within us, between us and in the world* (Ed.Kiehl). Einsiedeln: Daimon Verlag.

Williams, R. (2019). *Jung: The Basics*. London and New York: Routledge.

Wimborn, M. (2016) "Analytical Psychology and Science: Adversaries or Allies? in *Psychological Perspectives* 59 (#4):490–508.

Yehuda, R., Daskalakis, N., Birer, L., Baaer, H., Klengel, T., Holsboer, F., & Binder, E. (2016). "Holocaust Exposure Induced Intergenerational Effects on FKBP5 Methylation" in *Biological Psychiatry, A Journal of Psychiatric Neuroscience and Therapeutics*. September 1, 2016 80(5.80):372–380.

Chapter 13

Grace

Grace is what has enabled me to write this book. (How impressed you will be by that claim will, I guess, depend on what you have made of the book!) What I mean is, when I am 'in the zone' with writing, I find that I often wake with words in my mind which I dash to my desk to record. (This is known as hypnopompia as opposed to hypnagogic experiences – the reverse - which occur at the boundary between being awake and falling asleep.) Or dreams come to my aid. As I reported in *Jung: The Basics,* in the 1990s I awoke from a dream laying out the title and all the chapter headings for a whole book on dreams (which later became the chapter on dreams in *Jung: The Basics*). The knack is to grab these moments. It is a bit like recording dreams. Unless you do so straight away, they often slip away and are for-gotten. Even Einstein (and I am not comparing myself to him!) reportedly said "ideas come from God"! In a biography of Einstein we read:

> Einstein said his basic discovery came on waking up one morning, when he suddenly saw the idea. This had been going around and around at the back of his mind for years, and suddenly it wanted to thrust itself forward into his conscious mind.
>
> (1996 pp. 1)

In the period as I was preparing to write this book, I attended a discussion between novelist Philip Pullman and Lisa Allardice which formed part of The Guardian newspaper's Book Club series (28th May 2020.) Pullman said:

> the Muse needs to know where to find you! And, if you're sitting at your desk, the Muse knows where you are!

I found this to be a really helpful nudge. I see the inspiration generated by the 'muse' as grace.

Grace is rarely discussed outside of a religious context. And yet I would like to strip away the religious connotations here and concentrate on the simple way it arises no matter our belief system, if indeed we even have one.

DOI: 10.4324/9781003284550-18

It might feel like an embarrassing topic to raise. It has no rational scientific basis. What sensible person would take such a fanciful notion seriously? And yet … .

I suspect we will all have experienced what we might call unlikely coincidences. How do they happen? Some of these occurrences can be rationalised away, but other events can only be put down to an 'x' factor. Luck or serendipity does not cover it, for me. Many years ago I received a package addressed to me at the house of the man I was then secretly in love with, and with the post code of the society at which years later I would train as a Jungian analyst. How it actually got to me is another miracle altogether.

Grace is the ingredient we all search for in life (although we may not use that word) and, when people feel it is missing, it can leave a person feeling desolate, abandoned, forgotten, unimportant. Irene Clairmont de Castillejo suggests "love is a miracle that happens by grace" (1973 pp. 116). That may be where most of us experience the miracle that is grace. Some of the ideas I have touched on here, like peace, serenity, joy and kindness, need quiet to become known. It is more difficult to experience these aspects of life in the middle of a noisy din, in a pressured environment where your mind is whizzing. They can more easily make themselves felt when the mind is more calm and receptive. Perhaps it is the same with allowing grace to manifest. It sometimes feels as if life has to batter us over the head to notice the presence of grace. Synchronicities, and the ways in which these occur in divinatory practices are an example of grace intervening, as I hope I was able to show in chapter ten. Even then the occurrence of these manifestations are often brushed off as 'coincidence'. Yet, … … . I expect we have all at times experienced running into the right person at the right time; phoning someone at the moment they were ringing us; looking up to see the right book in your eyeline; hearing a tune on the radio which precisely captures your situation. These may all be seen as having meaning.

The singer Cat Stevens (now known as Yusuf Islam) tells a story that he was swimming in the sea in Malibu when he realised he was out of his depth and would not make it back. He offered up a prayer to God saying "if you save me, I'll work for you". In that moment a wave came and buffeted him towards the shore and saved his life. Stevens saw that as communion with God, being heard and responded to. This is one way in which we can recognise grace (this account is in a podcast interview with Russell Brand accessed 17th December 2020. See: https://www.youtube.com/watch?v=iQeCJqjPgRU

Sometimes grace just comes out of the blue, while at others it may seem to come when we surrender our will, bow our head, and allow something beyond our control to manifest. It arrives with no suggestion of merit. Its presence is inscrutable. It is simply a [divine] gift bestowed seemingly at random. It is usually a joyful and humbling experience. The joy may not necessarily be of the ecstatic sort, but may carry a sense that a higher power has shown its hand in your very own individual existence. Like in the example mentioned in

Chapter seven where I described sending unconditional love to someone who was psychically attacking me. These events have a numinous quality to them which cannot be explained. They are in the everyday but are experienced as if they have an added dimension. This is beautifully epitomised in Rap star Stormzy's magnificent *Blinded by your Grace* (Omari and Joseph 2017) which can be viewed on YouTube. (I particularly recommend the Glastonbury version where the artist looks lost in bliss.)

Grace is sometimes called a miracle. Sometimes the impossible does happen. You do not need an intermediary. We all have a direct line if we are open to grace, to inspire us, to assist, to move, to empower, to love us. Perhaps it is as simple as allowing our hearts and souls to be open to the possibility, although simple is not always easy. Sophisticated intellectual barriers can bar the way to such simplicity.

Grace can work by the appearance of people coming into your life. I suspect many of us have found love in this way. A person appears on your radar and perhaps keeps popping up in unexpected ways, so that it is hard to avoid a feeling that there is something/someone important being drawn to your notice until you pay attention. I know I have experienced that with the most significant people in my life.

For David Tacey, it is as if the light of consciousness:

> has been reduced but not extinguished by its association with darkness. It has become weaker, softer, more diffuse. It has become harder to see but is still possible to discern. It is as if the sun had been extinguished and instead of the gleam of Apollo or Phoebus, we have a new kind of radiance, a galaxy of little lights, a night sky of stars. To see these lights we must learn to see in the dark, discern glimmers of myth in dreams and moments of grace in the ordinariness of our lives. The divine light has been humbled and we have to humble ourselves to recover it.
>
> (2013 pp. 4)

Loneliness is a modern plague which bedevils so many. And yet perhaps we are closer than we know to the source of love and grace which can fill our hearts and souls in the blink of an eye. Even secular folk are wont to pray in desperate times. Yet I wonder how many actually expect a response? (Of course that might not come in a concrete way to fulfil your worldly desires, but genuine cries of the heart and soul are another matter.)

Grace is how the consciousness, that has more wisdom than all of us individual souls here on earth, communicates with us. You might feel it guides you, encourages you, nudges you in a particular direction. We must pay heed to these 'hints'. Grace will not insist or manipulate or force. The guidance is there for those with the eyes to see and the heart willing to accept the aid. To call it magic would be to trivialise it, although it may well feel magical. We need to be still enough to hear the breeze which brings the message; to be nimble enough to respond, and humble enough to know we need help.

You could wonder about the intervention of grace in analytic practice (and I do not mean because there is anything special about analysts as individuals!). Analysts often remark that the right people seem to turn up at our doors. The issues that arise in sessions are frequently uncannily meaningful in the context of the analyst's own life. Not necessarily identical, but it is interesting to note how often here is some similarity in the story, or affect needing to be coped with, or relationship dynamic, which makes the work intensely challenging on a personal level. This is a two-way process of course so that both parties need to feel there is a good match which essentially would entail some aspects of this 'underground' connection being present. (I am thinking partly here of Jung's gate diagram (1946 par. 422) where he talks of the unconscious to unconscious link between individuals which is when transformative work can happen.) That level of connection can create empathy, although, if the issues are not sufficiently worked through for the analyst, can create discomfort and defensiveness which has to be dealt with for the work to proceed.

Grace would be a way of describing the synchronicity which arose in the case of the suicidal patient mentioned in chapter eight who abandoned their attempt to end their life.

A fair question might be raised about the 'bad' things that happen in life. Where do they come from? Are they also manifestations of grace? Well, that is a really good question! If we think about the idea of us all having tasks in life, there are many ways to learn. And (as touched on in chapter nine when I looked at why things have to go wrong), it could indeed be that these 'bad' things need to happen in order for things to go right. But where/how would you draw the distinction? Can a 'bad' thing happen by grace (without any connotation of punishment or sin)? Can *anything* happen that does *not* have the 'blessing' of grace? Can man's Shadow (either personal or collective), override grace? Does free-will trump grace? These important questions really go beyond the scope of this study but are, I think, worth considering. Certainly, being open to grace and striving to live a life of integrity does not mean everything goes 'right'. Think of Psyche. Think of Job. Think of Homer's epic *Odyssey.*

Discussion topic

You cannot plan the arrival of grace (although you can fail to pick up on it.)

A suggested research project/discussion:

Can you block grace? Does it persevere until we wake up and notice it?

Parable

I will end with a story. A spiritual teacher I know used to tell a wonderful parable about the intervention of grace which runs as follow: A man is stuck in a flood out in a deserted location. He climbs up to the roof and prays: "God, please help me. I'm going to die unless you come to my aid!" A helicopter flies overhead and they call down to the man offering to lynch him up to safety. "It's ok" he says to them. "God is going to help me". They fly off. He prays some more. The water continues to rise and, as luck would have it, another helicopter is making a reconnaissance of the area and offers to lynch the man up and take him to safety. Again he turns them away and tells them God is coming to help him. He keeps hope alive. Amazingly a small plane then flies over. They see the man still on the roof with his exit points all closing off. He's clearly in mortal danger. They throw a rope down and offer to take him to safety. Once more he sends them away and says God is going to look after him. Sad to say, he perishes in the flood. When he gets to heaven and meets God he pleads with him: "Oh God. Why did you abandon me?" God replies: "Well, I sent two helicopters and a plane!"

❧

I wish you the wisdom and humility to spot the help along the way. May your life be filled with joy, peace, clarity and the ability to discriminate. May you fulfil your own journey to becoming a mensch – a real human; to 'being' as opposed to 'doing'. May your life be filled with grace.

References

Brian, D. (1996) *Einstein – A Life*. New York: Wiley.
de Castillejo, I. (1973) *Knowing Woman: A Feminine Psychology*. Boston, MA: Shambhala.
Jung, C.G. (1946) *The Psychology of the Transference*, CW16.
Omari, M. and Joseph, K. (2017) "Blinded by Your Grace" on *Gang Signs and Prayer*. Merky Records.
Tacey, D. (2013) *The Darkening Spirit: Jung, Spirituality, Religion*. London and New York: Routledge.

Appendix A

Question 1

Do you find 'soul' and/or 'spirit' spontaneously arise in sessions?

It depends on what you mean by these terms. For me, soul has a lot to do with emotion and emotions definitely arise spontaneously in sessions. For me, spirit, in addition to the religious sense, has also to do with being lively ('spirited') and, when things go well, that arises, too. Regarding the religious sense, whether soul/spirit arises depends on what sort of clients come and what their needs are. Some explicitly seek out a Jungian because they wish that the spiritual sides of their lives are also recognised and valued. Others, though, hardly know the meaning of those words.

'Soul' occasionally, 'spirit' less often.

It does occur, but rarely.

Yes I do. I like Mr Collins' definition as, among other aspects, "the essential part or nature of something", of one's lower case self, feelings personality. I think of spirit as the energy of life which enables people to reach the higher Self, to inspiration, and to the discovery of life's meaning.

Yes, soul and spirit do arise spontaneously in my sessions with patients, especially in response to their dreams.

Occasionally.

Yes.

Yes.

Yes.

Yes, I do.

(Continued)

Both words (in Spanish 'alma' and 'espíritu') arise with low frequency in the consulting room. A relatively small percentage of patients use this terminology. On the other hand, in certain circumstances, quite exceptional, I can make use of those words myself with a certain therapeutic intention, carefully contemplating what type of reaction or impact they will have on the patient.

Spirit spontaneously arises and particularly in my practice in men.

Yes.

Only if the client raised the concept spontaneously. I would not have raised it 'spontaneously' or otherwise.

I don't know what you mean by this question? Do you mean whether people use these terms or whether there are spontaneous paranormal manifestations in sessions ? Whose soul or spirit are you referring to..mine, the patient's or a transcendent energy/spirit e.g. the Holy Spirit? I would need to know what you mean by soul and spirit to answer the question.

Yes.

Yes.

Sometimes. Mostly it's 'spirit', 'soul' less so. It may arise when talking about 'nature' or 'the environment'.

Yes. (Of course you have not defined these terms here, so I don't know if what I mean by these things is what you mean)

If you mean the terms soul and/or spirit, brought in by the analysand, then for many people these are terms/ideas that weigh on them and often have driven them into an analysis. They may not use those words, but the essence of soul and spirit are often in the material. (Of course, soul and spirit are actually in the room from the first handshake of the first session).

Yes. More likely soul but spirit too.

Sometimes.

I think that the most helpful view of this is the idea expressed in the C of E liturgy that "when one or two are gathered... ...." then the spirit or whatever one calls it is present. Personally, I am neither a Christian, nor any other denomination, and I don't subscribe the spirit or whatever as "things, but as the experience is of a transcendent other. Ogden refers to it as the "analytic third". I think that it is more useful to think of it as the emotional connection between two people in the room, which apart from mirror neurons is the product of a logic peculiar to the unconscious and identical in emotional phenomenology, where two subjectivities become entangled. The experience is never absent; so if you believe in spirits, they're always there.

(Continued)

'Spontaneously' doesn't seem like the right word. As a Jungian, my subjective (although unuttered or not consciously intended) influence would colour the psychic field. There's an implicit invitation for such discussion. That said, I keep an ear out for avenues of discussion regarding soul/spirit.

Yes.

Depends on definition.

Yes.

Not in those terms unless the analysand is a churchgoer or was raised as one. The 'Guiding Presence' is palpable to me and helps determine if I even take a client, but I do not name it until the patient finds a personal image or word. 'Self' is often the Jungian term first used if the client is a reader of Jung. A 'Something' that is guiding the work has been discovered by many unless they are too mired in daily traumata. Usually by the time of termination, everyone has some sense of such guidance or they are not ready to sally forth on their own.

Yes, I often found.

Yes.

It sometimes happens within me when I am listening to a patient. I wonder about the child's spirit within them. 'Soul' isn't a word that comes to my mind but 'spirit' is when I am sitting with a patient.

Yes.

Replies to Research Questionnaire

Question 2

If so, how long into the work have such instances arisen (stating as many variations in times as you wish).

It varies enormously from the very beginning of the work to not at all. And from constantly (very rare) to sporadically.

A few times at the very beginning of the work, including in the initial consultation, (e.g. "I feel my soul needs something that it isn't getting and I don't know what it is". Several times some years in.

When it does occur, it might be present at almost all sessions.

A case from many years ago may illustrate how long illustrations of soul and spirit took to appear: a Jewish academic man came to start therapy with me. I could hardly find him behind glasses, dark beard and a full head of curly hair. He was

(Continued)

clearly depressed and only able to give me a little history, born in the United States, excelled at school, experienced no antisemitism. At age 14 he had a psychotic break, had seen a psychiatrist "but he did me no good". He complained that he was so anxious that he had trouble figuring out what furniture to buy for his apartment, whether he had time for a bike ride before teaching his class. Typically he would say something and then fall silent. He told me that his parents had emigrated from London before he was born, that he remembered one memory from childhood that whenever he skinned his knee or was ill his mother would see to him and then say: "There, there, you are alright now!" I felt his silences as daring me to intervene and help him though he said he didn't expect I could. I asked if London was where his parents had lived. He replied that it was a stopping off place from Germany and that he could never get them to tell him the whole story. I assumed the worst but decided that since he didn't know the family story, I would tell him stories about how people escaped the Nazis, how they walked across Europe to France hoping to find passage to America. He hardly spoke during these sessions but was transfixed. Each autumn when he went home for Thanksgiving, he would tentatively ask his parents to tell him their history but to no avail. One November he received tenure from his university and proudly called his mother to tell her. She said "Tenure? What's that? And do you know what day this is? It is Kristallnacht!" He was crushed and angry and determined to press on. While home for Thanksgiving that year, he sat them down and insisted that they tell him. His mother tearfully admitted that her brother and parents had perished at Auschwitz, that they did not have the date of their death so they could not say Kaddish [prayers for the dead] for them. This meant that therefore she unconsciously marked the dates of Nazi horror as a kind of penance. Their admission freed my patient up. He returned more relaxed than I had thought possible. He planned a difficult pilgrimage to Auschwitz by himself, complicated because the camp was behind the Iron Curtain at that point. He returned with a small jar of earth from the camp for me, thanked me and said goodbye. He was visibly moved and so was I. Since then his spirit has soared. He is famous in his field and has lectured and taught at universities all over the world. The work took four years.

I have had the terms appear in work with very new patients, if we are looking at their dreams. They also are present in sessions of patients with whom I've worked for many years.

I tend to introduce the concepts as early as possible in analysis, usually within the first 5–10 sessions.

Once arisen, they are often used/mentioned.

I would have liked you to have defined 'soul and spirit as we all have a different understanding of what this means to us. I can sense something deeper and beyond words evolving between us with some patients and supervisees. Usually it is with people I have developed an analytic in depth relationship with over many months, even years,

Do not know

(Continued)

It depends on the client, with some it could be often – every 2/3 of the session; with others it can be 2/3 times a year.

I don't quite understand the question. Maybe this question was already answered in the previous point.

On average within weeks following our initial session.

Quite early on into the therapy.

It varies and depends very much on the patient (and of course many patients never raise the subject).

Sometimes the first session, sometimes later on – these have regular presences in the consulting room, for me if not for my patients.

I can't say, it entirely depends on the patient and their spiritual interest.

Well – from immediately, as a reason for self referral, to never at all. Any variation is possible.

Could be the initial session or any time after that – there is no pattern.

Quite often in the very first session. This is a difficult question to answer, in terms of how long into the work. Sometimes with patients who stay a long time they emerge later in the work when the presenting concerns have improved and they get deeper into the work.

Do not remember.

It's just there: not a question of time.

No noticeable pattern.

2–8 minutes.

Anytime.

Throughout

Some sense of Self and Its guidance arises anywhere from the first session to years into the work, depending on severity of symptoms, personal history, and diagnostic patterns.

Sometimes they appear in our work or our dreams. 1–2 minutes or 1–2 seconds, because it is different in spirit and soul.

Such issues are extremely varied in time of arising; some not at all.

Unless someone has some experience (spiritual, religious or previous depth therapy) conceptually and intuitively, I find that patients are either eager to work or to become familiar and trusting of the process or take a couple of years to believe in

(Continued)

themselves sufficiently to 'share' their psychic journey. (Dreams and sandplay work helps and elucidates the process).

After 7 years working 4 times weekly with one patient. He had been abused as a child and he was wondering about the affect on his "soul". His word not mine.

Patient I had been working with for 6 years – also she had been abused as a child. She wondered about her "spirit" and also the "spirit" of her sister and felt them to be damaged.

Another patient 3 years into the work – her mother had left her as a child and she was brought up by her father. Her "spirit felt crushed". She was a practising Christian and started to question the impact on her of her mother leaving when she was age 3. This coincided with the number of years we had been working together. It also coincided with her thoughts about Jesus's ministry.

Male patient after 2 years – following death of mother – has been wondering about his inner spiritual world.

Another female patient 20 years – she has recently been wondering about her child self's soul – this has arisen as a result of working outside during Covid. She felt the soft breeze on her – recalling a moment in childhood.

Generally the topic only comes up after a considerable length of time. I have also met a lot of cynicism too. Particularly with ex Jehovah's Witnesses who have suffered sexual abuse. And with many of my patients it just has not arisen – at least not specifically with the use of "spirit" or "soul".

Different – as long as we can 'hold' it.

Replies to Research Questionnaire

Question 3

If soul and spirit arise in sessions, how would you tend to deal with such matters?

That, of course, depends on which definition of soul/spirit is used. I try hard to stay neutral and just be open to what the client wishes to share. Theological questions hardly ever come up.

I explore gently what the person using the term means, and what they are trying to communicate.

It is an important subject for me, so I give it much attention, **when** it arises. In my eyes it is about the most important subject for a human being.

(Continued)

In another case it took only a few months for the issue of soul and spirit to arise: a man in his mid 50's, well versed in Jungian ideas, a Classics scholar reading Greek and loving mythology consulted me. We are only on the telephone so getting a sense of each other took a little time but he raced through a short history as if to get on with the new life he imagines. (I call it seduction by Jung and we all did it). But his dreams placed him in the bottom chakra in a dream about being deep underground with the turnips and beets. The youngest of four children and the only boy, he felt sorry for his mother who had a debilitating illness. He felt compelled to help keep her alive though she died in her 50's leaving him with a mother complex of near compulsion to help women in need. In a recent dream one of the women he loves sinks into deep water. He tries to find a way to help her breathe while also finding a way to pull her out. In daily life he understands that his inner woman needs desperately to find her own spirit rather than projecting it onto outer women.

In this case I remark on his need to leap immediately to nearly any need that a woman may have and that his soul development seems to need to ruminate and not resist the slow growth of psyche. He has a brilliant mind and wants to hurry towards the many possibilities that he wishes for. He talks very quickly as if racing but is silent and very receptive to my interventions. I feel his fear which he cannot confront yet – at least with me – though he says that all the women in his family are suffering in one way or another and he feels compelled to help.

I deal with these matters comfortably and naturally, as the dreams come from the patients themselves or the patients bring the issues up; therefore, I'm not trying to impose a subject on them.

I introduce the concepts because I consider them to be foundational elements in my Jungian work; some of the most important concepts and framing ideas.

Depends if it is just a matter of speaking. I let it repeat or, if there is a spiritual connotation, I ask how they understand it. We come to a new path.

The patient and I both know it has arisen in the session, we become still, we wait, wait without hope, wait without thought, (T.S.Eliot) East Coker. Four Quartets.

I ask what the meaning of this 'event', Question is for the client.

I wonder what this means for a person and how my soul reacts or touch on.

If the patient handles this type of conception in order to understand himself, I adapt myself to it. Likewise, if I understand that the use of a more 'spiritual' or 'poetic' perspective, based in this kind of language, would help the patient's process of individuation, I can introduce these worldviews ('weltanschauung'), based on mythological and religious principles or on the work of C. G. Jung.

I would differentiate between soul and spirit with psychoeducation and soul and religion.

Openly.

Anything important to the client was important to me.

(Continued)

I would ask the patient to expand on their thoughts.

Embrace them, recognising we are touching on fundamental issues of deep importance.

Again, it depends on the patient's degree of spiritual interest or practice. Some patients want to explore their spirituality, others experience spirit through nature and talk about that, how they might want to develop their experience of nature. It may be talked about in terms of the environmental catastrophe. For others there may be a numinous experience, in the session or in a dream, and we explore that.

Pragmatically and situationally: as with anything else, it is to do with what it means to the patient, to me, to both of us, / what's going on in the transference / countertransference // I'd explore the meaning.

As with any other image, phenomenon that arises.

I might express interest and see if the patient wishes to take it further but when initially spoken about I might just register it and wait to see when it next arises.

In an ordinary way, the same as any material that emerges.

You notice what's there, Spirit, or in my terms, emotional connection and intersubjective symmetry (see Matte Blanco) manifests itself in the emotional relationship, whether that's a 'moment of meeting' (Stern) or malignant transference/countertransference interactions ('bad spirits', presumably), or whatever.

I ask for the person's understanding of the term. Unless invited to contribute my perspectives, and it seems appropriate to do so, I do not 'correct' or otherwise tamper with the person's understanding of the terms.

Rarely I comment it, but it always influences the therapeutic process.

With respect and as I deal with all other matters according to the individuality of patient.

On their own terms, as living archetypal energy fields.

The same as I would deal with any image – Casually, respectfully, enquiringly, depending on the circumstances. But the terms you are suggesting are more abstract and collective than the living images analysands discover/create.

It changes by itself.

I listen ... and if appropriate, ask for amplification or associations (as with a dream).

I tend to wait and see how the story unfolds. It feels more important to listen and see where their thoughts take us.

In short words – most with my students – mindful, respectful, touched inside.

Replies to Research Questionnaire

Question 4

Do you distinguish between dealing with 'soul' and dealing with 'spirit' in different ways?

Yes.

I feel more familiar/comfortable with 'soul' … I have a sense of what it means to me and feel it to be something close. I don't feel such a personal resonance with 'spirit' so if/when that comes up in a session I listen carefully to try to understand as well as I can what is meant.

I do, according to the beliefs of the clients.

I speak of soul when speaking of emotions that are not conscious eg when my patient's Jewish mother said "There, there you are alright now". I heard NOW and knew there had to be a THEN and that his young soul was longing for truth. In other cases I speak about spirit as being one's eagerness, excitement and motivation for more life changes, excitement about the work.

'Soul' to me is personal and 'spirit' is transpersonal, although the transpersonal is present in the Self.

This depends on the client and the level of sophistication I feel is appropriate for the person. I tend to use the concepts of yin and yang to elucidate the differences as well as Hillman's.

Depends on the patient. If she/he does it, I ask for their understanding of difference. If not, we come slowly to it later.

No.

Soul is nearer to 'psyche' whereas 'Spirit' is more a religious category.

And yes, and not, sometimes it could be difficult for me.

I understand that both notions can refer to different aspects of the human being. Both images are symbols that belong to the same realm but can express different aspects. The most evident associative chains are those usually handled in analytical psychology: Soul – Anima – Eros – Earth – Dionysus – Passion – etc. Spirit – Animus – Logos – Air – Apollo – Moderation – etc.

Yes and I have found, over my years of practice, that there has been a separation of a significant number of church going people that there has been a 'dropping off' in numbers in attending church going individuals. There seems to be a trend in society to talk about spirituality rather than soul.

(Continued)

Yes.

I would differentiate both from religion or religious practices.

I understand the terms soul and spirit in different ways but I don't know whether I deal with them.

No, not necessarily, but discussion of soul and spirit will almost inevitably lead to how the patient may understand the difference. I tend to see soul as belonging to the person (or me) – soulful, affectful ways of being that are non-ego; whilst I tend to see spirit as coming more from outside e.g. as inspiration, God, 'the universe' and so on.

As a Buddhist, I don't use the word 'soul' much. There isn't a 'soul' in Buddhism, and my patients don't often speak about 'soul'. Those that do, it tends to be in the context of their therapy training, e.g. Revision training places emphasis on 'soul' and 'soulfulness'.

Again, as I don't know your definition, almost impossible to answer. But, not really. I see them as synonyms.

I think of spirit as impregnating soul.

This depends on the analysand's understanding of the terms and on the situation in the field between us.

I am not sure about this. It depends on the patient and the context. I do think they are different.

Not particularly.

See Mysterium coniunctionis. In the first coniunctio, Jung is explicit that soul refers to emotion and spirit to intellect or thought. A major part of any analysis is connecting a person to their bodily emotional experience, whether this is a schizoid individual cut *off from it or a borderline inundated by what has not been 'mentalised'*.

My personal understanding distinguishes between the two, but unless the person make a point of distinction, I leave their definition of terms in place.

Yes.

Yes, I see them differently.

Yes, I see them differently.

It depends on the analysand and the meanings they give to the terms.

Probably, I think. To spirit, we may let is goes by itself or talk about them. But to soul, let it goes only by itself.

Yes and how or how much depends on the psychological sophistication of the patient and his/her curiosity.

(Continued)

No – I generally listen – and if I am unclear I ask them what they might mean by the use of the word 'spirit'. Maybe it's me but 'soul' isn't a word my patient's have used with me.

No.

Question 5 was a particularly sensitive question given that it is important for the analyst to be quite abstemious about revealing personal information so as not to interfere with the unfolding analytic process. Some practitioners seemed horrified at the idea of being transparent about personal beliefs with a patient, while for others this is the most natural thing in the world. Partly this is theoretical orientation; partly psychological type and/or personal style. There are of course no 'right' answers to any of these questions.

Replies to Research Questionnaire

Question 5

Are you transparent about your own belief system when these subjects arise?

Yes.

About 'soul' ... I don't speak from a belief system perspective or try to define it, (I can't!), but I might occasionally share my thoughts about e.g. how to nourish or care for one's 'soul' - particularly if working with someone who is alienated from themselves and living life in such a way that is damaging to them.

Yes, if asked.

When people ask what I believe, I draw them out about what the question means to them. Often I ask if they have ever been outside on a moonless night and looked up at the heavens. I tell them that I have had long distance pilots in my practice who tell me that they see UFO's all the time. Not menacing, just lurking. When asked if I believe in god, I say that I believe in the web of consciousness which is holding the universe together and however that came to be, I believe in it.

I am transparent about my own beliefs, but I make it clear that I'm not trying to indoctrinate patients or get them to share my perspectives.

Very much so because as mentioned earlier I introduce the concepts early in the analysis.

Depends on the transference-countertransference, personality, compliance.

(Continued)

Not by anything I say, as that would be intrusive. Yet I think there is an unconscious knowing that is transmitted between myself and my patient.

Yes, I am.

It is very relative. It depends on the uniqueness of each process.

Yes I am and I have no hesitation in sessions, to talk, particularly about Jung and spirituality.

If I am asked.

No.

I am not transparent about my belief system with patients.

I would not volunteer this information, but also would not hide it if I thought it was relevant and might be helpful.

Pretty much – I don't give a lecture about it but I name things as soul, or a soul connection, or spirit or spiritual, as they arise and as seems relevant and appropriate.

Only if asked directly. One or two patients have come knowing I'm a Buddhist. If patients talk about mindfulness, meditation etc I respond in a way that means I know something about this. In my consulting room I have some small Buddhist artefacts which are sometimes commented on by patients.

If I feel like it. no rule. Again, depends on what it might do to the transference / countertransference.

I am an anthropologist having studied religious practice in shamanic cultures, when these topics arise I will tell what the shamans I have worked with have told me.I am clear about what Jung says about these issues if it is appropriate—in the 'education' aspect of our work. But I do not offer my personal beliefs or experiences. Especially with these images of soul and spirit I think it is essential that the analysand comes to his/her own conclusions and has his/her own encounters with anything transcendent, not muddied by a transference projection.

Rarely unless I feel it is appropriate.

Sometimes. I think soul and spirit are part of life

Yes: where relevant. Mostly not. A Buddhist patient who knew perfectly well I wasn't a Buddhist told me that I might as well be; and I have treated Anglicans, Catholics and Jews, often with reference to theological conceptions, sometimes non-believers too.

No, but not opaque, either. I tend to not let my personal 'cosmology' (in Shamdasani's use of the term re Jung) enter and, rather, if 'necessary', point toward the analytical psychology point of view.

(Continued)

Not always ... sometimes there are patients who would'nt want to know anything about it.

Depends on situation and person.

I don't consider it a 'belief system' because I experience these as part of psychic energy.

No, unless the analysand asks, and then I explore why he/she needs to ask, and/or what is their feeling/thought/imagination. This can be very useful in exploring the transference. I might be more forthcoming if I sense fear of being misunderstood or not being met on the transpersonal dimension. But I would not talk about my beliefs, instead wonder what they are projecting from their past experience that makes them feel they would not be companioned/understood in our analytic relationship.

Yes.

No. Although on one occasion a patient pressed me re my own spiritual views and I eventually said, "Maybe, it is important to you to feel that I consider spirituality important". It felt a bit of a cop out but it felt important to keep the focus on her. I actually found it very challenging not to tell her my views as she really was pressing me.

I cannot understand this question! Do you mean: if I am aware – ? what do you mean by 'belief system'?

Replies to Research Questionnaire

Question 6

Would you tend you introduce these topics into the work?

Up till now I have not had the impression it would be appropriate to introduce these topics but I'm happy to deal with them if they come up.

No.

Yes, it happened. I worked with a child of about 11 who had questions like: where do we come from, what is our goal ? it was clear to me that there was a need of talking about spirituality and religion.

Yes, but not unless a person is curious or receptive. I wait to assess where they are with esoterica.

I introduce these topics when dreams seem to call for it, or if patients bring them up. For example, if they're discussing going to church now or the religious views of their family when they were growing up.

(Continued)

Only if there is no better word, or if the patient used it before in a colloquial way.

No. They introduce themselves if the time and the attitude is right.

Yes.

Yes, I do. It could be in various options or by chance.

In my opinion, the patient's experience of synchronicity is an opportunity to get into these kinds of issues. Another occasion that can lead to these considerations is the patient's contact with death, for example, from a recent loss.

Yes but in an open and unbiased manner.

Yes.

No.

I try not to introduce concepts (or language generally) that the patient has not brought first.

I might do so if for example a dream or synchronistic experience led us in this direction.

'If appropriate' – if that is what I feel the person is struggling with.

Not unless the patient is edging towards it.

No. Whatever for? If they are going to arise, they'll arise. 'introducing' sounds like 'being in a hurry'.

If there was an indication from the psyche of the analysand that these matters were arising.

If they were in dreams or implicit in what is being said. Otherwise not.

Possibly.

If helpful.

Generally not, although as mentioned in the first question, it's in the air of my practice.

Yes, more and more.

Not usually.

Yes, if I felt they were pressing to be made conscious and given space and a name. If not, then no.

NO. I try to follow the analysand's needs and dream process. I do not feel analysis is a tool to impose or even teach about my beliefs, but an opportunity for the analysand

(Continued)

to open to discovery of their own relationship to the transpersonal in whatever form it arrives from their own Self via dreams, imaginations, etc.

I didn't want to talk about them, but I had to face them when the visitor did.

Again that depends on the needs and wants of the patient, tempered with my knowledge and experience.

No.

Of course!

Replies to Research Questionnaire

Question 7

How do you find people respond to these ideas?

Since they bring them up and I am not pushing any particular belief or notion, I've not encountered any problems.

I don't generally introduce them. Although I remember responding to someone who hadn't used either term by saying that what they were describing felt to me to have been 'brutalising of [their] soul'. They looked initially a bit startled but then became pensive and said, 'Maybe'. Eight years on they referred again to the same event that I had suggested was 'brutalising' and reflecting on it that time, they acknowledged with real heaviness, 'It was very fucked-up', and shook their head remembering the 'soul-destroying' scenario in which they had been a willing participant many years before - before they had learned how to take better care of their soul.

In a very open way – sometimes it feels like they are relieved the subject comes up and can be talked about.

When people are ready, I find them excited and hopeful. These days, with nearly a year of devastating problems all over the world and panic here in the States over the total insanity of the Trumpists, people who are calm and realise that human extinction is possible and even likely if we don't act decisively and soon are energised and welcome change. It is a spiritual experience for some friends and family as well as patients to lovingly care for strangers, for the environment, for composting, gardening, feeding the birds and especially to loving life itself.

The responses are usually very positive. I recognise that patients who did not have a Jungian background might be less comfortable with these topics.

Quite well because it frames the work.

Depends. I adapt if they prefer not to walk that path.

(Continued)

There is a particular quiet in the room, and sense of mutual understanding, a kind of waiting and experiencing of something bigger than both of us.

Open.

Clients over 40 are more often to respond to these ideas.

In general, the response is favourable. Obviously, in many cases, there can be an initial reaction of scepticism, but with the necessary care, many times it can be enriching for the patient.

I find people respond well, but where and when depends on relevance and interest is notes in sessions.

Openly.

This question assumes I would have introduced these topics.

I don't introduce them so my patients don't have anything to which to respond.

There is no general rule or answer to this question. Every patient is different, which is what makes our work endlessly interesting!

Well – often relieved, pleased, or deeply moved to be talking on this level.

I don't introduce ideas.

Which ideas?

No pattern—each individual is different.

Sorry. I am not sure how to answer this.

Fine if they are in tune with what is being said.

They seem to have found them helpful.

Positively.

Usually they respond in a positive, perhaps even curious manner ... the 'new' patients have seen my homepage and choose to come to my office, because of my work with spirit and soul (in a shamanic way).

It varies.

With relief.

I do not provide such terms as they are usually considered a churchy imposition of language. My job is to accompany the client on her/his discovery of the images and terms in her/his personal journey. Often an animal, known wisdom figure, or dream image appears to deepen the search towards what might become such a guiding Self image. Analysands of various religion backgrounds then have no problem going their

(Continued)

individual ways and enlarging and personalising their experience of 'non-ordinary, non-rational' phenomena.

Most people don't believe the soul but they cannot tell you why those things happened.

Again, I find the response varied.

I felt Question 8 was important because in general terms diversity is rather poorly dealt with in Jungian trainings (although the situation is improving). I was interested to know how many people notice such differences as well as whether any difference may be discerned which would be highly significant. I was especially interested to discern if there were any cultural variants geographically. The data does not provide any statistically meaningful result but I do think this could be a really fruitful and interesting area for future exploration.

Replies to Research Questionnaire

Question 8

Do you notice any perceptible difference in responses along gender, class or cultural lines?

Not in general. I have not had many clients in which spirituality was a big issue for them. They have more pressing problems. I need to make it clear that I work more as a therapist than as an analyst.

No … male and female patients of different classes and cultural backgrounds have used 'soul' and 'spirit'.

No, women and men are interested.

I am finding that younger people of all classes are tuned in in passionate ways to Greta's message, to gender fluidity, to anger at their elders unless the elders are on board with the need to change utterly in order for life to go on. The middle-aged people seem to ignore (repress) their fear and keep on buying things and thinking that we will get back to 'normal' after Covid and all will be well again. Among the cultured so-called 'elite' there is a lot of sadness about the loss of so much – museums, opera, symphonies – my daughter-in-law is a cellist with an orchestra and she is out of work.

I have not experienced gender differences or class differences. I have not worked with patients from non-Western cultures.

Hard to say because my practice is mostly with men.

(*Continued*)

Yes. More mentioned at 'low' and 'high' social classes. The least mentioned in middle-class. Also more in non-Protestants.

It beyond gender, class or cultural lines, it just is.

Yes, religious people like to talk about this.

Don't.

No, in my clinical practice I have not noticed significant differences in relation to these characteristics. However, I can assume that they do exist.

Yes in all of these areas.

No.

Again, this question assumes that I would have introduced them.

No, again I can't generalise.

Not particularly, very difficult to generalise.

No.

No.

No.

I suppose that because I am concentrating on the individual I don't necessarily think in more general terms.

No.

No.

Hard to say. I was about to write something about young people not using such concepts but that's not true, in my actual experience. I do find that many of my analysands come in pre-loaded with projections onto Jungian work as being oriented toward 'spirituality'.

No.

I haven't.

Not really.

No; though people brought up with church terminology and in church dogma often have more difficulty finding their own, individual path and supporting its images and requirements.

Maybe, elder people, more easy to think it true, I think in China. The more you live in the countryside, the easier it is to believe.

(Continued)

No.

That's a good question. When I was working in Luton I noticed differences – I worked with a lot of different ethnic backgrounds and mostly working class and many who went to Church – often Irish or black African/Carribean. They were always open to exploring spirituality. Definitely, class and culture play a part. Gender – hard to say.

Only in cultural lines.

Replies to Research Questionnaire

Question 9

Are there any other matters you would wish to raise?

Psyche is soul and we are engaged in the care of souls, but not explicitly.

Let me say, Ruth, that I can't think of a better thing to do than for you to write about this so important topic. Thank you for asking us. I hope I haven't overwhelmed here but I have so enjoyed responding to you.

Spiritual issues seem more pressing now than they were for my patients thirty years ago.

I might add that I have reformulated Jungian psychology for myself based on numinous/sacred/Big Dreams in relation to Native American vision quest, sweat lodge, and pipe experiences put within the context of complexity theory as elucidated by George Hogenson and my description of Hermes as the god of complexity theory. Synchronicity and spiritual concepts are therefore integral aspects of this formulation.

Our patient is the boss. We are giving them service, so their terminology is the key of good communication.

This can be a numinous, awesome experience. It cannot be put into words and cannot be made to happen, it is a living felt experience.

No.

I think that analytical psychology is an excellent way to introduce and bring the patient closer to the consideration of these dimensions of being.

No.

No.

Those who have experienced more profound early trauma seem to be particularly open to these levels and ways of thinking and being although, having said that, some

(Continued)

of those people specifically do not mention them. My understanding being that this relates to whether they have a sufficient degree of ego-functioning so that they can cope with and think about these experiences; whereas those whose ego-functioning (capacity to contain and think about experience) is severely disrupted keep away from this kind of experience more fervently, lest they are overwhelmed and lose themselves completely perhaps. For these people (in the latter group), these ways of thinking and being might emerge later on, yet you discover that they have been there all the time, they have just been more concerned about being able to function and deal with people on a day-to-day basis.

It's interesting your survey doesn't refer to 'religion'. In a survey I heard about I think from the Royal College of Psychiatrists, years ago, all the people practising a religion identified as 'spiritual' whereas those who identified as 'spiritual' were not necessarily practising a religion. So 'religion' is a wider area, according to this survey.

Some kind of definitions of what you are asking about would be cool.

The concept of embodiment, which entails participation, is helpful with patients. My basic premise for what we are trying to facilitate: learning to be effected, while maintaining the engagement with life.

Soul registers the effect, as well as giving effect.

The patient may (it does happen) ask directly using the terms 'soul' and 'spirit'. I answer: our work together has the important element of 'with' – with soul and with spirit. Our work is not 'about' – about soul and about spirit.

No thanks. Except to say thank you for sending me this.

No.

My favourite of Jung's works to teach is CW 11, *Psychology & Religion*.

No.

I wonder why you are using church terms to narrow and suggest an old bottle on the fresh new, individual wine of our practice.

Hope to see your study result: ☺))

I think in my work so far with patients what has chilled me the most has been the duplicity of church people or so-called 'pillars of the community' or parents or grandparents or teachers who have tampered with the delicate 'spirit' of a child or teenager. I think that is what is most concerning for me. And looking back on the 100 or so people I have worked with all of my patients have been damaged by the non thinking, selfish 'spirit' of a person close to them. It's made me more wary of the damage I can also do to a patient. That I need to be constantly working on my own essence of being – checking my motives for the work I do, my work ethics and keeping maintenance on my own 'spirit' of being.

(Continued)

Yes: the role of the introverted basic-functions* of the person – because I experienced that these functions are leading deeper than the extraverted functions – so I call them 'the depth-function' (at Jung et al. in past: 'minor function') * sense-function, intuition, feeling, thinking I am convinced that everyone of the four Basic-functions has its own access to spirituality.

Appendix B

Transcript of online meeting with Dr Terence Palmer on 24 August 2020

Bio: Dr Terence Palmer has a degree in Psychology from Canterbury Christ Church University and a Master's degree in the study of Mysticism and Religious Experience from Kent University. He has been a hypnotherapist for 20 years and a spirit release practitioner for 12 years. His doctorate was awarded by the University of Wales at Bangor for his thesis on the scientific conceptual framework and research methods of nineteenth-century researcher F.W.H. Myers. He is the first practitioner to be awarded a PhD on the topic of Spirit Release Therapy in the UK. Terence is a member of The Society for Psychical Research and The Scientific and Medical Network, and he is a Fellow of the Royal Society of Medicine. Dr Palmer is an active lecturer in encouraging UK institutions to take up the challenge to test the efficacy of Spirit Release Therapy under controlled conditions.

RW: Thank you so much for agreeing to talk. I have to start by saying that I'm coming from a slightly ignorant position in that I'm at quite an early stage of researching Myers and I have not even been able to get a hold of your book as it was unobtainable when I tried a couple of times. So, I apologise that I do not have that information already. But I hope that will not take away from the sort of things I wanted to ask you anyway.

TP: It's Cambridge Scholars Publishing. There are two versions of it. There's a hard back and a soft back version. The hard back version is for the serious researcher, and the softback version has been edited down for the lay reader. And of course naturally it is less costly. It is an expensive book. It's £52.

RW: Oh, normally it is an identical version but just in different cover.

TP: No, the soft back is edited down. It is a third smaller. I've taken out all the scientific references so that it is easier to read.

RW: I see. OK.

TP: They're very different prices. But you can claim a discount and get 20% discount by putting in the discount code in with your order direct from the publisher.

RW: What discount code?

TP: The discount code is 'spirit20'. That's what makes it easier to get it direct from the publisher.

RW. That's fine. One question which is not directly about what I wanted to ask you about your work, is that I've come across in the past some research where people write a message and put it on top of a wardrobe so somebody obviously cannot see it. They are lying on a bed and they can read it from where they are. Do you know where I can find that work as it is a long time since I came across it and I cannot track a reference.

TP: This is an example of out of body experience.

RW: Yes.

TP: So, if you research 'out of body experience' – OBE – that is just one example of how it can manifest. Quite simply, the spirit leaves the body. It can go anywhere. Experiments have been conducted with patients undergoing surgery under anaesthetic. Or rather, cases have been reported where a patient undergoing surgery can describe exactly what is happening in the operating theatre whilst they have been under anaesthetic. There's a relationship between a 'near death experience' and an 'out of body experience'.

RW: Yes, yes.

TP: The difference is that, with a near death experience, with the patient under anaesthetic, the body actually dies. The brain stops working. But then they come back. An out of body experience on the other hand can be experienced at any time by any person. And there is a huge amount of evidence. Just research 'out of body experience' or astral travelling. It's huge.

RW: Do you know the work of Anita Moorjani who's talked about her own near death experience?

TP: No, no. I don't find it helpful to read personal accounts. Because there are actually so many. So many. I prefer to access serious research. If you haven't got a copy of the book in front of you. I've made references to this in my book, so let's just have a look. I'm just going to check the index for out of body experience.

RW: Oh, don't worry. I can look it up later.

TP: I know it's in here. I'm just trying to find it in the index. Out of body experience – there are one, two, three, four, five, six, seven references to out of body experience.

RW: Brilliant. Lovely. Thank you.

TP: So, you will find it in there.

RW: I was kind of interested in how you came to this work.

TP: It's my life's task.

RW: Yes.

TP: It's what I came here to do.

RW: Yes, I understand that.

TP: But I didn't realise that until I reached maturity. Because you go through life being influenced by your environment, your parents, your education. And then there reaches a time when you stop and go 'hang on a minute', what is this all about, Alfie! When you start observing an alternate reality from spontaneous experiences, and you ask these fundamental questions. It is then when you start asking fundamental questions, that you start getting answers to those questions. And that happened for me – it started around about 1990, I think. 30 years ago.

RW: It began with spontaneous experience, and then you met spirit guides? Would that be a way … .

TP: It's a long story. It's a long and detailed story and part of that story is in fact written in the preface to the book.

RW: Oh, OK.

TP: Where I explain how the book came into being. In 1990 I was a conference and exhibition organiser through the 1980s and towards the end of the 80s – this was the age of Thatcherism –

RW: I remember it well.

TP: There was an economic boom, and then a catastrophic collapse of the economy. So, my business was a victim of that catastrophe. So, when I'd lost everything I'd worked for, I found myself homeless and penniless saying to the universe – 'what's happening here!' And that's when you start getting answers, and that's when I started experiencing what could best be described as mystical experiences. Hearing voices, witnessing possessions, stuff that I had never been exposed to ever before. But now, because I had nothing to occupy my mind, I was wide open. And I started asking questions and then I started getting answers. In answer to my questions, the result of my questioning was a book that was inspired by spirit and that book is the first one I wrote is called *The Tao of Natural Cycles: How natural cycles affect you, the economy and the shape of history* (2014 Kindle). It's still not available in hard copy because basically I haven't had time to get round to it.

RW: Well, publishers might be a bit wary of this kind of area I think.

TP: No, there are publishers that do specialise.

RW: Yes, there are places like Watkins …

TP: There are several publishers that would do it. But it's a question of time you see. The easy part of writing a book, is writing it. Especially if it's inspired by spirit. If you're being used as an instrument of communication, it comes easy. It just flows through. The hard part is getting it published. And that is in finding the right publisher. They are there. This [*The Science of Spirit* Possession] is published by an academic institution because it is a scientific thesis.

RW: That's the result of your PhD, isn't it.

TP: Yes. But the *Tao of Natural Cycles,* I just – that was published actually 20 years after it was written. Because, as I was writing it, I was reading it. And I was asking myself – where's all this come from? So, it took me 20 years to get the evidence to support what was being written. And this was before I even got a degree in psychology. This was what motivated me to get educated. Because, before then, I hadn't been to university. I went to university at the age of 53. And that's what inspired me to do it. What I've discovered since then is that, every step I've taken since I began my questioning, every step I've taken I've been guided down a road and I had to take three separate avenues of education in order to get the full picture. I had to go to university to study psychology which introduced me to mainstream psychological thinking and scientific method. But that was not the full picture. I didn't learn anything about spirituality from psychology. I had to go to a spiritualist church for that. And I also had to learn, I had to formally study hypnosis because I needed to understand the relationship between the conscious mind and the sub-conscious mind. And different levels of dis-associative thought. And, again, I didn't learn any of that from psychology because it's a taboo subject in psychology.

RW: And so were you using spirit guides in hypnosis?

TP: Not then, no. These three avenues of education eventually coalesced to form a complete whole. And I learnt about spirit guides from the spiritualist church. Not from psychology and not from hypnosis. So you see the three avenues provided different educational information. They didn't provide me with a complete picture. You have to use all three.

RW: Is the spiritualist church – is that connected to the Society for Psychical Research?

TP: No. The Society for Psychical Research was formed in 1882, and Frederic Myers is one of the founding fathers. And the reason it was formed was to investigate – at the time (in Victorian times) spiritualist seances were very popular. They were popular in society; they were a social parlour game. They were popular in the theatre and it was a fashionable thing to get involved in. But the Society was formed because serious thinkers and serious scientists wanted to know if there was any scientific validation to it. Or whether it was just nonsense. This is why the Society was formed. So they conducted serious experiments to investigate spiritualism and Myers' own book was for me the essential outcome. Have you got a copy?

RW: No, I haven't yet.

TP: You need that. You need that.

RW: I will get that. Yes, thank you.

TP: This is very, very edited. This is the edited – the summary – of 20 years of Myers' work. His own work was published by the Society. It's still available in the archives and it amounts to something like 20,000 pages of research, research method and work. And this is why I had to do a thesis on it. I had to go through all that in order to get a rounded picture of how Myers conducted his research. And what I found is that yes, it is scientifically validated, but I also found that that knowledge has been shelved and side-stepped by modern psychology which, to me, is absurd. Because – I like to use the euphemism of the elephant in the room. We live in a physical universe, a physical world, a three-dimensional space, but we are multi-dimensional creatures in a multi-dimensional universe that people – that science in the mainstream – chooses to ignore. Even though the evidence is staring them in the face.

RW: Yes, I agree with you. Some people simply aren't interested in looking more deeply.

TP: No, well then that's their look out. I have no time for people who are not interested in looking more deeply. I'm only interested in sharing information with people who are willing to listen, and are willing to learn. So, I don't try to convince anyone. I will only engage with those people – like yourself – who are willing to listen and to learn. As there's so much to know. It's huge.

RW: I mean this is only one strand of what I'm doing, but like you're saying – it's a lifelong thing. I mean these things don't come from nowhere, do they.

TP: No, they don't.

RW: I mean I hadn't really been thinking along these lines when I sat down to do this piece of work at all, but now – so many different strands of my life are just coming together in this, so I can't ignore it.

TP: Well this reinforces what I was saying to you earlier. I had to engage in three different avenues of education. They come together, they coalesce. It's not just one strand of knowledge. It's many. And they come together – it's like putting a puzzle together. All the pieces start to fit, and then you get the big picture. And you can't ignore it.

RW: Did you know Joe Benjamin by any chance?

TP: No. Who's Joe Benjamin?

RW: He was a psychic we used to go and see years ago – well more than 50 years ago. He used to do a meeting once a week. There was a big hall in Kentish Town in London where he would hold meetings. And people – as you were saying earlier about the beginning – for some people it was a bit of a parlour game, and for others it was really wanting to commune with people they'd lost. So that was probably my first meeting with this stuff, after my dad died. I mean he must be dead by now (Joe Benjamin). He was getting on then. He was just a very interesting man.

TP: There were obviously many. There's no shortage of mediums. I'm familiar with some names. The ones who interest me are those who have been investigated scientifically. Edgar Cayce. Have you heard the name Edgar Cayce?

RW: Yes, indeed.

TP: Very important psychic medium. And Chico Xavier from Brazil. Chico Xavier – a Portuguese speaker – uneducated, virtually illiterate. But he wrote 450 books as an illiterate man! How did he do that? They were channelled – this was automatic writing. Again his work is referenced. So, these are important mediums and psychics who have contributed to scientific knowledge. For me, those are the important ones. I bump into people who are psychic every day. It's very common. People have the gift of spiritual communication from childhood and it's knocked out of them by their parents and by society. They're told not to be silly, and it's suppressed. And it emerges again in their adulthood and then they need to explore it. So we are, as human beings, and this is what Frederic Myers states from his research, and he states it quite categorically – very clearly – he says we are a spiritual being that possesses a spiritual form.

RW: Well, that's exactly what I say. Yes, exactly that.

TP: So, if you're going to apply this knowledge to health, you have to begin with the spiritual health. Everything that happens in the spiritual world, filters down into the physical.

RW: Yes. One thing I was interested to know is how you experience the guidance you get. Do you hear it in words, or intuitively, or in visual clues? I was just wondering how it manifests for you.

TP: Well for me. I don't see or hear spirit, so I'm not mediumistic in that sense. I don't communicate with the spirit world. But I know that I'm influenced by spirit because I will experience an irresistible compulsion for example. An irresistible impulse to either travel somewhere, to go somewhere, to walk into a particular bookshop, or to read a particular book. I'll give you an example. My very first example of this was when I was living in a tent in the mountains of Crete. I was living as a hermit when I began to discover this. I had an irresistible impulse. I had first of all a name going round and round in my head. It had no relevance. Well, it was my middle name – James. My father's name was James. But, in that context, in that situation, it didn't mean anything. I thought 'what is this'? It was going round and round in my head. And then I had an irresistible compulsion to go to my tent and rummage around in my pack and in my pack was a book that was a gift to me from a dear friend in Germany and I've still got it. I've got it here [King James Bible]. It was an irresistible compulsion. I had to go and find this book and I sat down and it fell open – would you believe – at the *Book of James*. Then I was astonished. So I read and this is what it said. I've still got it. Here it is: "If any of you lack wisdom, let him ask God that giveth to all more liberally and upbraideth not; and it shall be given him". That was my first message from the spirit world. It came through a compulsion. An irresistible compulsion. It came from a name. And I didn't hear a voice. It was just an idea.

RW: Did the line you read, did that mean something significant to you?

TP: Immediately. Immediately. I knew – I didn't understand – I knew immediately that that was a profound discovery, a profound statement. And I knew it meant an awful lot but I didn't know then, I didn't understand how much. But what it means is that – I like to use this as my first bookend. [He holds up the King James Bible and his book, *The Science of Spirit Possession.*] You've got a book shelf, and you've got bookends holding your books in place. This is the first at one end, and this is on the other. And everything in between, every question I have ever asked has been answered. Can you believe that? Now, that is a profound statement to make. *Every* question I have ever asked, has been answered. All I have to do is ask the question. So, when I teach the method now that I use for healing and spirit de-possession, I teach – and I've got 100 students – I teach my students now to ask the question. Because if you don't ask the question, you can't get an answer.

RW: Absolutely. And the right sort of question.

TP: So, let me give you an example. People who are desperate, right; in their desperation they'll put their hands together and say "dear God, please help me". But what they need to do is ask a question. What they need to do is say "why is this happening to me?" Then they will get an answer, an explanation and they will be guided to the answer by a compulsion. And that's how it works. Another way of putting this is, it is often said in religious language, "God helps those who help themselves". So, what happens is that you'll get a compulsion to follow a particular direction, to go down a particular street or go into a particular bookshop, where you'll be given information that is going to be helpful to you to learn. But it's not going to be made easy. You have to work for it.

RW: Do you make a distinction between the spirit world and God?

TP: Between the spirit world and God?

RW: So, when you're asking a question, say..

TP: Well, for me to answer that question you need to define what God is.

RW: Yes, indeed. It sounds as if you're seeing it in religious terms, if the Bible is meaningful to you.

TP: No, I'm using religious language for people who like to use religious language.

RW: Personally I don't relate to that at all.

TP: No, I don't. I don't use religious language in my day to day work at all. But many people do. So, what we have to do is to use the language of the person we are talking to.

RW: Yes, agreed.

TP: So, in my education, it began with the compulsion. And the answer to my question just happened to be in the Bible. Now, that does not make me a religious person. And it doesn't mean that I refer to the spirit world as God. That's what was written in the Bible. I didn't write that. That's what I read.

RW: Yes, of course.

TP: My understanding is that each and every one of us is an autonomous spirit that has free will, and, when we discard the mortal coil and leave, consciousness goes back into the universal pool of consciousness. Some people might like to call that God, the universal pool of consciousness. Within that universal pool of consciousness we all exist, all of us.

RW: Well, that was another strand that I was interested in asking you about, although really it is about your beliefs. Because religious people often talk about – or I should say some of the monotheist religions – they talk about meeting your relatives in the afterlife and stuff like that which for many people like me would be the epitome of a nightmare. I don't believe that the individual ego carries on in the afterlife.

TP: OK. Let me stop you there. What I have learnt is that belief is irrelevant. It doesn't matter what you believe. And I'm going to read to you now a quotation from Myers that starts off my book.: "My discussion I may say at once will avoid metaphysics as carefully as it will avoid theology. For somewhat similar reasons I do not desire to introduce the philosophical opinions which have been held by various thinkers in the past, nor myself to speculate on matters lying beyond the possible field of objective truth" and I'm going to pick out two words from this that I find particularly important: The philosophical opinions. Opinions are beliefs, and we all have individual opinions and individual beliefs. And these are to be avoided. Speculation is guessing the possibilities. Beliefs, opinions, speculations and ideas are irrelevant.

What we need to do – and this is what appealed to Frederic Myers – for me, to get answers, is you have to get beyond the opinions of men. You have to get beyond the speculations of the philosophers and you have to find out what is real, what is true. So, you have to get beyond belief, expectation and the power of suggestion. And this is why it's important to understand how hypnosis works. Because, when a person is in an altered state of consciousness, in a trance, they are highly suggestible. So false memories can be implanted, so you need to get .... How do you get behind all that so that your information is not contaminated by the power of suggestion? And this for me is what Myers did; his method did that. And this is the method that I use to get answers to my questions. I bypass the expectations, the beliefs and the power of suggestion by accessing the spiritual mind of the person which is way beyond their conscious awareness, and then you get to the truth of it. Which is fascinating. But of course these ideas are challenging to mainstream.

RW: Absolutely.

TP: The easy part of my work is really bringing relief to the suffering. That's the easy part. The hard part is explaining to the medical profession how it's done. And it's quite simple. It's very simple how it's done. You can take a person who's been suffering their entire lives, diagnosed with psychosis, put into mental hospital, and we can discover a solution for them in less than an hour. It's a question of asking the right questions.

RW: You work at that interface with psychiatrists a lot, do you?

TPL: No. We have one psychiatrist. Well, we have three psychiatrists who endorse our work. Four actually, or five? Interestingly they're all retired. As it's a taboo subject in the ... They're free to express themselves because they're retired. So what we're looking for in the research is a psychiatrist or psychiatric clinic that's willing to put these methods to the test under controlled conditions.

RW: How do you distinguish between psychosis and spirit possession? You intuit it?

TP: I don't. I don't distinguish the difference. I ask the question of spirit. I say to the spirit, "Is this person sovereign?" Are they the sole occupier of their physical body? Are they the legitimate spirit occupying .... that's what sovereign means. Is this person sovereign, yes or no? If they're not, it means they are being influenced by a discarnate spirit and without any further ado, without any discussion, or any negotiation, we just ask for them to be removed.

RW: I see.

TP: Which is a completely different thing to exorcism. You don't engage the spirit at all in a battle. That's all nonsense. You just ask the spirit realm to remove it, and it's removed.

RW: And what if it's not?

TP: It is. It's the power of spirit; removes it. You just ask, and it's removed. Simple.

RW: But, what if the spirit that's possessing the person is stronger than the one you're asking?

TP: It isn't. Because, the powers of light are stronger than the powers of darkness.

RW: Oh, there's a subject!

TP: So, you go up the hierarchy. Again, we avoid focussing on theology or metaphysics. We just ask the question, Is the question answered? But at the end of the day, where is the evidence? Where is the proof? Is there evidence? The evidence is in the outcome. You just ask for the interfering spirit to be removed, right? And you go back to the patient – how are you feeling now? Did it make a difference? But it's all done beyond their conscious awareness. 50% of our cases are in North America. We have cases all over the world, so we're not in direct contact with the person. We're not delivering suggestions to them.

RW: Understood.

TP: We're working beyond time and space, so is this person hearing voices? OK. Persecutory voices, telling them to kill themselves and all this business. Psychiatry gives them drugs to suppress the voices; it doesn't take them away. What we do, we say to the spirit world, "remove the agency of these voices". And then we go back to the patient and say, "are you still hearing voices, yes or no" and they give us the answer. And that's how we have the evidence.

RW: And what about when it's psychic attack from somebody living?

TP: Yes, we can deal with that as well. That's dealt with in the same way as a curse is dealt with. You put a reflective shield around the person so that the negative energy impacting on them is reflected back to its source. Back to its sender. And that makes it stop. That's how that's dealt with.

   Lots of questions; lots of answers. It's taken me 30 years to get answers to these questions. They don't come easy. You have to go, you have to find a way of asking the right question and find a way of addressing the question to the right source of information. And without knowledge, without understanding, you could call that God or Allah or whatever religion you choose to follow, but we are dealing with universal forces here that are beyond that. Because religion is man-made.

RW: I 100% agree with you.

TP: So, we're dealing with universal forces.

RW: Do you have a view on Karma and reincarnation?

TP: It is my understanding that we've all lived many, many lives in the past and this is where our knowledge and experience ... and we've had many cases – and again my knowledge and experience comes from working with cases. Not just my own personal experience, but the experience of many, many others. I've got a book here somewhere ... I'm looking for a book that's written by a friend of mine in the United States, who's a surgeon. His name is Charles Tramont. So, if you're interested in questions of Karma and past lives, then I would recommend this book: *From Birth to Rebirth* (2006).

RW: Wonderful. I'll look that up. Thank you.

TP: He's a surgeon. Charles is a retired obstetrics surgeon who spent his entire medical career delivering babies, and working with birthing mothers. His second book is called *What's Missing in Medicine?* And what he discovered by using hypnosis for birthing mothers for pain-free birthing, is that they would spontaneously remember past lives. So that's what his first book is about. And the second book, they would also spontaneously reveal the discarnate spirits that were attached to them. So, he wasn't following guidance from anyone. He was discovering this himself accidentally just by working with his birthing mothers. So, his ideas are not influenced by other practitioners or other philosophers. He is a very, very nice man. Lovely man, Charles.

RW: I was interested in something you said in the interview with Mishlove, that you're in touch with Myers now, and I wondered if you could say a bit about that.

TP: Yes, a dear friend of mine – Stephen Shapiro – was until recently (he died last year). Stephen was a senior advocate, a lawyer in the Supreme Court in the United States. He lived in Chicago with his wife and family. He was a very highly respected lawyer. Now, his wife was a medium. And he would work with his wife on communicating with spirits and between them they published twelve books. Because of his profession he published under a pseudonym. He published under the name John and Martha McGuinness. And during his conversations with people in the spirit world, he came across Frederic Myers so he wrote to the Society for Psychical Research in London – and of course I'm a member – and asked for the Society to provide validation for his discovery in his communication with Myers. One of the members, Trevor Hamilton, had written a biography of Myers. So, I became very closely connected with Trevor and Stephen investigating these communications with Frederic Myers. And all the evidence showed it to be true that he was actually having conversations with Frederic Myers. What I found particularly encouraging was that, during these conversations, and unbeknown to me, Myers was talking about my work! Because I was reinforcing his work. So, I had acknowledgement and encouragement from him from the other side. Unfortunately last year Stephen was shot and killed – he was murdered. And I've since had communication with him from the spirit world. His experience ... and Trevor Hamilton is continuing to write about Stephen Shapiro and his work. In fact, he contacted me only last week and said I need to publish some more stuff on Stephen's work, but I need approval from his family because the family will be mentioned. So, there's an ongoing project you see. Stephen's connection with Frederic Myers. But Frederic Myers did state in his own words before he died, he promised that he would continue his work from the other side, and there is evidence that he has. Another book written by Saltmarsh – you may be familiar with Saltmarsh?

RW: Yes, I've just got that.

TP: Where he investigates the cross-correspondence with Myers which is very, very important. Again, providing evidence that Myers promised he would provide. Interesting isn't it?

RW: It's brilliant, yes. I mean this could ... every aspect I go into, it could be a book in itself.

TP: It's huge, isn't it.

RW: Massive.

TP: You mentioned when you introduced yourself to me that you were a Jungian psychologist. Are you familiar with the fact that Jung referenced Myers' work in his own PhD thesis?

RW: Oh yes.

TP: Myers influenced Jung's thinking on the Collective Unconscious. Myers called it something else. He called it the subliminal mind.

RW: I saw that he influenced Freud as well. Freud was a member of the Society for Psychical Research which I found very strange as it's not him at all.

TP: Well Freud was such an egotist. He wanted to make a name for himself. He wasn't interested in investigating the truth. He wanted to create an idea.

RW: Well, I don't think he understood it.

TP: He didn't.

RW: His paper on "The Uncanny" just doesn't get the uncanny at all.

TP: He didn't understand it at all. But this is something that is very, very common, that I witness today with students of mine. If they have a desire within themselves to be recognised, then the ego comes to the fore and you can discount their work. Because then they are missing the point. The importance of doing this work is humility, and of course Freud had no humility.

RW: Well, that's my mantra, I have to say. That is the number one requirement in the work.

TP: It's very sad that mainstream psychology and psychiatry adopted Freud rather than Myers. Because Myers was the forerunner of all of them. Well, he was the initiator of scientific investigation, into these phenomena.

RW: I think that's a bit too advanced for medicine. But maybe things are changing.

TP: It was 150 years ago!

RW: But the rational mind is determined to keep hold, I'm afraid.

TP: Well, you could call it the rational mind. I prefer to call it ignorance. In the true sense of the word, they are ignoring it.

RW: Yes, I agree.

TP: And false teaching. I mean medical students. Young people who want to be doctors, they go into medical school in their early 20s and they are indoctrinated in the way they are made to think. And they are taught to believe, taught to think that this is how you heal the sick. It isn't. It's false teaching.

RW: Well Western medicine is a very narrow field.

TP: They go through their entire career of medicine and it is not until they retire and have another look at it, like Charles Tramont did. This is why he called his book *What's Missing in Medicine?* He's an expert. He's trod the path; he's walked the walk and he knows from experience that what he was taught as a surgeon was wrong, and he says it.

RW: Well, it's limited. It has a very narrow scope, Western medicine, unfortunately.

TP: It's limited to the physical. But in addition to the physical you've got the mental, the emotional and the spiritual. It's like a pyramid. You have to start at the top. And deal with problems at the source, at the spiritual source. And doing it that way is very simple.

RW: Well I don't know if you have to start there, because I don't know that it matters where you start. But it has to incorporate all of those levels.

TP: Well, for me my journey of discovery started with the physical to arrive at the spiritual. When I discovered that I had the gift of healing physical pain. Hands on healing – which nowadays is called Reiki. But that's where I began. So, I've been led down this pathway of education which has drawn me to the spiritual. Yes, you can't start at the spiritual. You have to start at the bottom and work up. Has this been helpful, Ruth?

RW: Yes, it's been very helpful. Thank you. Very interesting. What I'll do is I'll turn it into something and I'll send you what I would propose to put in so if you wanted to comment or change anything, I'd be happy to do that.

TP: Let me ask you. Why are you doing this? What project is it part of?

RW: It's a new book about spirituality but it incorporates lots of things. First of all I talk about 'what is a spiritual perspective', and it goes into mantic practices and synchronicity, and what's the point of existence and suicide and stuff like that. And then it ends with this piece about spiritualism, ghosts and the paranormal; at least that's the penultimate chapter and then there is a chapter on grace. So, it's quite wide-ranging.

TP: You're dipping in a toe into a huge ocean of knowledge. You just mentioned suicide. You may be interested to know that there are dark forces who use - these inter–dimensional species – that use the energy, the life force of human beings, as a commodity. Just like we use energy. To us – energy like electricity, any kind of power is a commodity. We use it in our daily lives. Milk from cows is a commodity, an energy which keeps us alive, in much the same way that the energetic life force of the human being is a commodity that's traded on inter-dimensional markets. It has value. So, how do these inter-dimensional beings harvest human energy to trade on the inter-dimensional markets? They harvest it by encouraging people to kill themselves because the moment the spirit leaves the body, the spirit is free; the energy is available to be captured and traded. Now there's an idea for you to explore. Suicide.

RW: Well, what you're saying is – I don't know where to start with that. Trading … .?

TP: We've discovered this from the experience of working with spirit and encountering inter-dimensional beings who actually do this. So, these are not my ideas. I haven't learnt anything about this from books. Other than stepping out into the real world of psyche and spiritual and mental health to find out why people commit suicide.

RW: When you say species, you sound like you mean more than spirits or souls.

TP: OK, let me put it this way. How many species of insect do you suppose there are on planet earth?

RW: Yes, lots.

TP: It's infinite isn't it. And this is just one planet in an inter-dimensional multiverse. So, when people ask me how many types of spirit there are, how many different types of insect there are on the earth … . It's commensurate. So, we're dealing with new species all the time. And that puts our existence into perspective.

RW: Well I've got a very interesting bit on perspective. Yes.

TP: For me, and as I was writing my thesis, I came to realise that perspective is everything.

RW: Absolutely.

TP: Your perspective is how you perceive things and how you view the world. If you change your perspective, you see it differently.

RW: Well, let me push you a bit on this, as I find this idea of inter-dimensional species rather difficult. What would you say is the purpose of them harvesting these suicides?

TP: It's a form of energy. Why do we milk cows? Because they provide us with energy. So, there are inter-dimensional species that milk us for energy. And if you have no knowledge of these things, no awareness of these things, then you're vulnerable. So, we're all vulnerable.

RW: I've got enough trouble with people milking my energy here!

TP: This is the elephant in the room. Just because you can't see it, doesn't mean it's not there.

RW: No, indeed.

TP: What we have to do in our work, is to send out recovery teams to recover the stolen energy that's been taken from people and bring it back. So, suicide is the outcome; it's the objective of – you take someone who has negative experience, who suffers from depression, they go through life with a very, very low negative vibration. They're vulnerable. And that negativity will be costly, ramped up, reinforced to take them to the point where they can't tolerate life any more. They take their life and spirit leaves the body and the dark forces capture it as soon as it leaves the body.

RW: But, given that energy cannot be created or destroyed, so, what would be … .

TP: Who said that?

RW: That's Einstein.

TP: That's the theory of third law of thermo-dynamics.

RW: So, what would be the need of these inter-dimensional species to appropriate energy?

TP: Well, why do we need to milk cows?

RW: Well, a physical body needs to be fed with something.

TP: You see in this discussion, and it takes me back to Myers' observation discussing theology and metaphysics and so on. We can explore all these ideas that we are influenced in our discussion by our earlier knowledge, our earlier thinking, which is probably irrelevant. And that's a difficult pill to swallow.

RW: Well, we can only come from where we come.

TP: That's right.

RW: You have to understand it through what you've got.

TP: Yes. It's a leap of faith to step outside the box and say, right, here we are going to discover something completely new, completely different to what we've understood before. And this is what makes it difficult for mainstream science to accept. Because it is a solid box they've trapped themselves into, the three-dimensional box. But you're on the right path. The trick is asking questions and not assuming you've got an answer. It's huge.

RW: Some of this is going to be going further than I have scope to deal with, I think.

TP: You can only take small steps.

RW: Yes. Anyway, that needs work.

TP: And it takes time. I've got several books waiting to be published on the back burner. It's a question of time. This is why I don't do one-to-one therapy any more because it just takes up too much time and I don't have the time to prepare for it. When people contact me. People contact me because they want to talk about their problems. And actually I just don't have time for it as there's just so much to do on the research side.

TP: [When I'm working with someone] Now I don't find it helpful at all to be aware of past history. All I'm interested in is, is there a problem. What is the cause of the problem? And how do we deal with it? So, my suggestion to you is that, if you need answers, you need to ask the question: is there something that's impinging on my spiritual health, yes or no? If yes, can it be dealt with, yes or no? Can it be dealt with now please? And again, reinforcing what I said earlier, it's not the individual, it's not the therapist, it's not me, who has the answer to those questions. The answer to those questions comes from spirit, so you just need to know how to ask spirit those questions. You could do it yourself if you know how to do it.

TP: You have to do it every day. Every morning. It needs to be a part of your daily routine. When you get up in the morning, if you're going to step into the world, you wouldn't dream of stepping outside your front door naked would you. It just doesn't make sense. You need protection for all sorts of reasons. So, that's a part of your routine. You have your breakfast, you do your ablutions, you get dressed, before you step into the world. Similarly, you need to go through the daily routine, the habit, of putting on your spiritual protection. Like an overcoat.

RW: That's a really good way to put it actually.

TP: If you go to my own website, you should have access to it. Go to the psychic defence page, it explains to you various methods you can use in one of my interviews with Jeffrey Mishlove, I talk about this psychic self-defence. It's a daily habit; a daily routine. If you apply that daily routine, you can keep yourself safe. And, if there's anything attached to you, you go through the protocol, you go through the routine, and you clean it up, clean it away, like brushing your teeth. So, you just need to follow it. Don't just read it: understand it, apply it; use it every day. Well, it's a resource. A lot of questions you have will be answered by the information we have available. It's protection; it's free to use. Do it while you're brushing your teeth. Make it a part of your routine. That's how long it takes. We do it every morning, to keep yourself safe. There's a lot to think about.

RW: There is. There's a lot here. I really appreciate your time.

TP: Good luck with all you do.

RW: Thank you. The same to you.

References

https://www.amazon.co.uk/s?k=terence+palmer&ref=nb_sb_noss_2

https://www.amazon.co.uk/Tao-Natural-Cycles-natural-economy-ebook/dp/B00KYPB6B8/ref=sr_1_2?dchild=1&keywords=terence+palmer&qid=1598305397&sr=8-2

https://www.amazon.co.uk/Whats-Missing-Medicine-Unleashing-Subconscious-ebook/dp/B07BLP1VL4/ref=sr_1_1?crid=1RX9QLMZDYE7I&dchild=1&keywords=whats+missing+in+medicine&qid=1598290481&sprefix=What%27s+missing+in%2Caps%2C156&sr=8-1

https://www.amazon.co.uk/Human-Personality-Survival-Bodily-Death-ebook/dp/B07JBJNTSY/ref=sr_1_1?dchild=1&keywords=f+w+h+myers&qid=1598305556&sr=8-1

https://www.amazon.co.uk/s?k=trevor+hamilton+myers&ref=nb_sb_noss

https://www.google.com/search?q=chico+javier&oq=chico+javier&aqs=chrome..69i57j46j0j46j0l3.4463j0j7&sourceid=chrome&ie=UTF-8

List of useful resources

There is a vast literature on the topics covered in *Exploring Spirituality* so the following is really just a little taster of where you may like to explore further.

Recommendations for future reading

Bloom, W. (2011) *The Power of Modern Spirituality: How to Live a Life of Compassion and Personal Fulfilment*. London: Piatkus.

Cayce, E. (1999) *A Search for God*. Books 1 and 2. Virginia Beach, VA: A.R.E Press.

de Chardin, T. (1965) *The Phenomenon of Man*. New York and San Francisco: Harper Colophon Books.

Dossey, L. (2009) *The Power of Premonitions: How Knowing the Future Can Shape Our Lives*. London: Hay House.

Henderson, J. L. (2005) *Thresholds of Initiation*. Wilmette, Illinois: Chiron Publications.

Moody, R. (2001) *Life After Life*. London: Rider Publishing.

Mulhern, A. (2012) *Healing Intelligence: The Spirit in Psychotherapy – Working with Darkness and Light*. London: Karnac Books.

Tacey, D. (2001) *Jung and the New Age*. London and New York: Routledge.

Tacey, D. (2004) *The Spirituality Revolution: The emergence of contemporary spirituality*. London and New York: Routledge.

Thurston, M. and Christopher, F. (1992) *The Edgar Cayce Handbook For Creating your Future*. New York and Toronto: Ballantine Books.

Wohlleben, P. (2018) *The Inner Life of Animals: Surprising Observations of a Hidden World*. London: Vintage.

Young-Eisendrath, P. and Miller, M.E. (2000) *The Psychology of Mature Spirituality: Integrity, Wisdom, Transcendence*. London and New York: Routledge.

Resources

Department for Psychosocial and Psychoanalytic Studies at the University of Essex in the UK runs a suite of prestigious degree courses on Jung and psychoanalysis (some of which may be accessed virtually). This includes a Centre for Myth Studies. See: https://www.essex.ac.uk/departments/psychosocial-and-psychoanalytic-studies

Institute of Noetic Sciences See: https://noetic.org/

Manifesto for a Post-Materialist Science See: https://www.opensciences.org/ where you will also find the The Institute for Research on Extraordinary Experiences (INREES).

Pacifica Graduate Institute in California run Masters and Doctoral Programs in Depth Psychology, Mythological Studies, and the Humanities. See: https://www.pacifica.edu/

Quechelah Medicine Community® See: https://www.quechelah.org/

Scientific and Medical Network See: https://scientificandmedical.net/

Society for Psychical Research See: https://www.spr.ac.uk/

The Galileo Commission See: https://galileocommission.org/

End plate

I will end with a little humour, a most Jewish way to end. However serious the matters I have covered are, humour is often a good way to leaven the weight. (Although I was brough up Jewish, it is not my practice. However, the humour most certainly tickles my funny bone.)

The Lotus and the Mishpokheh (Yiddish for whole clan)

The Principles of Jewish Buddhism

- Let your mind be as a floating cloud. Let your stillness be as the wooded glen. And sit up straight. You'll never meet the Buddha with posture like that.

- There is no escaping Karma. In a previous life, you never called, you never wrote, you never visited. And whose fault was that?

- Wherever you go, there you are. Your luggage is another story.

- To practice Zen and the art of Jewish motorcycle maintenance, do the following: get rid of the motorcycle. What were you thinking?

- Be aware of your body. Be aware of your perceptions. Keep in mind that not every physical sensation is a symptom of a terminal illness.

- If there is no self, whose arthritis is this?

- Breathe in. Breathe out. Breathe in. Breathe out. Forget this and attaining Enlightenment will be the least of your problems.

- The Tao has no expectations. The Tao demands nothing of others. The Tao does not speak. The Tao does not blame. The Tao does not take sides. The Tao is not Jewish.

- ☯ Drink tea and nourish life. With the first sip, joy. With the second, satisfaction. With the third, Danish.

- ☯ The Buddha taught that one should practice loving kindness to all sentient beings. Still, would it kill you to find a nice sentient being who happens to be Jewish?

- ☯ Be patient and achieve all things. Be impatient and achieve all things faster.

- ☯ To Find the Buddha, look within. Deep inside you are ten thousand flowers. Each flower blossoms ten thousand times. Each blossom has ten thousand petals. You might want to see a specialist.

- ☯ Be here now. Be someplace else later. Is that so complicated?

- ☯ Zen is not easy. It takes effort to attain nothingness. And then what do you have? Bupkes! (Zilch)

(These are extracts from *Zen Judaism: For Your, a Little Enlightenment* by David M. Bader (2002 New York, New York: Harmony Books).

Index

Note: Page references in *italics* denote figures and in **bold** tables.

Milton Keynes UK
Ingram Content Group UK Ltd.
UKHW021928271123
433384UK00005B/66